MANY FACES~MANY SPACES

MANY FACES~MANY SPACES

Artists in Ontario

DEY-BERGMOSER, OLGA M.
co-author

MAJUMDER, KHALETUN
co-author

COULTER, ELIZABETH J. (BETTY)
editor

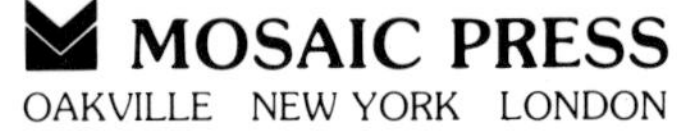

MOSAIC PRESS
OAKVILLE NEW YORK LONDON

DESIGN: First Edition Book Creations

CANADIAN CATALOGUING IN PUBICATION DATA
Dey-Bergmoser, Olga, 1938-
  Many faces, many spaces

ISBN 0-88962-350-3

1. Ethnic art — Ontario. 2. Art, Canadian — Ontario.
3. Art, Modern — 20th century — Ontario.
I. Majumber, Khaletum, 1942-   . II. Title.

N6546.05D4 1987   709'.713   C87-095052-5

Published by Mosaic Press, P.O. Box 1032, Oakville,
Ontario, L6J 5E9, Canada. Offices and warehouse at 1252
Speers Rd., Unit 10, Oakville, Ontario, L6L 5N9, Canada.

Published with the assistance of the Canada Council and
the Ontario Arts Council.

Mosaic Press expresses its thanks to the Multiculturalism
Directorate of the Department of the Secretary of State for
its generous support of this publication.
All the views expressed here, however, are those of the
authors and editors.

Design by: First Edition Book Creations
Typography: Michael J. O'Leary
Printed and bound in Hong Kong

ISBN 0-88962-350-3 cloth

MOSAIC PRESS:
In the United States:
    Riverrun Press Inc., 1170 Broadway, Suite 807,
New York, N.Y., 10001, U.S.A..

In the U.K.:
    John Calder (Publishers) Ltd., 18 Brewer Street,
London, W1R 4AS, England.

CONTENTS

PROLOGUE

Since to view expressions of our culture is to have an insight into the soul of our nation, here, for your reading and visual enjoyment, is a collection of representative work by a magnificent cross-section of Ontario artists of the most varied ethnocultural backgrounds.

Read of their struggles to attain recognition and of their successes eventually leading to public acknowledgment.

Some have brought their local art from their homeland to contribute to the Canadian art scene while others have given a distinctive flavour to the art here, influenced by the impact of Canada – the land and its people – coloured by their own ancient traditions and interpretations of life – all of them being equally eager to share their cultural heritage with the people of Canada.

These artists happily express their thanks to Canada, the country they proudly and lovingly embraced as their new homeland, offering this colourful floral bouquet as a tribute to Canadian hospitality, friendship, values, traditions and to the opening to them of an unlimited horizon of opportunities.

FOREWORD

Art is a statement.

In whatever medium an artist chooses, his or her work is a statement about the artist as an individual, about the culture in which the artist lives, and can be an expression of despair or hope, of defeat or inspiration. It may be a view of the moment, or a timeless message.

Whatever statement an individual artist may make through his/her work, he or she also holds up a mirror to society.

As we look into those "mirrors" in this incredible book, "Many Faces, Many Spaces — Artists in Ontario", we see a Canadian society reflecting a great diversity, vigour, individuality, and a colourful sense of time and place.

Not in this book is to be found the stolid statement of collectivist art which some of the totalitarian states of this 20th century have produced. Nor do we find here the crassly commercial product designed to placate the senses with blandness, or become high price-tag objects of manipulated consumers in the trumped up world of art marketing which Thomas Wolfe describes in his book "The Painted Word".

Instead, this book, through the art and text alike, displays the vibrancy and vitality of individual artists, each of whom is the inheritor of a particular culture and values, now transposed and being actively reinterpreted in the dynamic Canadian context. In this sense, this valuable book "Many Faces, Many Spaces" is a snapshot, taken in the mid-1980s, of a Canadian artistic tradition in transition.

This transition began when the first artist in Canada gave visual expression to his feelings and interpreted his surroundings, and it will continue for so long as Canada is a country.

For instance, if one thinks of the paintings of Cornelius Krieghoff, an exemplar of the Dutch School of art, his paintings of Quebec landscapes present a strong European atmosphere, even though the scenes he depicted were on this side of the Atlantic Ocean. Then, when the Group of Seven began projecting onto canvas the rugged and unrefined beauty of the Canadian scenery, in strokes and colours that seem "wild" in comparison with the works of the Dutch masters, we begin to see an important new stage in the evolution and transition in Canadian painting. It was this evolution — which continues today — that permits an artist the freedom and scope to express the intrinsic and unique character of Canada, unencumbered by techniques or attitudes borne of other cultures, of other times, and of other places.

Yet those other cultures, those other techniques, *are* a part of Canada, too. This is the delightful paradox of Canadian society, a new society, a society that evolves by blending many faces and many spaces into a uniquely different pastiche. There is no other society like ours.

Canada will continue to defy comprehension by anyone who does not understand this central reality of our cultural evolution.

To understand, first look into the mirrors in this book.

The artists depicted in these pages represent a vibrant new wave in this continuing Canadian saga of blending different cultures into a unique Canadian expression.

Olga Dey and Khaletun Majumder and Elizabeth J. Coulter have displayed tireless and persistent effort and motivation in bringing such a monumental project as this book to culmination…in holding this mirror up to us all.

Patrick Boyer, M.P.
Etobicoke-Lakeshore

ACKNOWLEDGEMENT
to the Secretary of State Department
MULTICULTURALISM Directorate

*Our heartfelt thanks to all those
idealistic Canadian artists who
have so generously donated their
time and given us free access to
their material.
It is indeed a privilege and pleasure
to be able to serve the arts community.*

*In gratitude:
Khaletun
and
Olga*

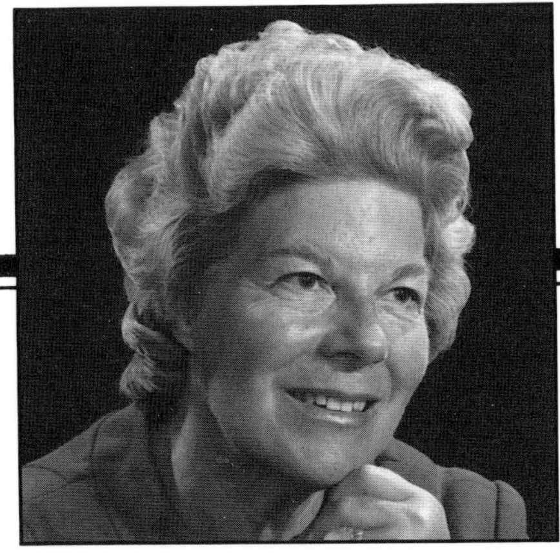

Editor Elizabeth (Betty) Joyce Coulter
author, columnist, editor, broadcaster and creative writing instructor

Born on a homestead to pioneering parents in the Peace River Country of Northern Alberta, this lady, who has a warm heart and contagious smile, now lives in Toronto where she is busy promoting talent in people of all ages.

Her book, TODAY, STARTING POINT FOR THE FUTURE, published recently, is a spiritual treasure chest for anyone to explore and in which to find consolation and strength.

Betty also writes a column in the Etobicoke/Advertiser Guardian, a weekly community paper; is the publisher/editor of the 32,000 copy publication, THE SPIRES, a cultural community focus, and is the hostess of a cable television program, CULTURAL CRISSCROSS.

A truly third generation Canadian with sparkling eyes full of joie de vivre, Betty is also the idealistic promoter of Canadian talent. She works with novice writers, helping them to improve their articles about people with various artistic skills, thereby encouraging all the arts. Being herself a talented writer who lives by the values she advocates, she sets an example to be emulated and shows that, although writing is usually done in solitude, one can, nevertheless, successfully lead a full family life and maintain friendships at the same time.

She believes in tight but daringly colourful writing spiced with innovative concepts and ideas – no unnecessary padding. Idealism, enthusiasm and talent alone are not enough, she feels. You need commitment, too.

This writer is highly self-motivated and falls into the category of those who burn the midnight oil, yet are always cheerful and accessible to sharing others' joys and tribulations.

Faith and love for people seem to be her prime movers. Her faith inspires her and endows her with special strength which she radiates. Yet she never flaunts her beliefs or tries to force them on others.

Her popularity with people is such that they comment: "Everything about her is encouraging."

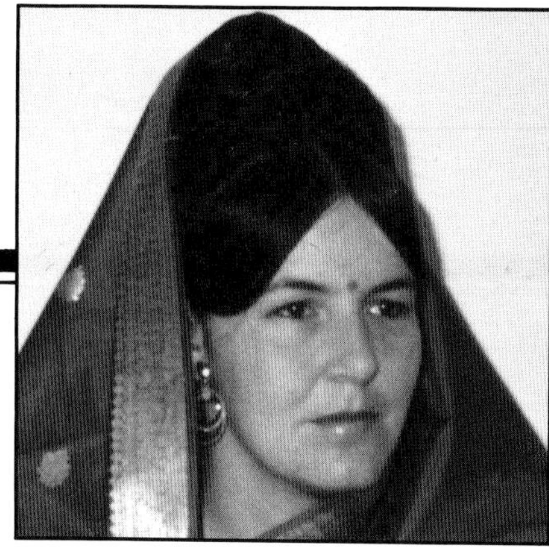

Olga M. DEY—BERGMOSER
Canadian author of truly multicultural and multilingual background,
born in Holland,
to German parents,
proud mother of a Eurasian daughter
multilingual translator: German/French/Spanish
theoretician in Portuguese/Dutch/Latin
November 1974 — B.A. with A-standing U of T, Toronto
Octover 1975 — APUS Scholastic Award for academic excellence
November 1978 — scholarship (tuition fee refund)
November 1978 — M.A. U of T, Toronto
volunteer instructor of Spanish at the University Settlement House in Toronto
(November 1964 to April 1965 inclusive)
1976 — VIP hostess at the Montreal Olympics
1976 — hostess for the TORONTOLYMPIAD, the Olympiad for the Handicapped
Publications:
hardcover   December 1978
paperback   December 1979
ltd. edition   April 1981
PEOPLE, a collection of short stories
travelogues, short stories, interviews (authors and artists)

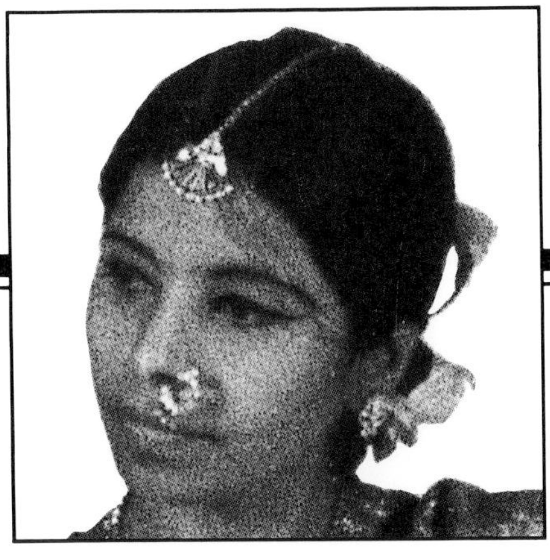

Khaletun MAJUMDER
B.A., B.A. (Hons), M.A.

educated in Canada, India and Bangladesh
Studied at the University of Western Ontario,
University of Dacca, and Oxford School
She is a freelance illustrator, dancer, writer, fashion designer, and choreographer.
Currently teaching at the Ontario College of Art
Recent publications include her illustrations in:
Bannerji, Himani   TWO SISTERS
Dey, O.   UNDER THE SPELL OF INDIA
Khatun, Jobeda   KOOLI OF BHADHURABAD GHAT
Khatun, Jobeda   TREASURE OF HEAVEN
Khatun, Jobeda   TWO WORDS
and   THE BEGUM, a monthly magazine.
She has directed more than 79 dance programmes since 1970 and has chore-
graphed more than 235 dances which include SPELLBOUND, a Canadian Show, pro-
duced and directed by Ivan Reitman, with magical direction by Doug Henning.

with our special thanks
to Betty Coulter,
author, editor, and promoter
of Canadian arts and – above all –
a truly wonderful friend
who idealistically edited the entire book

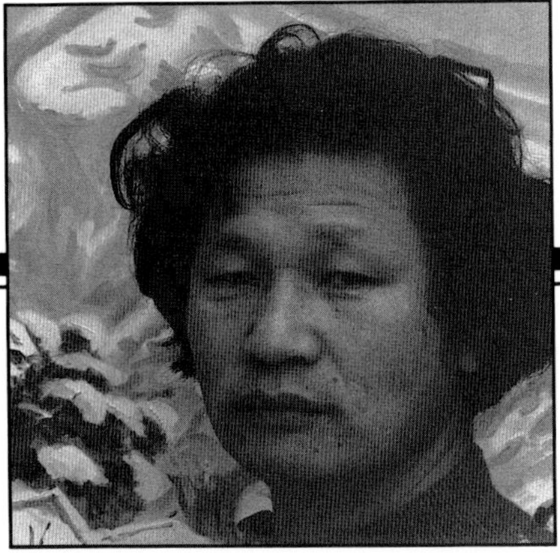

SEUNG WAN AHN

a most prolific artist who ranked among Korea's five leading painters

(born on April 9th, 1948, in Seoul, Korea)

This unique artist combines subtly stated details with sweeping grand-scale landscape composition of a dynamic forward thrust. The impact of his grandiose settings is almost over-powering, creating a strong bond of familiarity between the artwork and its viewer. One cannot help feeling as though having been under the spell of such a sight at some time or other in one's life while aboard a plane coming in for a landing.

No wonder, then, that Seung Wan, a restless person whom nothing and nobody can stop in his creative drive, always felt compelled to paint ever since the age of 15. He made art his main profession, teaching on a full-time basis at high school and on a part-time basis at a college. His artwork was featured in three one-man shows and numerous group exhibitions. His sole hope and ambition is that he may contribute something to this world by means of his art.

Sitting by a lake or at the foot of a mountain, leaning against a tree, this painter does all his work right on location, no matter whether under a scorching sun or pelting rain. Maybe this complete submission to the raging elements is the secret factor behind the startling freshness of his landscapes. Never yet did Seung Wan try to recreate mood and setting from photos. For him it's HERE and NOW. It's right on site that he captures a panorama in all its intriguing aspects and facets, carefully preserving a certain feeling and mood.

With skilful strokes that come easily as a result of endless practice, he creates the forms and shapes as he sees them and tinges them with the colouring perceived by his creative mind, awakening a sense of distance and impelling movement. The viewer instinctively senses that this man climbed mountains, crossed valleys and is deeply attached to the land and its soil.

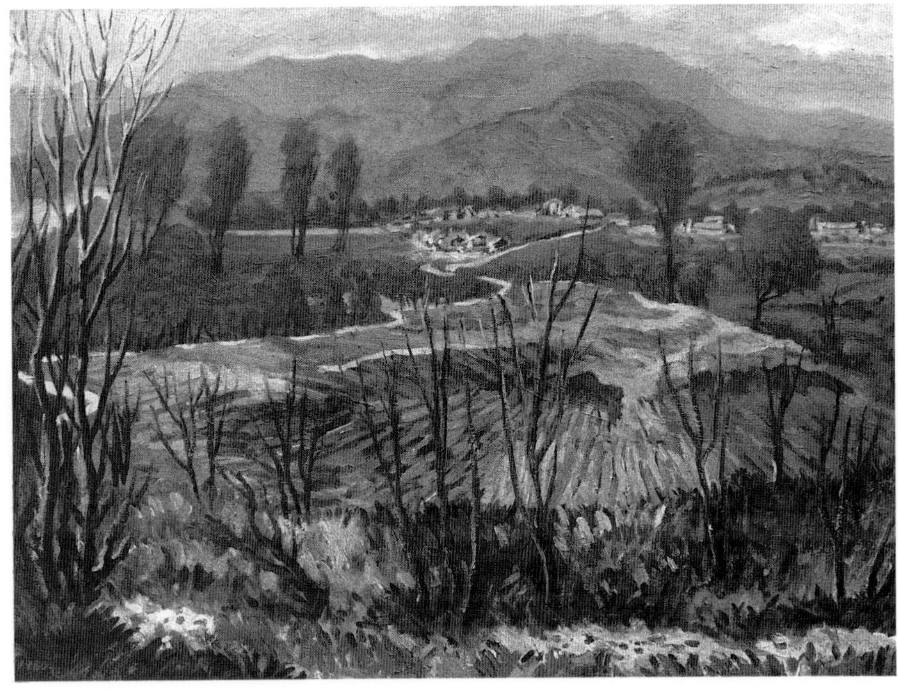

Yet his powerful compositions never lack coherence. There may be a grand-scale mountain massive in the background stretching in one direction, interspersed with an almost island-like undulating countryside in the centre. Yet the spatial unity of the shifting optical planes is preserved and balance reinforced by a foreground with the same directional movement as the background, the rocks in the backdrop now reduced to the size of boulders in the foreground.

Ahn also makes amazing use of the warm orange colour by placing bushes – done totally in orange and resembling licking flames – in the foreground. They seem to be speedily burning away, shooting sparks up trees and even up to the thatched roof of a cottage – a carefully disguised artistic expedient adding urgency to the scene. To Seung Wan, the colour orange actually symbolizes a well-balanced relationship between two poles of attraction.

This talented artist feels equally at home with watercolours, pastels, oils, and acrylics as well as in the various genres such as portraiture, still life, and landscape painting.

Rhythmic swirls on mountain slopes impart a sense of action. Yet the impact of the majestic mountains is softened by homes almost buried underneath snow – roofs sagging under their white load, as if ready to collapse at any moment – and branches stretched out like frail arms rein-

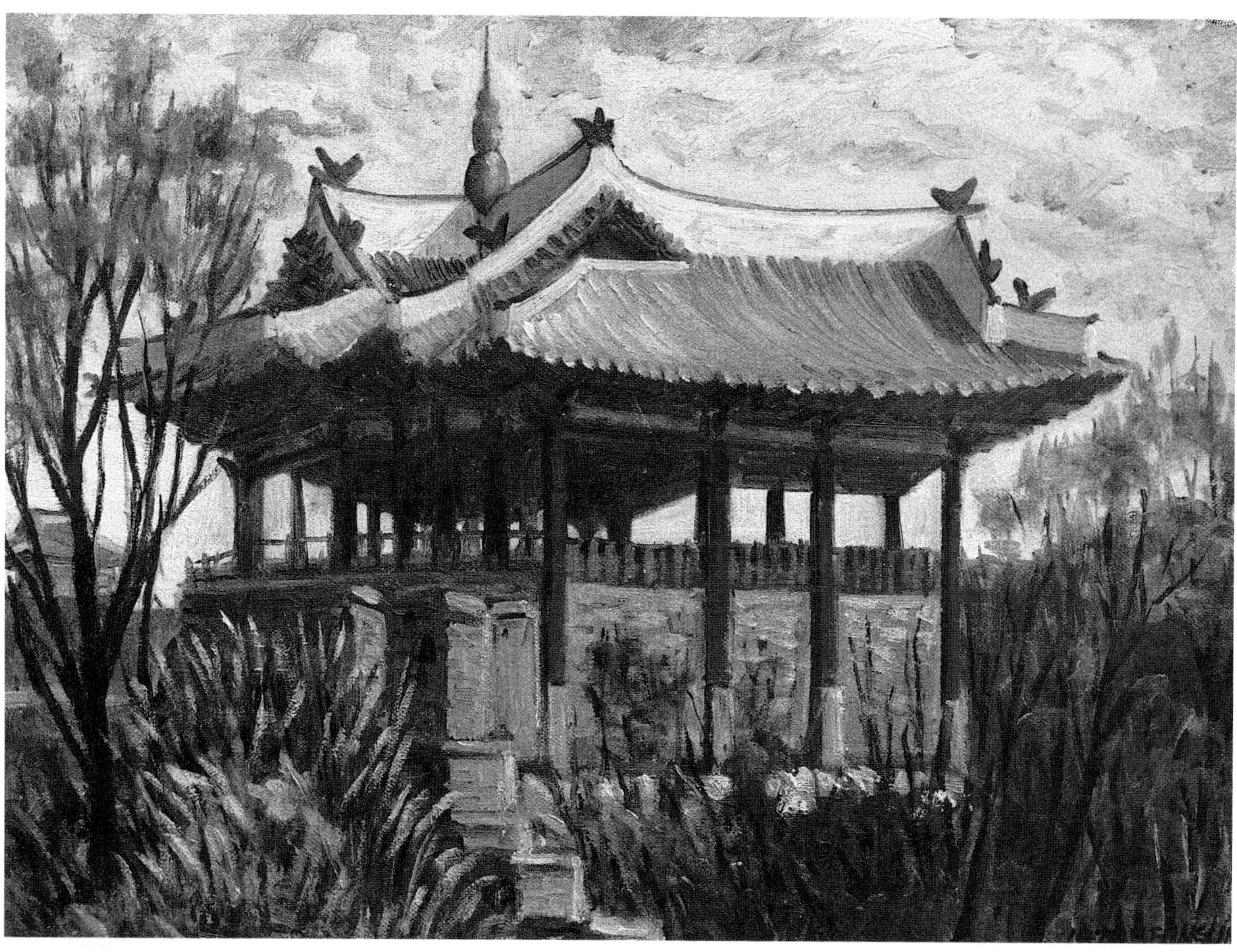

forcing this skilfully conjured feeling of fear and warning. And the snow-covered mountain peaks make us think of the ash-white heads of wise elders.

Seung Wan is clearly fascinated with summits piercing the sky. They seem to represent a challenge and recur in many of his paintings.

In one of his landscapes, a small pavilion perched atop a fortress wall is the central element of his composition. The painter applies the unusual technique of showing us a figure, wrapped in a white shawl, seeking refuge from the blowing wind, indicated – at the height of abstraction – by merely a dot implying motion. He makes us focus, first of all, on the magnolia blossoms swaying in the wind and, then, on their direction that is, so-to-speak, in sympathetic unison with the movement of the figure.

Gradually, the minute detail of the blossoms recedes into a more distant slope in the centre with its blooming tree-tops forming a pink vault that – by contrast – makes the mountain range in the background look all the more dramatic. The painter is extrememly economical in using but one dark green line to separate the foreground and centre from the backdrop – the orange-brown colour of the wall blending into the mountain slopes on the left and gently fading out in the background.

Just like the breathtaking mountain ranges, pavilions and temples recur in his paintings as well. However, they involve a marked switch in his colour scheme to more sombre shades of anthracite and sepia in order to highlight the delving into the past. This foreshadows the potential threat of man-made structures succumbing to the inevitable march of time and becoming overgrown with weeds.

Of course, pavilions used to hold special significance in Korea where they are to be found in the most secluded scenic spots — on slopes and in glens. Poets and scholars would temporarily retire to them in order to dedicate themselves fully to their studies and philosophical discussions and … to imbibing wine.

This artist's work clearly reflects his deep love for people and nature, having resulted in a sequence of oil paintings depicting familiar scenes of his native land — the countryside in its striking changes brought about by the four distinctive seasons.

In this painting, the grey roofs of the shacks in the foreground and the purplish-tinged grey of the mountains in the backdrop serve as strong connecting and balancing elements.

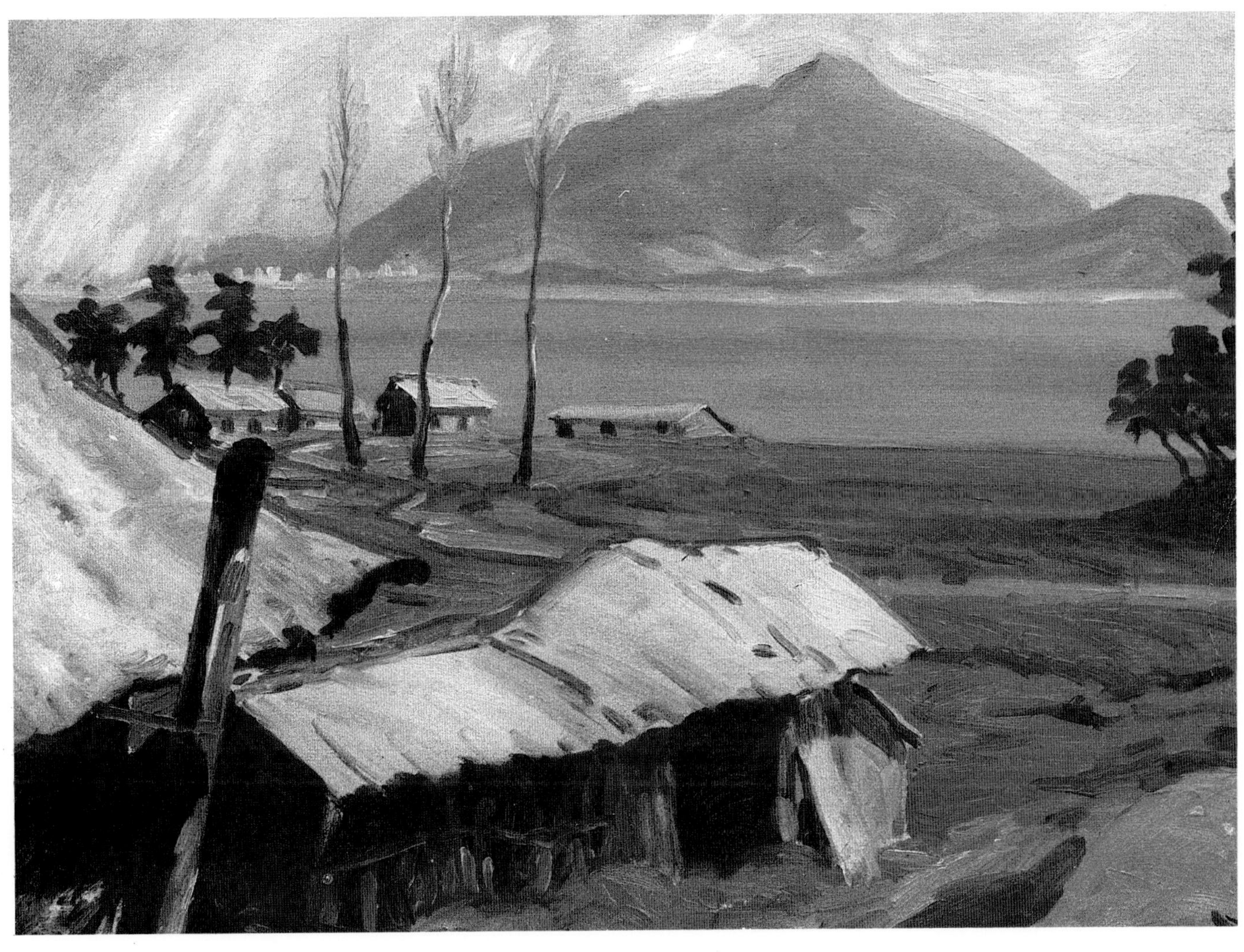

SEUNG WAN AHN

There are those striking paintings where the symbol of war looms spatially and thematically, first and foremost, over otherwise peaceful communal settings bustling with daily life activities. The visually presented dichotomy is startling, yet not disturbing, for life goes on and the nests, homes of birds — and the houses, homes of people — create a certain emotionally reasurring stability despite the large canon in the foreground that is totally ignored by a peacefully grazing cow so close to it.

Some of these paintings are bathed in warm orangey hues, and the sweeping roofs – done in an intensely bright red – attract the viewer's attention. To Seung Wan, red is a very meaningful colour symbolizing the sap of life, growth, youth, red cheeks and glowing health, sunshine, and progress.

Whereas his landscapes usually reflect a mood of serenity and peacefulness, his floral paintings evoke a soothingly mellow quality inducing a very comfortable state of mind in the beholder.

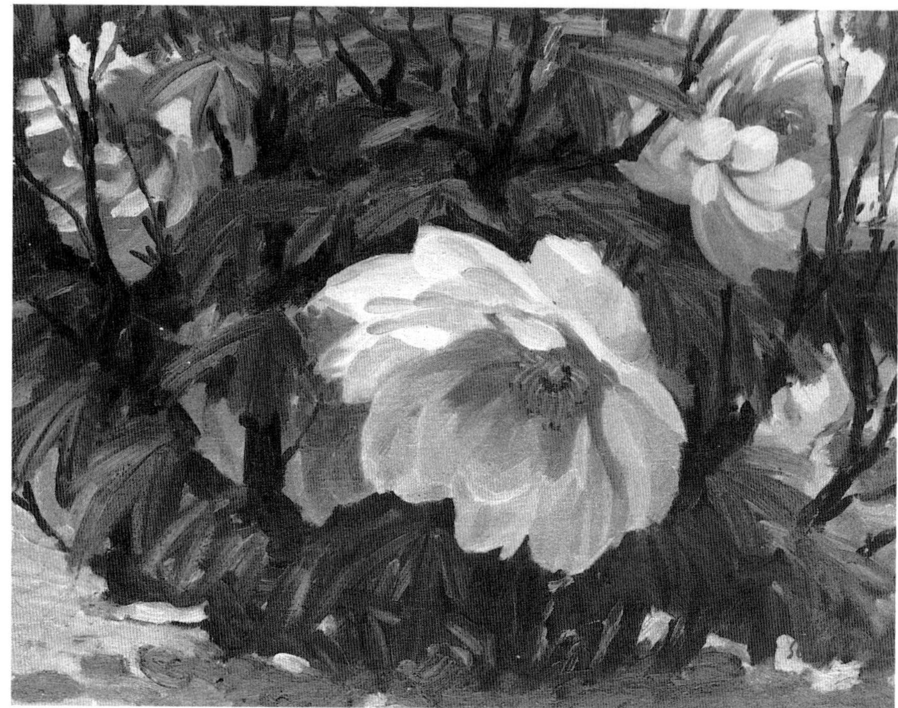

The luxuriance of the various shades of green in petals and leaves is contrasted either with the rich, soft pastels of shy flowers or with coquetish shades of pink. One can sense that the artist himself derives great sensual pleasure from the fragrance of these flowers and the beauty of their richly varying colours and shades. The touches of his brush reveal a particular tenderness for every individual flower. All seem to have a character of their own, ranging from the timid to those bolder ones lusciously opening their petals to the world to be caressed by a breeze, titilated by solar rays and kissed by the bees.

Suddenly in March 1984, when still back in Korea his work, for the first time, showed vibrantly brilliant, explosively electrifying, almost orgiastic colours that are deeply, emotionally charged.

And, now, although but a short time in Canada, he already has had two exhibitions at the Bridgestone Gallery in Toronto, a one-man show & joint show with Key-Min Lee.

At this moment he is only able to paint on weekends and holidays, or whenever he gets time to sneak away from his studies and job. However, he intends to dedicate this summer to painting in the Rockies.

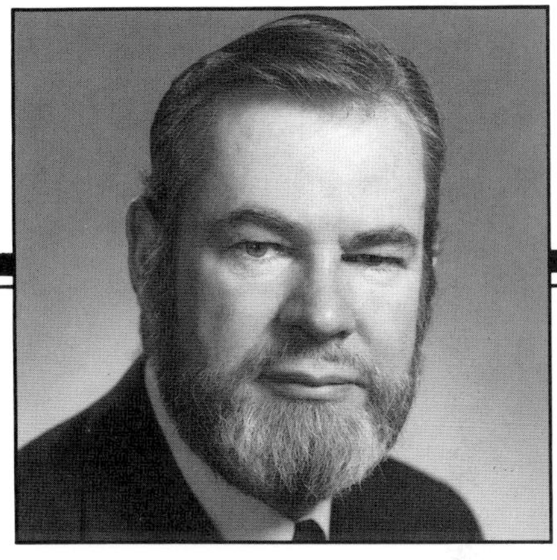

KEN BELL

A strikingly handsome man of admirable bearing; a happy person with the unmistakable face of an artist emphasized by a strong, grey-flecked beard;

excerpt published in the 1982 Spring issue of THE SPIRES Cultural Community Focus)

One of the 1st five photographers awarded a Master of Photograpic Arts (MPA).

Ken Bell, who lives in Etobicoke, is one of Canada's most versatile and gifted photographic artists. His work triggers a gamut of emotions in the beholder. He combines a unique discrimination with special sensitivity and lets his pictures do all the talking. In him one senses the true artist who fuses craftsmanship, imagination and ingenuity with creative talent.

Furthermore, he is the successful author/artist of seven books, and his photographic artwork has been featured repeatedly in THE CANADIAN MAGAZINE: PROFESSIONAL PHOTOGRAPHERS OF CANADA, INC.; NATIONAL NEWS; CANADIAN PHOTOGRAPHY; MACLEAN's; LIBERTY; THE STANDARD and other publications.

How did such a success story come about? It all started with a simple Kodak camera given to Ken by his sister for his 16th birthday. Initially, he took snapshots of his classmates and fellow Boy Scouts until one day in August, 1930, he spotted an R-100 British dirigible majestically sailing over his backyard.

He got a picture of it and, surrounded by his enthusiastic friends, developed it in a small darkroom his father had built for him in the basement. That shot won Ken a prize at Central Technical School, a prize that had tremendous impact on his life and professional orbit.

Ken, who studied to be an architect, had already been accepted by the School of Practical Sciences at the University of Toronto when the Depression thwarted his plans. Other priorities suddenly developed. He had to subsidize the family income and was fortunate to find a job in photography. He worked for several studios, gaining experience. Starting as an apprentice, he familiarized himself with many phases of the field and thus came to know it in depth. He regularly changed jobs to con-

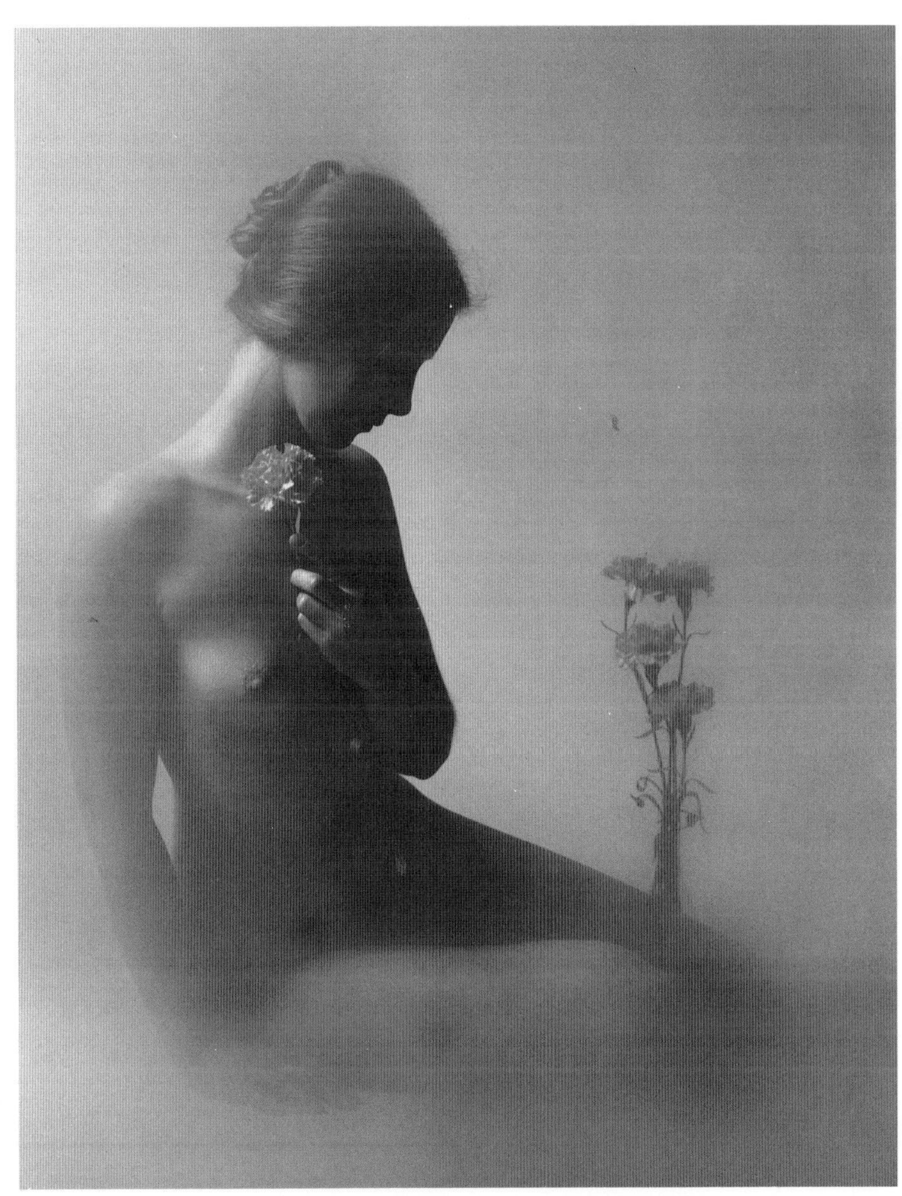

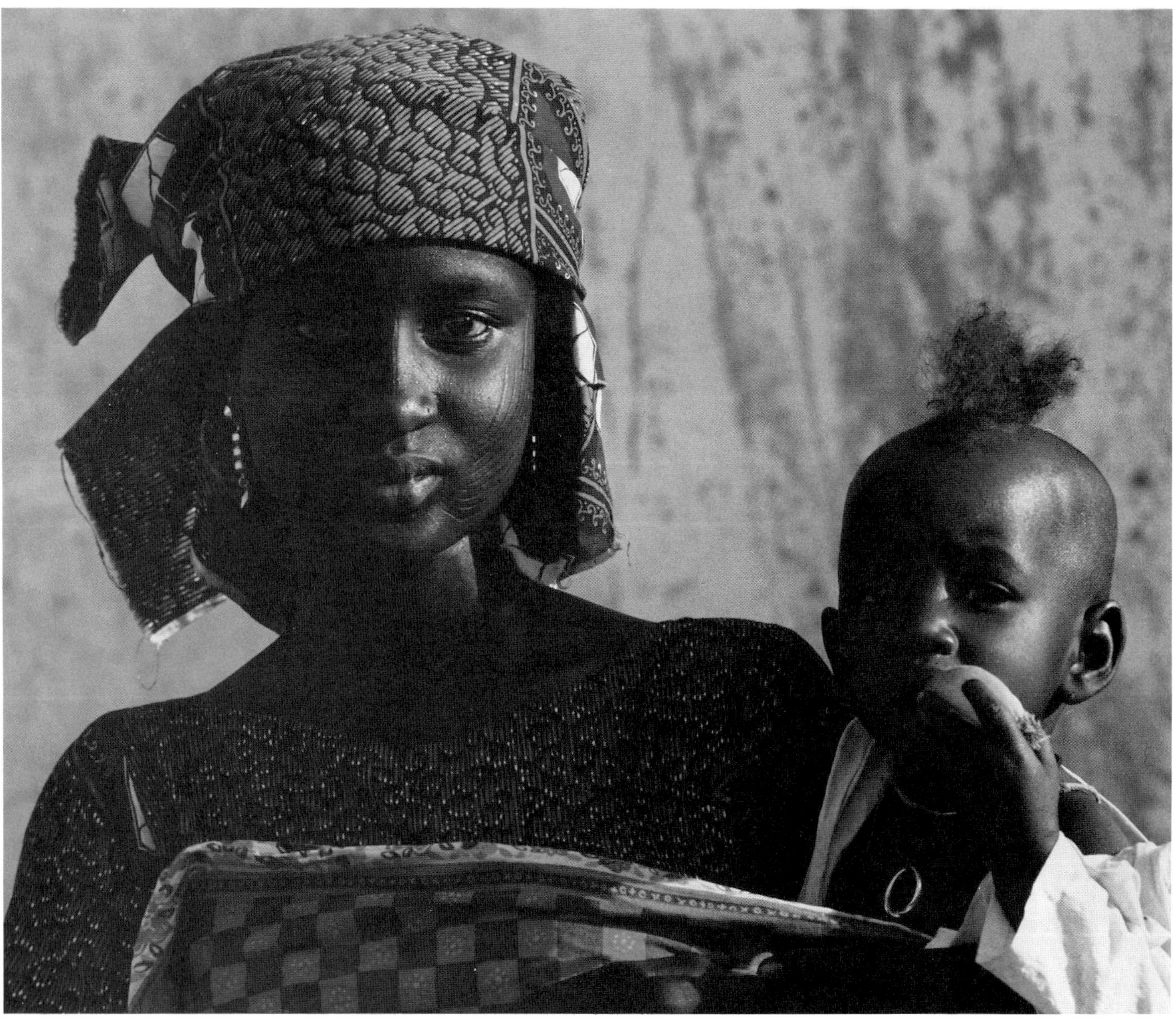

tinue learning and gathered more diversified experience.

Apart from commercial and advertising photography, Ken also did editorial work, covering special events such as the Canadian National Exhibition. He rose to the position of director at several studios.

Ken left the safe confines of a commercial studio and plunged into the turmoil of World War II. As a young Lieutenant he was assigned to the Film and Photography Unit of the Canadian Army, serving as Public Relations photographer in Ottawa. He spent over a year photographing Canadians becoming soldiers, paratroop training, mountaineering and jungle fighting, and took photos for promotion and publicity all across the country.

In early 1944, Ken went Overseas with the army to prepare for the invasion of Fortress Europe and landed in Normandy on D-Day. His art proved to be fantastic for his morale. It helped him to keep busy with his camera while many troops just crouched and waited. Bell captured the history of World War II in pictures which are preserved in his book "NOT IN VAIN". The cruelty of war and the horror of wanton destruction are shown in black and white, and twenty-five years later the same people and places are contrasted in peace. Skilfully, Ken Bell contrasts the battlefield of war with the billowing seas of golden wheat now in their place, juxtaposing the dead, lying face up on the beach, with lovers being caressed by the sun on that very same beach.

Yet in the havoc-wreaking war, Ken

Bell finds rays of hope in
— a soldier carrying his wounded comrade,
— babies being born amidst the inferno of death,
— the intact sculpture of Virgin and Child (Church of Carpiquet)
— a symbol untouched by the ravages of war, and
— the rainbow, a sign of reconciliation between God and man.

In 1945, following the end of the war, as a Major he commanded the Film and Photo Unit in the Occupation of Germany.

In 1946 he returned to Toronto and set up a studio in partnership with Gordon Rice. By 1949, he had opened Ken Bell Photography Ltd. and did much editorial work for MacLean's, Chatelaine and other magazines, continuing with editorial and fashion work until the present day.

Following the war he joined THE ROYAL REGIMENT OF CANADA and in 1962 was promoted to Commanding Officer of his Regiment with the rank of Lieutenant Colonel. He is a Director of the Royal Canadian Military Institute, and an honorary life member. He is also Chairman of the Board of the "THE FAMOUS PEOPLE PLAYERS", the famous black light theatre group.

Meanwhile Bell had many assignments. He travelled extensively throughout the Caribbean where he focussed on fashion, featuring the models with elan and flair. However, Africa seems to hold a special place in his heart. He made five trips there to produce his book on Cardinal Leger, and whenever he mentions that continent, his eyes take on a special glow. He returned there many times to photograph the Nile, the Sudan, and South Africa. He loves the people of Africa who still have "moving stories in their eyes!" Africa is a continent that keeps on luring Ken.

This versatile artists needs continuous variety in his work. He is not limited to any specialty such as fashion or architectural photography, but has an infinite repertoire.

From its founding, Ken Bell functioned for 25 years as official photographer to the National Ballet of Canada, resulting in a book: A CELEBRATION · THE NATIONAL BALLET OF CANADA.

What does he have to say of the outstanding people he has photographed?

THE QUEEN MOTHER: There is nobody nicer than she is, in this world.

PRINCE CHARLES: He is graced with special charm and simplicity, with a warm and genuine interest in people irrespective of their station in life

SOPHIA LOREN: She is beautiful, even with glasses. She and Nana Mouskouri have done more for glasses than anyone else in the world.

Ken knows neither racial nor religious bias, nor does he profess any particular religion or creed. Instead, he feels respect for all beliefs. He is impressed by the architecture of the different religious shrines and takes in the particular atmosphere. He believes in "Some Force" so great in time and space that it would burst a human brain trying to figure out the mystery.

What is he doing at this time? His present studio specializes in advertising photography, food publicity, fashion and editorial work. As well, he has been teaching at the OCA since 1973 (his specialty: advertising photography). Ken particularly enjoyed the warm rapport with the demanding students whose questions kept him on his toes. He was also happy with

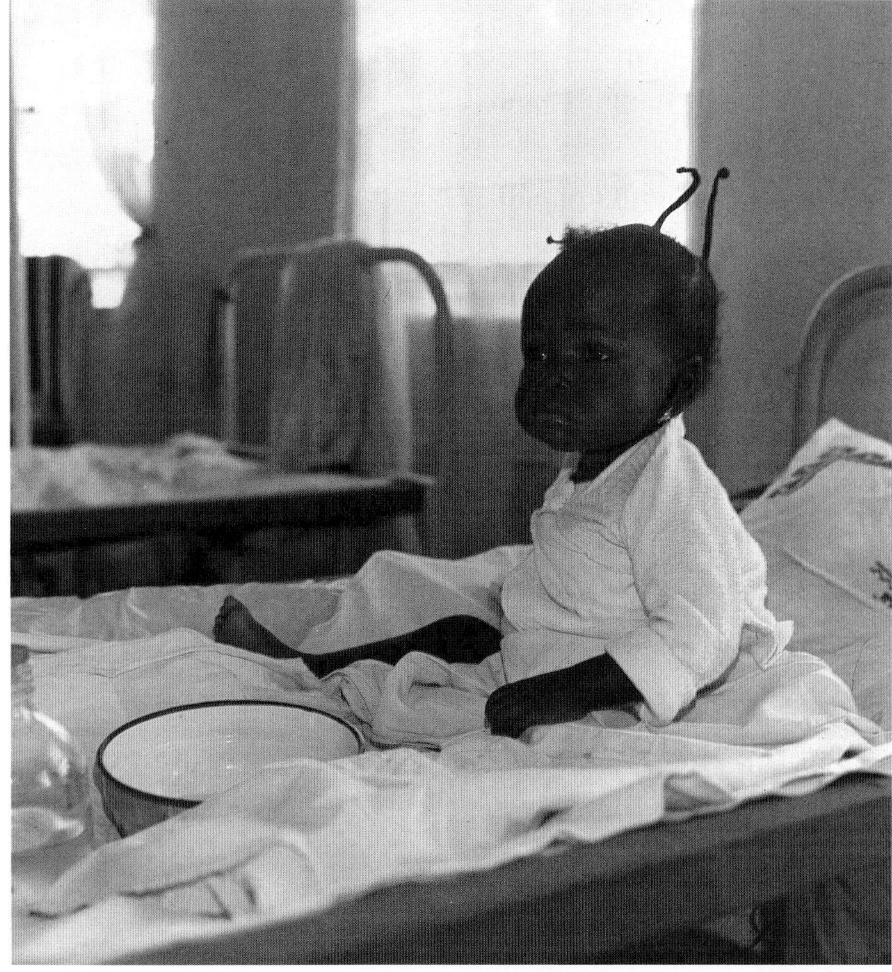

KEN BELL

the wonderful artwork they produced. The bulk of student mail he receives from all around the world, is clear evidence of his quality as a teacher.

Ken, who is creative and innovative, feels that a good photographer must have discipline and be willing to work innumerable hours beyond regular duty. He must really love his art because it is hard work apart from the challenge and excitement. Besides, a good photographer must have a combination of talent, flair, solid background in composition and a feeling for people. In addition, he will need an awareness and appreciation of colour, highly developed professional skill and technical ability combined with persistence and infinite patience. Despite all the work, he will feel greatly rewarded once he has overcome the initial obstacles and witnesses that others enjoy his work.

Ken responds to wholesome competition and greatly values peer group recognition.

He was awarded Fellowship in the Royal Photographic Society in the Spring of 1986 for consistent excellence in photography.

The First Lifetime Achievement Award was conferred upon him in the spring of 1986 by the Can. Association of Photographers and Illustrators in communication (CAPIC).

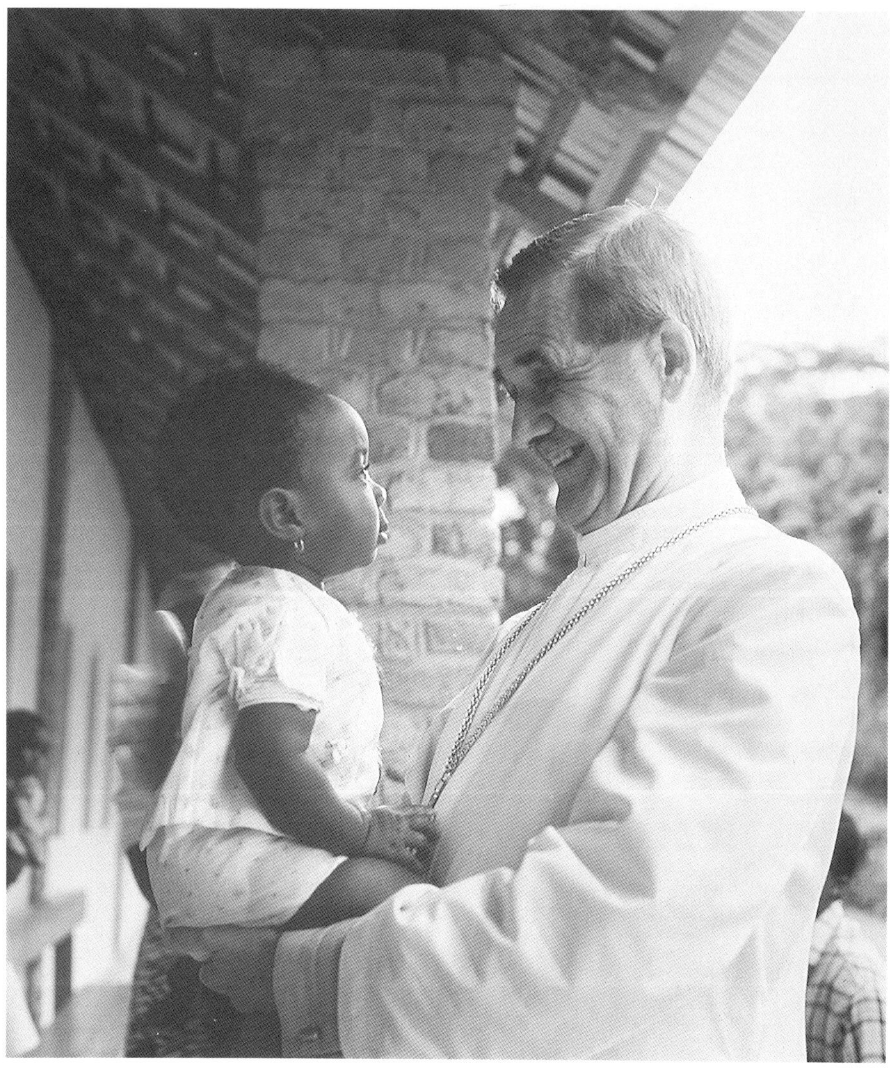

Canadian Paul-Emile Cardinal Léger (from Montreal) with patient friend Lisa at rehabilitation centre for infant African polio victims in Cameroon.

PUBLISHING CREDITS:

1951	CURTAIN CALL — 5-year retrospective
1973	NOT IN VAIN — 25-year retrospective
1974	COLLECTING CANADA'S PAST — English and French versions
1976	OIL LAMPS, THE KEROSENE ERA IN NORTH AMERICA
1976	A MAN AND HIS MISSION: Cardinal Leger in Africa
1978	A CELEBRATION – THE NATIONAL BALLET OF CANADA
1983	100 YEARS ROYAL CANADIAN REGIMENT: 1883-1983

JOHN BOYD

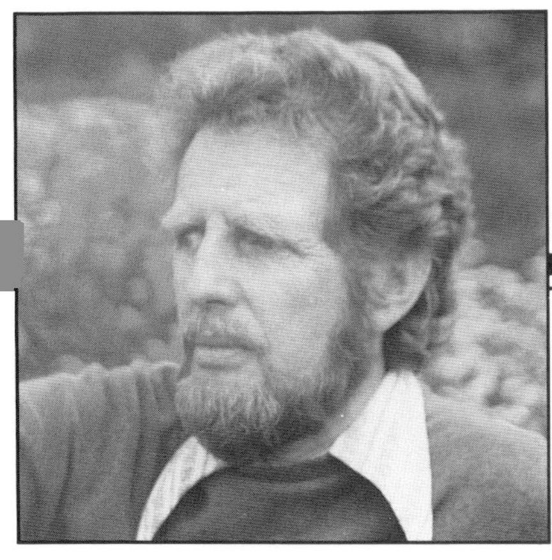

YOU ARE STILL SEARCHING FOR THE ULTIMATE IN LIFE? …John Boyd may help you to develop your own potential

Meet this unique blend of artist and philosopher – an exponent of the NEW AGE philosophy for a tired world –

(excerpt published in the 1981 Fall issue of THE SPIRES Cultural Community Focus)

John Boyd, a man of regal bearing, is six feet tall, has deep blue eyes with a direct, kind gaze and wears an artistic curly beard that frames his face and gives him a most distinguished appearance. He is one of those striking persons who makes an impression wherever he appears.

Here is a man who feels at home in many cultures and even displays the particular mannerisms of each. When he converses in English, he is somewhat more reserved and so are his hand movements, but when he switches from English to Spanish – in a sonorous voice that really carries – his eyes sparkle and he makes ample use of gestures.

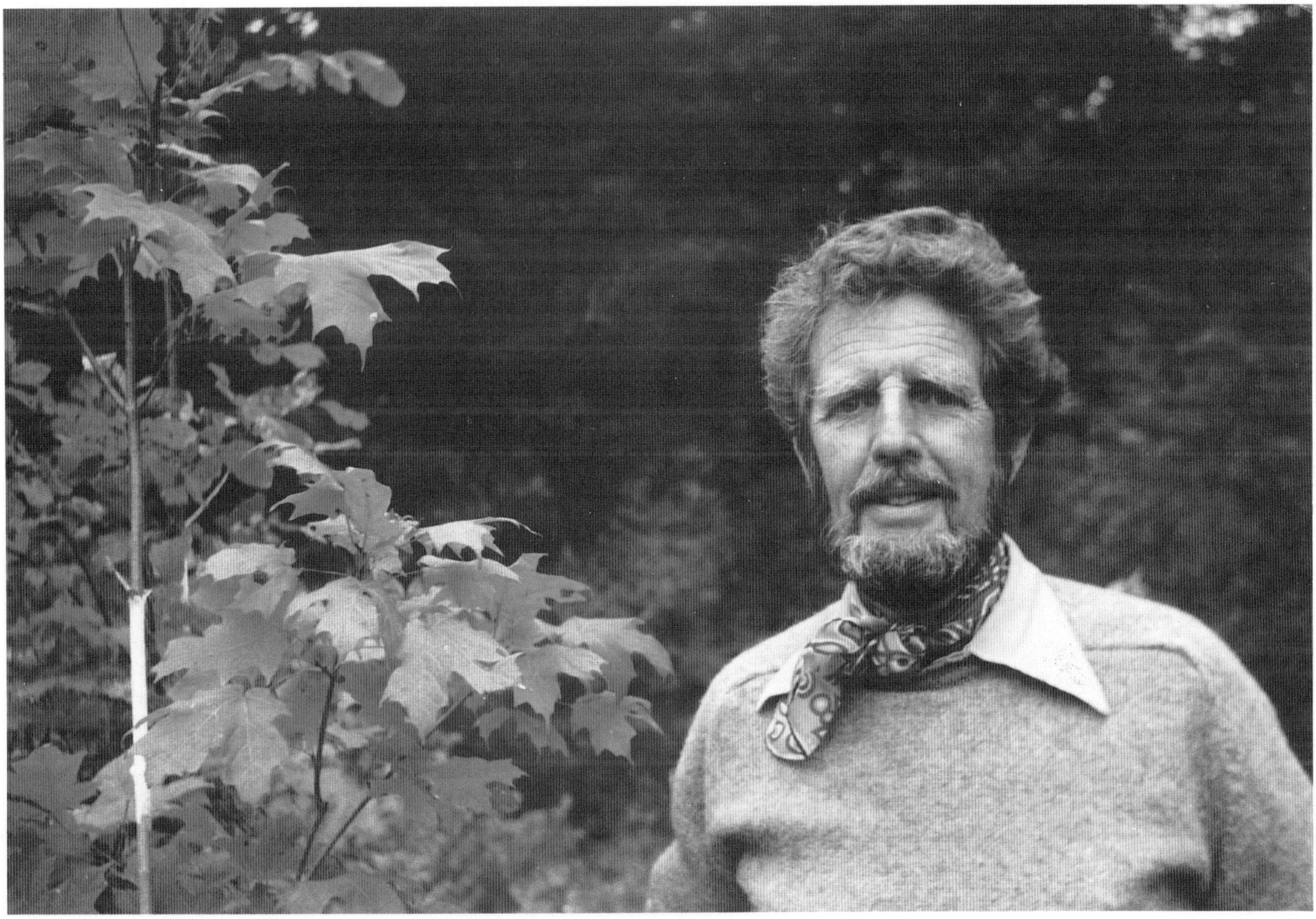

Another aspect that is obvious to everyone is his love for people, an inherent kindness that shines through – a caring in no way impeded by insecurity – for John Boyd would appear to have reached a level

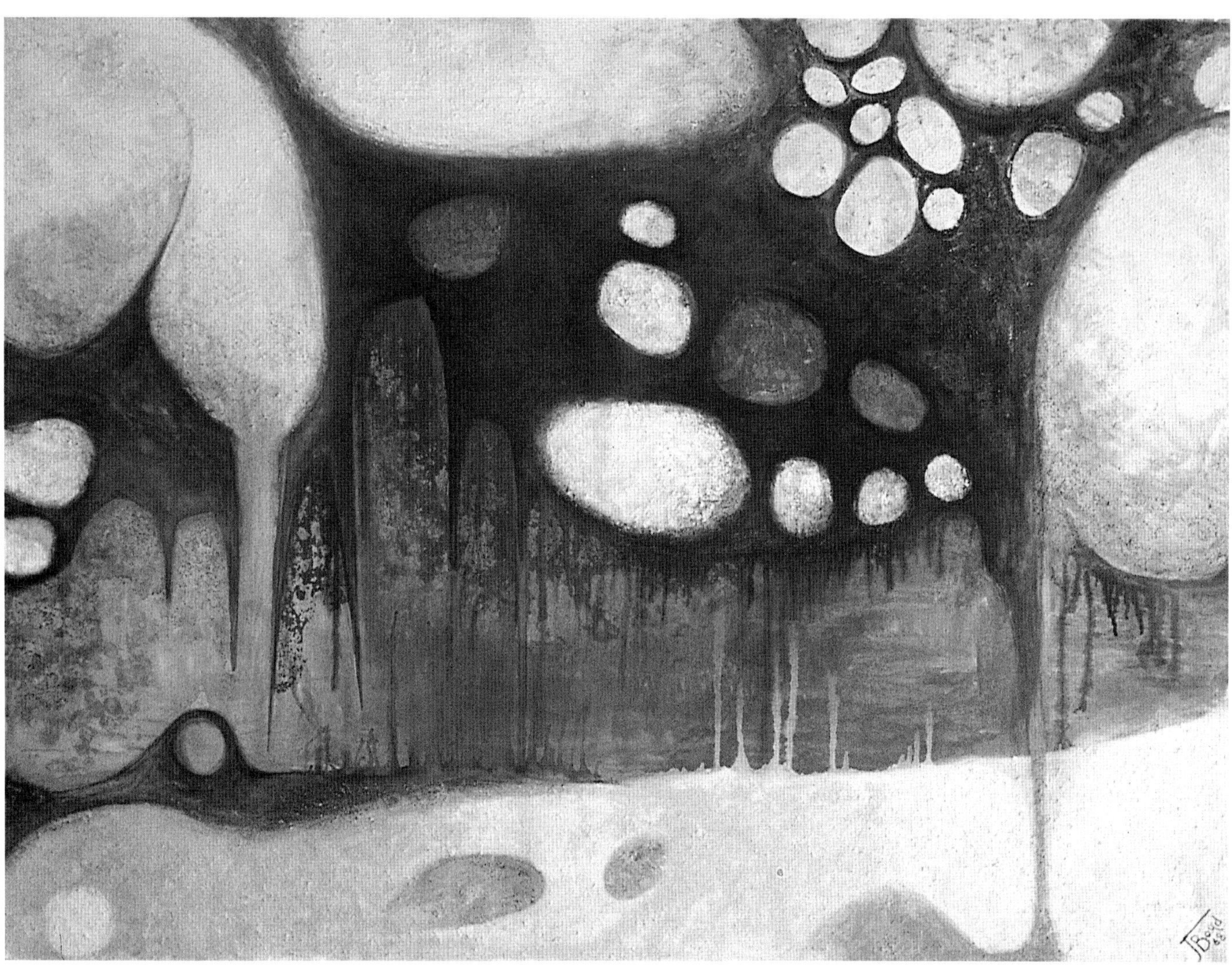

of consciousness where the external differences of role, prestige, image and position are minimally important.

Besides, John is a person who is hard to label. He is always in a state of flux, having sought to divest himself from the need to have authority, position or power. He has been increasingly interested in taking full responsibility for his own life and consequently has given up seeking the guidance of any father or guru figure. He has achieved much personal contentment, not in a self-satisfied or smug way but by finding his own inner peace and personal identity.

How did this Renaissance or New-Age person acquire such an enviable frame of mind? Who or what awakened his interest in uncertainty and his eagerness to step into the unknown? We have to turn for a moment to his colourful background and to the exciting challenges he encountered in different parts of the world. John Boyd was born in 1926 in Spain of English parents, but completed his secondary school education in England where he subsequently enlisted in the RAF. He attended Durham University as a pilot officer and returned there after the war to pursue an honours degree in geology.

He then underwent training as an art teacher at Goldsmiths College in London and taught in several schools, clinics, and hospitals for retarded, delinquent, and seriously disturbed children. He was granted a year's leave of absence to attend the London Institute of Education where he was awarded a special education diploma for work with emotionally disturbed children.

But who influenced him? For one, he felt strongly inspired by the Summerhill School in England, that was run by A.S. Neill, where the rule was teaching without the use of force or coercion but by applying the principles of trust, enthusiasm and caring. Summerhill was basically an educational experiment in applying freedom and love to the process of helping children to grow up with a healthy balance between the mind and the emotions.

John Boyd had his passion for life awakened by Ethel Manning who wrote about the exciting people in her life and among them: A.S. Neill. John wanted to meet Neill and it was on one of his hitch-hiking excursions to do so that he met Eileen, the women who later became his wife.

In 1957 John's particular interest in the field of emotional maladjustment brought him to Canada, as the founding principal of the school within the Thistletown Hospital Treatment Centre for seriously disturbed children. Later he joined the Etobicoke Board of Education as their Assistant Supervisor of Psychological Services.

After a one-year stint back in England, he returned to Etobicoke in 1961 to teach art, and served on the creative arts committee of the Ontario Curriculum Institute. In 1967, he took a Sabbatical Leave and spent the entire year with his family in Mexico. There he earned his Master's Degree in Fine Arts from the Instituto Allende in San Miguel de Allende.

Later he gave up teaching, taking an early retirement, but still remained an educator. For 4½ years he was the co-director of the Abraxas Personal Growth Centre, a therapeutic country retreat.

He has served on the Board of Directors of the Consumer Health Organization of Canada, being active in promoting the wholistic health concept of self-help, promoting the idea that discourages any undue dependency on external props or drugs. He left Abraxas in order to look for what there is beyond the confines of sickness and to explore the more spirtual pathways that lead to self-awareness and human unity.

Boyd is also a practising artist whose work is found in many private and public collections. He painted for many years, doing mainly traditional scenes and, later on, more abstract work, delving into symbolism.

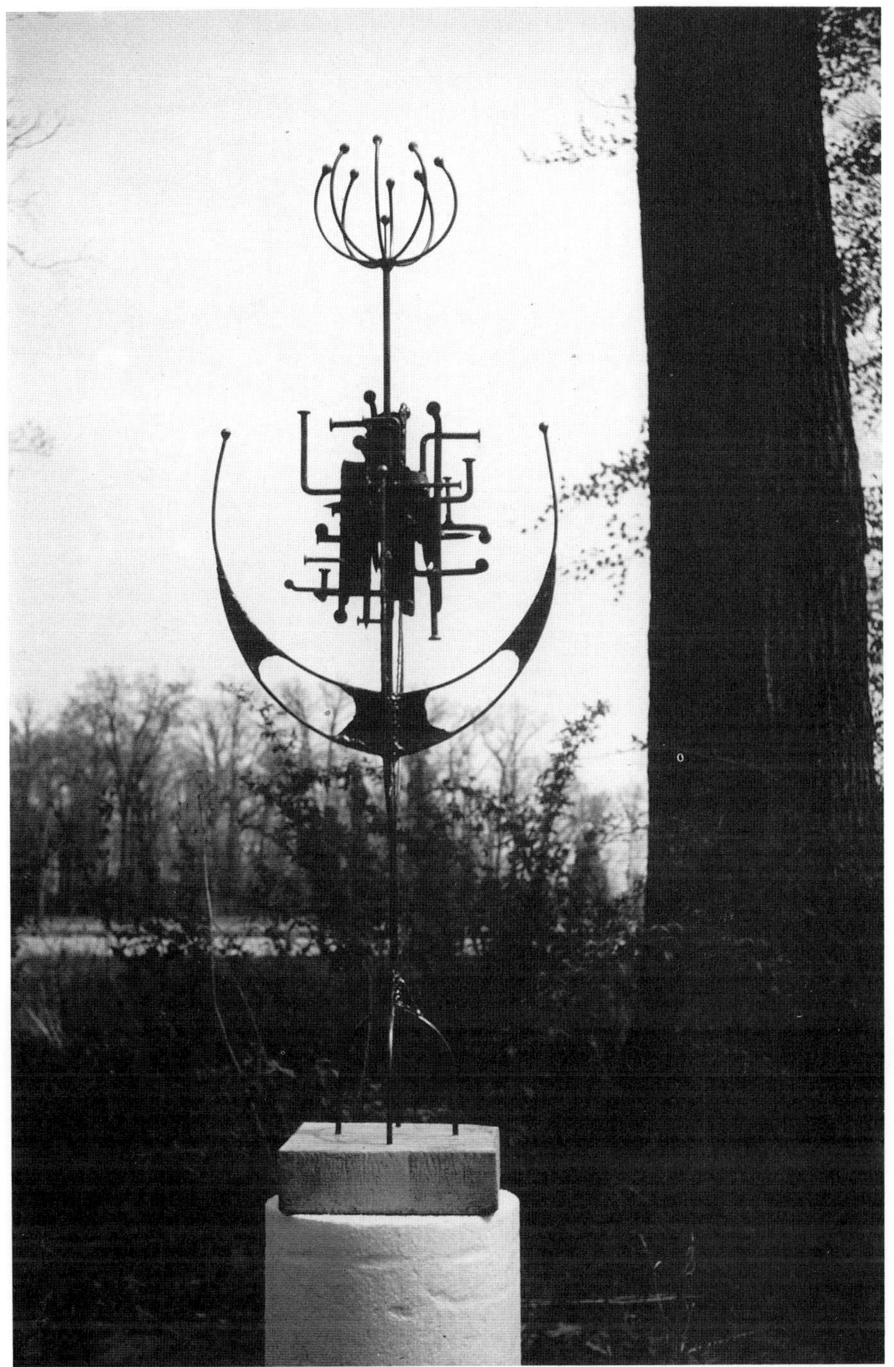

JOHN BOYD

He is also a sculptor and in this art form was engaged in a most intriguing project. He totally dismantled his old Cadillac, once used to take him to Mexico on his yearly pilgrimages to renew his soul. He planned to translate that patched-up old Cadillac into an art show. To that end he spent two months within the confines of his backyard, uncovering the technological wonders of this magnificent car much as an archaeologist digs to discover what is hidden. He actually finished 18 out of the originally planned 150 art pieces, but had to abandon this undertaking due to moving and the lack of space in his new home.

Over the years, Boyd became more and more involved in exploring the unknown and applying positive values to everyday life. Rethinking and reassessing, he became an exponent of the NEW AGE philosophy, a leaderless movement without group identity – a philosophy that gradually refines itself – his involvement in psychotherapy and the human potential movement all opening up tremendous vistas, He enjoyed the extreme satisfaction of applying his newly found insights, and in giving up the more traditional methods of teaching and preaching in favour of a more synergistic way that was practical and yet very much rooted in the uncertainty of life.

This New Age thinker spent a great deal of time on the two basic questions: WHO AM I? WHAT IS THE PURPOSE AND THE MEANING OF LIFE? Besides, he had the courage to do exactly what he wanted to do – to use his hands – with a sense of caring. With a tremendous strength of conviction he set up a handyman service to do anything within the limits of his competence, even at the risk of temporary impoverishment.

John Boyd is not a passive emissary of life but an active do-it-yourself man. It is not surprising that he is a sought-after speaker by various organizations and church groups. He talks on love and its relevance to life.

This highly diversified man also has had his own television show on Channel 10, i.e.: CONVERSATIONS WITH JOHN BOYD, as well as LET'S TALK ABOUT IT, co-hosted with Betty Coulter – a show that ran for two seasons and attempted to involve the public in some kind of in-depth dialogue about life's values.

Besides, he is writing a book provisionally entitled BEYOND RAGE or FOR THE LOVE OF LIFE. His emphasis here is on love and its profound relationship to the crippling factor of fear. He makes us aware that love is the greatest of all human resources, urgently in need of reactivation in our present-day world.

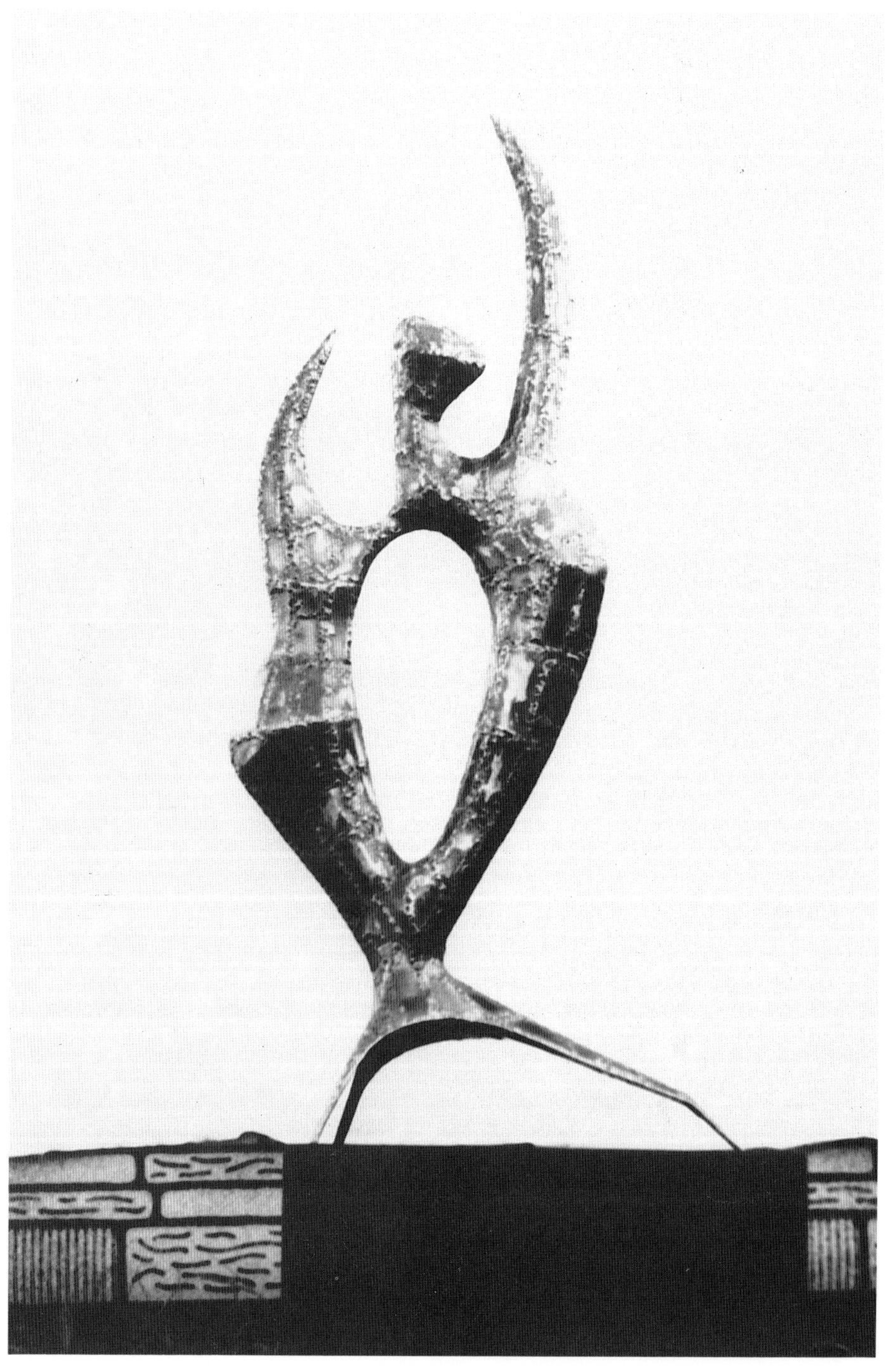

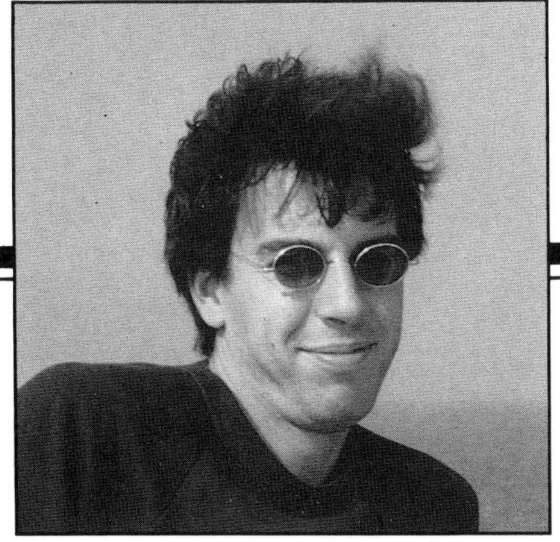

ALEXANDER BULZAN

prolific energetic painter, medical illustrator, innovative advertising designer

Q: What inspired you to be an artist?
A: I was born an artist. There was no question about it. There was no hesitation about it.
Q: How about your schooling?
A: I first attended a boarding school in Montreal. I was there for four years. That school was strict, regimented, but it gave me a good structure – not only as an artist, but even more so as a person. It taught me morals, manners, values – those things that are really important. I find that many people dont' know very much about these qualities anymore.

Everything else after that had a great deal of influence and impact on me, but not as much as the four-year period at that school – I guess because I was very young then. So, coming from a Roumanian and Greek background, I learned French.

Thereafter, I attended an English school that was completely different where I learned the English language.

Until 1971 I was going through structured academic classes like most people in high school, and in 1971/72 I started discovering painting through a teacher. Maud Paradis helped me to forget those views and allowed me some freedom of expression. I guess you might call that liberation from fear and inhibitions. I always wanted to paint and draw and express myself through music. I enjoyed music and rhythm – art being more than a form of two-dimensional expression – but there were still many things telling me to go in an academic direction. It was always a risk and, somehow frightening for me to think about going into the Arts. I am sure people in my situation go through that.

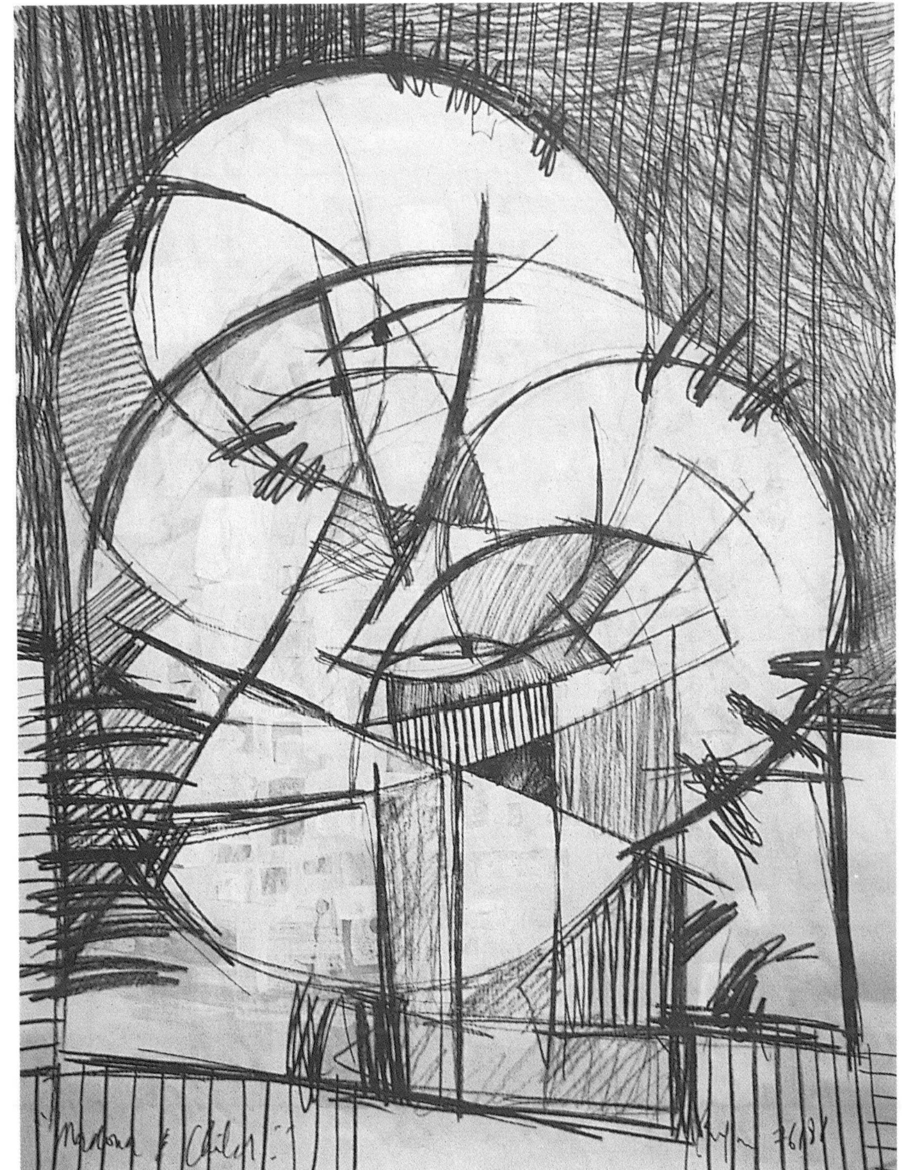

MADONNA AND CHILD 1976

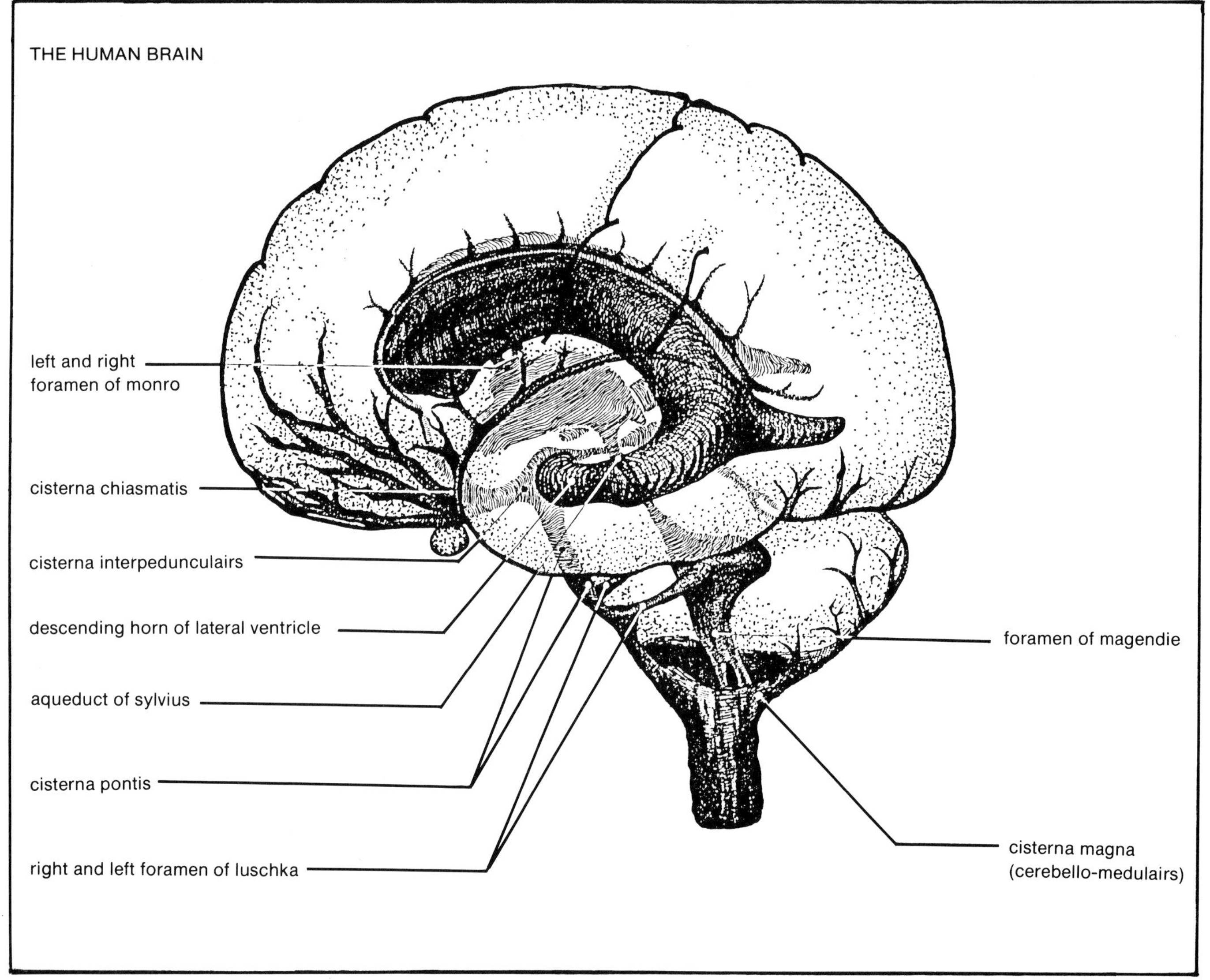

An introduction to the Study of Disease.
7th edition & 8th by William Boyd and

Huntingdon – Sheldon publ. by Lea & Febiger
Philadelphia, Pa.

Q: Were you exposed to pressure from your parents?
A: No. My mother always encouraged me to go into the Arts. It was rather a pressure I felt within. I, myself, was afraid to do it and so much so, that although I was in Fine Arts when I finished my schooling, I worked as a draftsman for an engineering firm.

I decided to go to night school, studying Fine Arts at Vanier College of Montreal five days a week for one year.

I used to work from nine to five as a draftsman and attended classes from seven to ten every night, five days a week. For some reason, I then decided to go into something really academic – dentistry. So I went into Health Sciences at a CEGEP in Montreal. In the Queen's educational system in Montreal, you have to go to a CEGEP first before you can enter university. I took sciences for three quarters of the year 1975.

Our building being a few storeys high, I was waiting for the elevator going upstairs one day. I got into it with a Chinese girl whose name I later discovered, was Anna. She carried a portfolio. Yet there were no artists what - so - ever in that building. On the contrary, people had to come from the Arts Building to ours in order to take Humanities and English. When I got into that elevator with all my science books on my way to the library, there I was suddenly faced with that girl carrying her portfolio. We were the only ones in the elevator, and the door closed. I sort of looked at her and said something brilliant like: "Oh, you must be an artist?" She smiled. Then I asked her where she went for art. She said: "Delormier campus – an advertising-illustration type of school." I was really interested. I wanted to do something – some art – but I wanted the structure.

At that time, I did not understand why

people painted stripes on canvases or conceptualized art. I did not understand anything about fine art then. All I knew was that I wanted to do art – something structured, even as structured as medical illustrations or something like that. The elevator was going up. So I just went to the Registrar's Office on the top floor and enrolled on the spot. Just like that, I transferred.

So, the following September I was in commercial art doing illustrations, and I loved it. Then I went to Europe. When I came back I was in such a good frame of mind that I would do three times the amount of work necessary. At the end of the year, when everyone had a panel of their year's work, I had several. I did not have to think about it – it just flowed, and it was exciting. It was a most productive time. I was doing exactly what I wanted to do.

Soon, after two years, having read and heard about OCA, I again took the elevator and changed. That's the route I took to Toronto.

Q: What did your parents say?

A: They did not fight my decision but obviously they were not happy, that I was that far away. I have been here for six years.

Q: Would you like to comment on your being in Toronto?

A: When I first came, it was great. I was as free as anyone could possibly be. Being in a different city was a whole new experience for me. I had to do my laundry, cook, buy groceries, budget money. It was good, although I was also sad – something that showed in my work – because Toronto was so different. It took me about a year to get settled, and some good friends helped. Friends are so important.

It was nice being in an environment full of eccentric people. OCA, at that time, it seemed to me, was full of crazy people; paintings were all over the place. Everyone was doing something. So, OCA was a good experience.

I originally intended to go back to Montreal but I somehow liked Toronto and the freedom I enjoyed. I liked everyone. And I just happened to get a job. I guess part of it was skill but a lot of it was luck, fate maybe. I could be in Australia right now, but I'm here!

Q: What do you aim to achieve through your art?

A: I like to think of myself as a design problem solver. I read once that my name, ALEXANDER stands for HELPER OF MAN.

Q: In which way are you going to help them in design? Is it by way of teaching?

A: The teachers I respect are those who don't whip you into shape but help you unfold your potential. A good teacher has so much to give – so much time and so much energy. Of course, it is helping the teacher himself, to dedicate all his time and energy to his students.

Q: Do your believe in mental or physical strength through freedom?

A: Yes, in mental freedom, first of all. Physically, some people need freedom – some don't. To me, the all-important thing is mental. It is so important because people have ideas inside and they have to put them on paper or just get them out. Sometimes you feel afraid that someone is going to laugh at you. You don't want to do it but if you don't, you go crazy. You have to to it. That's why you need freedom. Everyone who understands what I am saying, knows exactly what I am talking about – I mean, it's not something you can easily put into words.

Q: Are you different from other artists you know?

A: In graphic art, right now, I am exactly the same as other artists — but I am not the same as a lot of people because I am living a lot. There are many people out

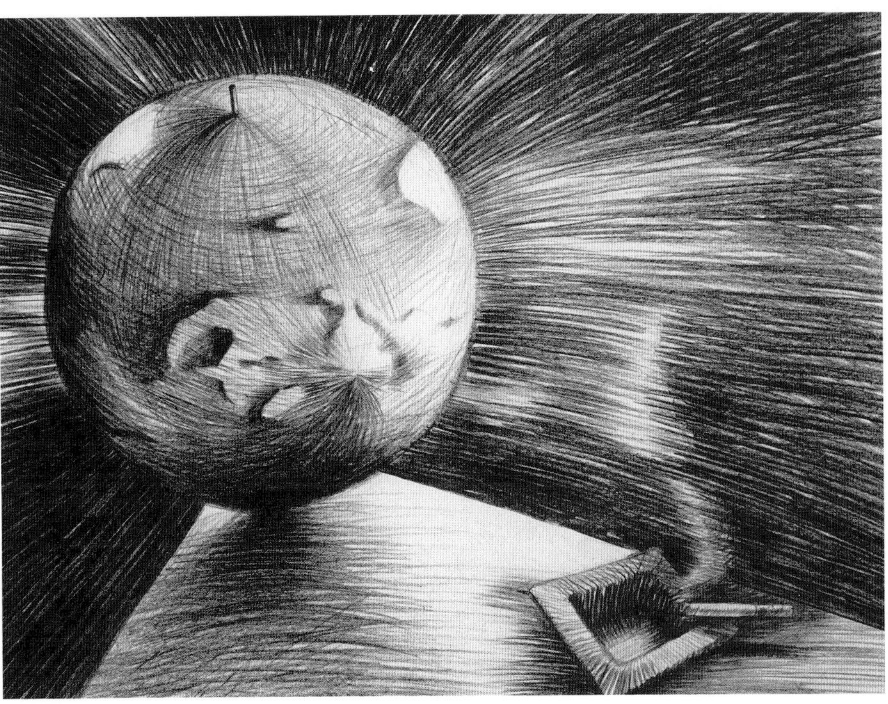

UNCONTROLLABLE URGE
1984 photo by Chris Gosso

there — a lot of talented people. In this field, it's hard to be different; yet some day I am going to be.

Advertising is business. It's not pure enough for me.

Q: As an artist, what would you like to do?

A: You are talking about freedom. I would like to design buildings. I would do whatever anybody would give me an opportunity to do.

Q: Do you have any hobbies?

A: Yes, music and anything that gives me energy like walking on the street. I like walking. I like music. I don't think of it as a hobby though. I don't play the guitar – I just make a lot of noise, but it gives me pleasure. Everyone should have a noise-maker in the house. Seriously, that's what you need.

Moving is healthy, too. I watched the movie, FAME — something about the Performing Arts that no other art can touch —a lot of energy. That's the new way and I like it.

Many artists from OCA, in the past few years, have become musicians. There are lots of bands out there and even if you think of musicians like David Bowie, John Lennon, and others, I guess you'll find — when looking into their background — they all came from the arts schools. They

realized something. You can hang stuff in a gallery and have people come to look at it, but if you are not there to explain it, it can't possibly explain itself the same way — what's missing is the energy that was there when it was painted or built. It's something that can't be duplicated. Performing artists do it over and over —ideally, full of energy every time. You are expecting too much from people — that they go to an art gallery and understand some of the things they see and I don't think you can expect that from them.

Q: Do you dance?

A: Only in my head. I am serious. Don't laugh at me. It's really important to know.

Most people go through life not knowing what is good for them or what they are good at. That's really unfortunate and quite sad that there are people who go through life not enjoying what they do. Enjoying one's life — to be happy — should be everyone's top priority, I feel. I am fortunate enough to know what I want to do, irrespective of whether I succeed at it or not in the eyes of the people around me. That does not really matter to me as long as I die with a smile on my face. That I will have because it is something that I control; something nobody else controls. I may not have enough money — I may not

have what people think I should have — but I will have my smile on my face. I'll probably die underneath a pile of paintings, I hope.

Q: Do you have any favourite artists?

A: I have favourite artists. I think that the artists today have come a long way. At one time, it may have been enough to do 'nice' pictures. Today, conceptual art — not necessarily the end product, but the thought process, the psychology involved — is interesting! Fascinating!

I like Picasso — as a person. I don't really like waking up in the morning, doing five stretches before lunch and three pieces of pottery, sculpture, and two paintings by the time he went to sleep. I like the fact that he could sit down and do all that. If he could have lived for 300 years — he would still be doing the same.

I love Matisse because, even though he could not hold a pencil in his hand when he got old, he had enough strength to pick up a pair of scissors and do cut-outs — the strength behind it — it's just not human! To a regular human being, the loss of his hands would be so devastating, but to someone who is truly an artist it does not matter even if he loses his sight. In art, all you need is your head — a good head, a good brain.

TRAVEL USA — "A little invitation from the folks next door."

TRAVEL USA poster — promotion to encourage Canadians to travel to the USA

photo by Mohammed (Mitu) Khaledul Hacq

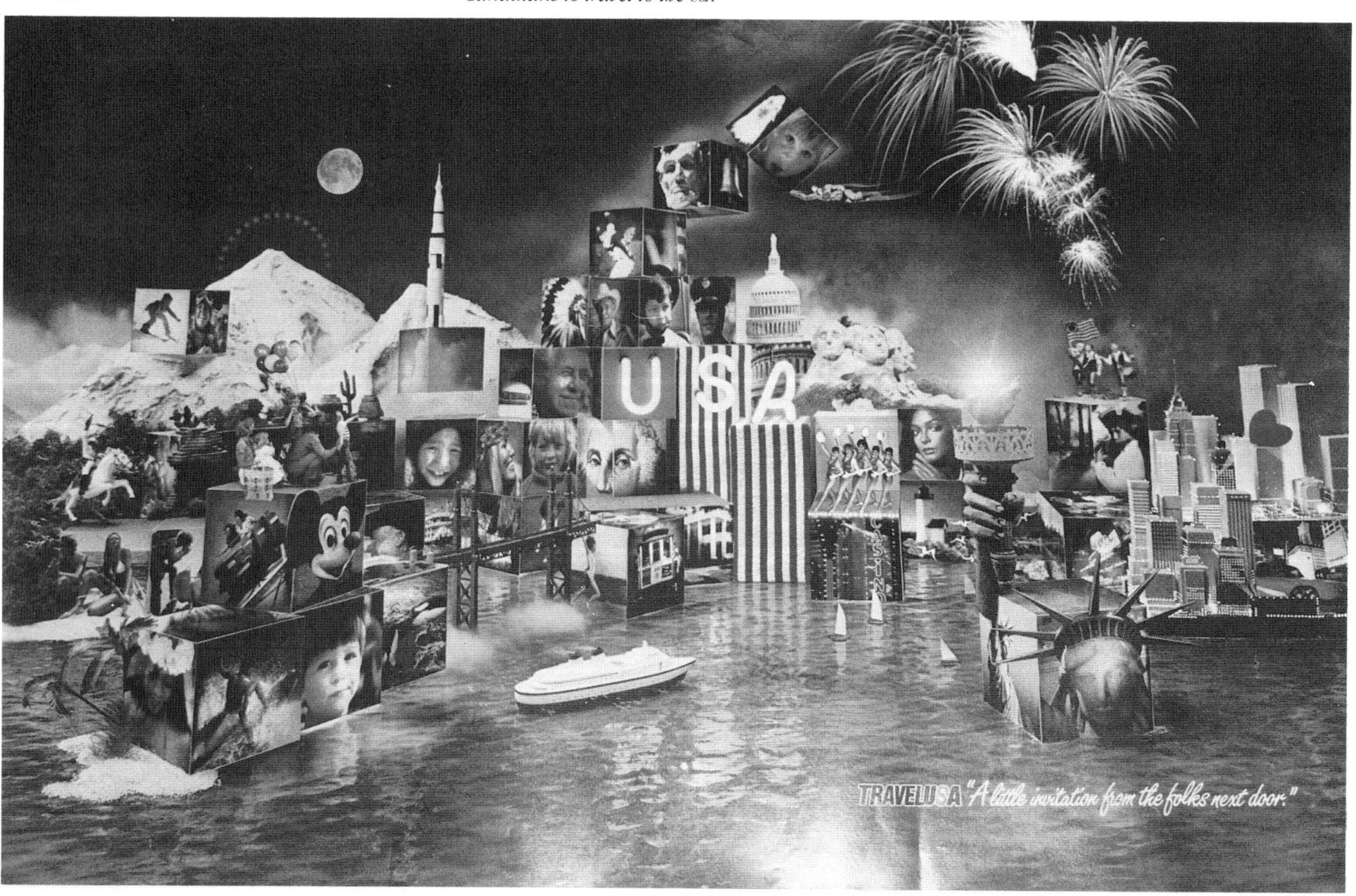

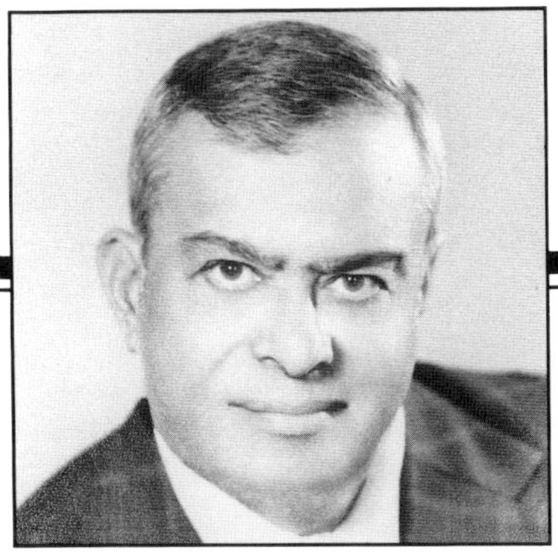

LADIS DA SILVA

exponent of realism, with special emphasis on Canadian native art

(excerpt published in the Summer 1981 issue of THE SPIRES Cultural Community Focus.)

Ladis, who was born in Zanibar in 1920, spent about twenty years in Kenya. He came to Canada in 1968 where, that same year, he had a one-man show at a Bank of Nova Scotia branch in Mimico.

His talent was initially inspired by the breathtaking African scenery with its glorious sunrises and sunsets. It was brought to fruition by sincere dedication combined with a relentless working discipline, supported by the loving and persevering encouragement of his parents.

Ladis, who also writes, illustrated his own book entitled THE AMERICANIZATION OF GOANS, and also drew the cover for LEGENDARY GOA featuring a sepia-tone rendition of the old church of Chandor. This clearly reflects the painter's faith, for the church is lovingly sketched in great detail and placed amidst a setting teeming with lush growth, the focus being on the church with all the branches and leaves swaying towards the sacred shrine as if to heighten the emphasis. Although but a small-scale sketch, the viewer is immediately familiarized with three of Ladis' greatest assets: flawless perspective, structural unity, and exquisite texture.

The illustrations for THE AMERICANIZATION OF GOANS reveal salient facets of the painter's personality, i.e. his love of nature and his love for people. Ladis, who considers Africa the Garden of Eden, being blessed with an abundance of wildlife of myriad species with the law of LIVE AND LET LIVE reigning supreme, drew the animals from first-hand studies in the jungle. He was simply fascinated by the fact that, although wildlife is so plentiful and varied, the animals live, in general, without causing clashes. All of them have their different characteristics; yet all subordiante themselves to a higher order — ethnic rivalry being unknown among them.

THE GIANT ARAB DHOWS BEING REPAIRED AT THE ZANZIBAR CREEK is another fine example of magic realism, dhows, boats, caravels, and Portuguese galleons being this painter's special forté. Ladis knows how to create a three-dimensional effect without impairing the overall fluidity.

Interviewer: I see you do mainly pen-and-inks nowadays, enhanced by the wash effect. When exactly did you leave your oils and water colours behind and adopt this technique?

Ladis: There can be no question of wilfully adopting a technique. It was rather a unique coincidence that brought about the use of this medium.

I had started painting in the early morning and was so absorbed that I did not even notice the rain setting in. It caught me totally by surprise. When I felt the first drops, I was furious and feared the rain might have ruined my work, but to my amazement, I found that — on the contrary — the splashes had given the painting a new form of life. Dismay was followed by the joyful excitement of having detected a new effect.

I guess in my case changes were brought about, mainly, by circumstances. I started out with water colours and oils at St. Joseph's Convent School in Zanzibar where I was given excellent training and unlimited scope.

A mangrove swamp on the East Coast of Africa with a small craft (in the background) sailing into the lagoon.

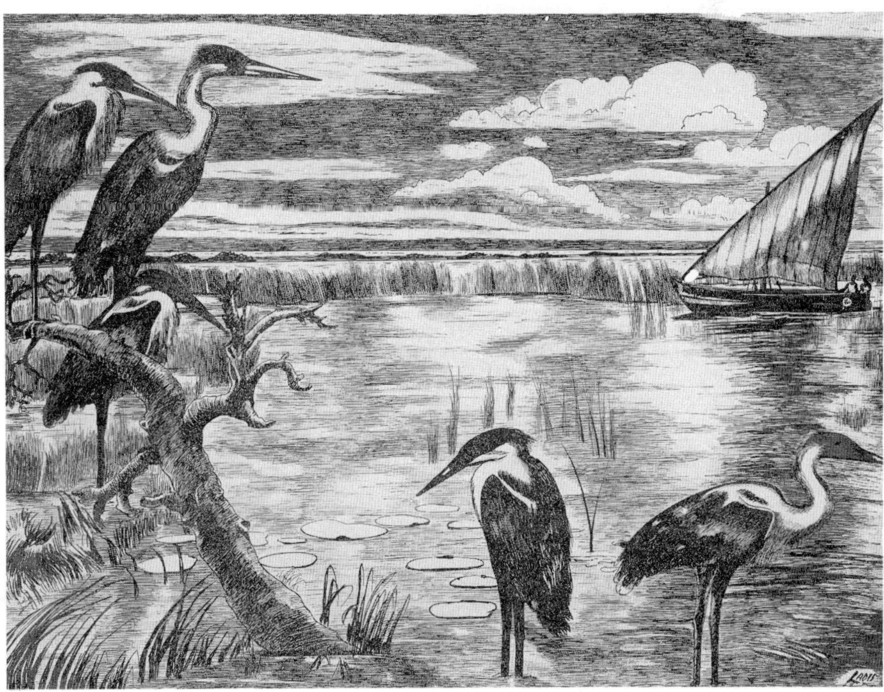

LADIS DA SILVA

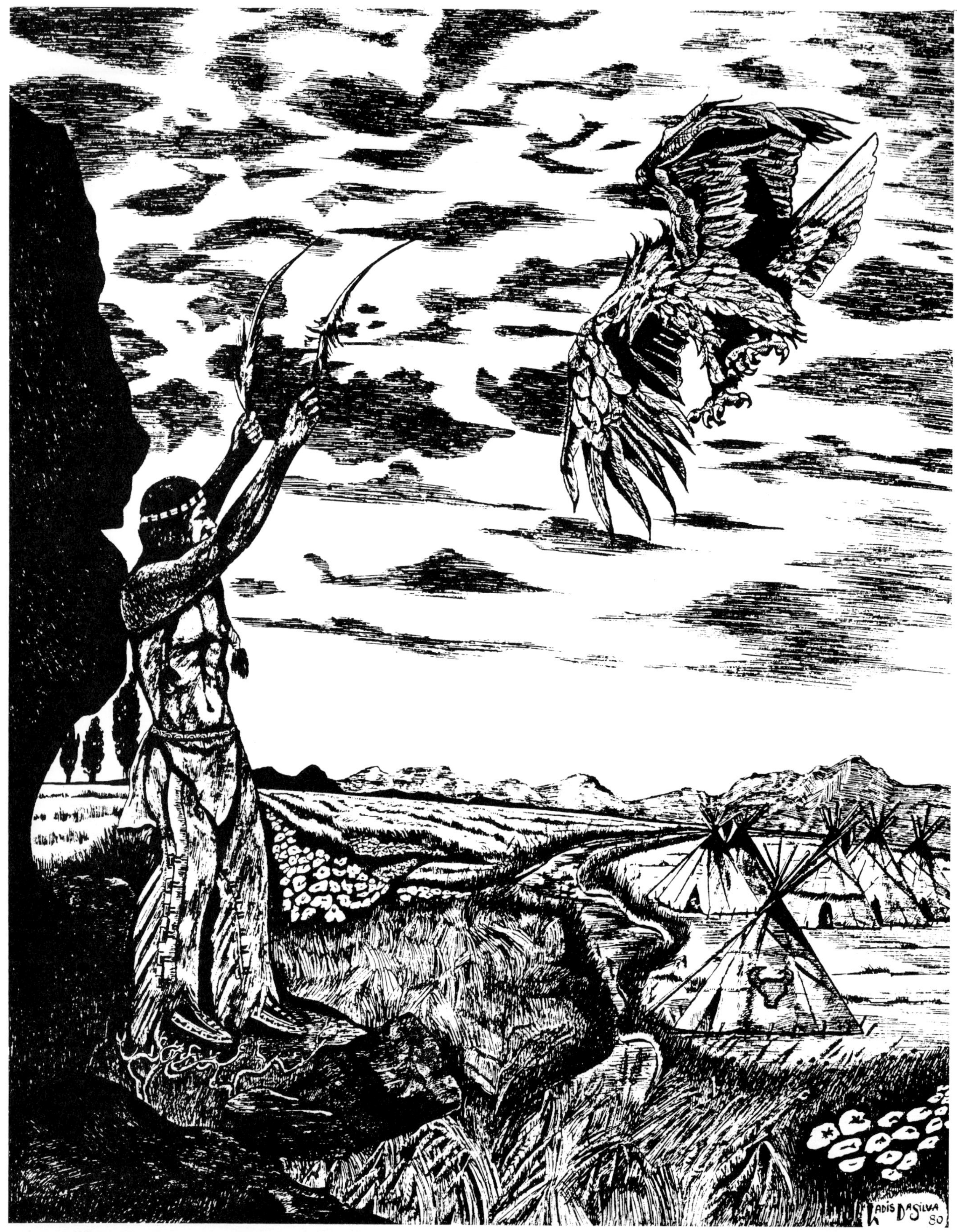

Chief caught in the act of worshipping the sun god, raised feathers being part of the religious rite. The soaring eagle holds special importance as central inspirational life force, standing for everything virile and courageous.

photo by Elizabeth Verkoczy

During the war years, for instance, when there were shipping problems, I specialized in Christmas Cards for the VIPs of the Military Forces. From time to time I also did graphic design work for major enterprises.

I also did calendars, on commission, for wealthy art-loving clients, and numerous drawings on parchment that were subsequently used as lampshades. Then, towards the middle of the Forties, pen-and-inks became an important medium for me.

Interviewer: Did you belong to any arts societies or clubs in those years?

Ladis: Not only as a member, but I was also the founder of several arts and crafts societies on the African continent.

Interviewer: Did you participate in any shows?

Ladis: I had several one-man shows and also group exhibitions in Zanzibar and Kenya.

At times, those glorious African settings still surge in my dreams and, all excited, I then paint them next morning from my carefully stored mental notes.

interviewer: When do you feel most creative?

Ladis: Mainly under hardship or deprivation. It makes my creative juices flow, acting, so-to-speak, as catharsis. It releases suffering and relieves agony.

Interviewer: When was your last exhibition in Canada?

Ladis: I participated in the art exhibition at Harbour Front in August 1982, held under the auspices of the Goan Overseas Association.

Interviewer: Do you follow any particular routine?

Ladis: Well, I usually paint seven days a week from 9 in the morning until 10 in the evening. I start, stimulated by the chirping of the birds, and put in breaks only for church service and meals.

I do not need artificial background music nor any other stimulants to keep me going for hours on end. I thoroughly enjoy painting.

Interviewer: Trees seem to be one of the motifs constantly recurring in all your work.

Ladis: Yes, because to me they symbolize life in its multi-faceted stages. Trees are useful to the land and beneficial to man, affording shade to the weary wanderer.

Interviewer: Your latest paintings seem to concentrate, exclusively, on Canada's native peoples.

Ladis: It all started back in Zanzibar when I was still a little boy. In those days, I would enjoy watching wild west movies and also felt inspired by the Canadian native folklore.

As soon as I came to Canada, I purchased as many books dealing with North-American Indians as I could find, for an in-depth study. Having met Chief Dan George at Massey Hall some years ago, I felt a strong bond with the native peoples whom I like for always thinking of their brethren first. I was so fascinated that I stayed on reserves for first-hand immersion.

I listened to their elders and observed them doing their handicrafts. My pen sketch illustrated the January, 1981, issue of the international monthly magazine, GOA TODAY, featuring an article of mine on Chief Dan George and the Canadian Indians.

REFLECTIONS

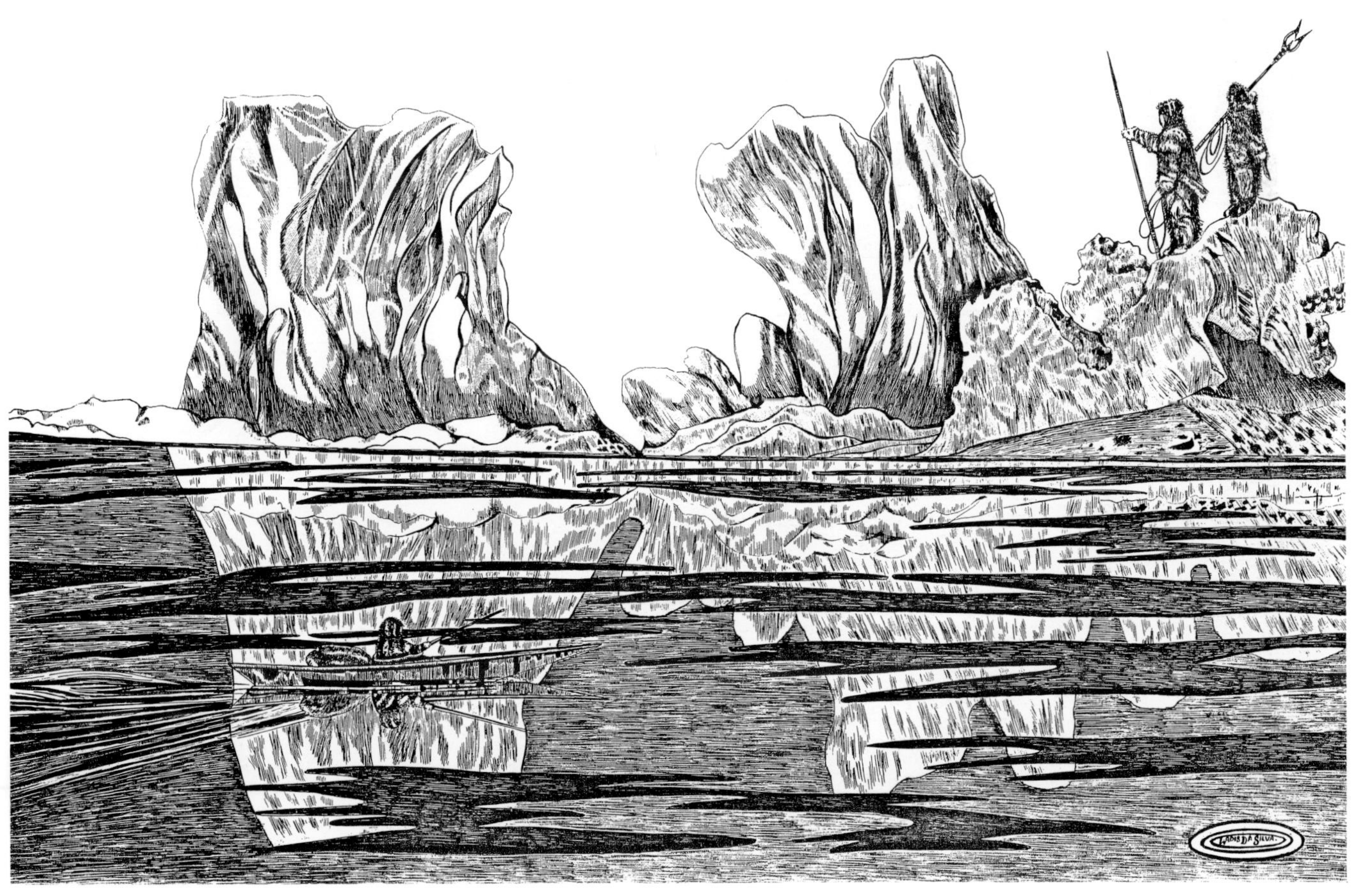

LADIS DA SILVA

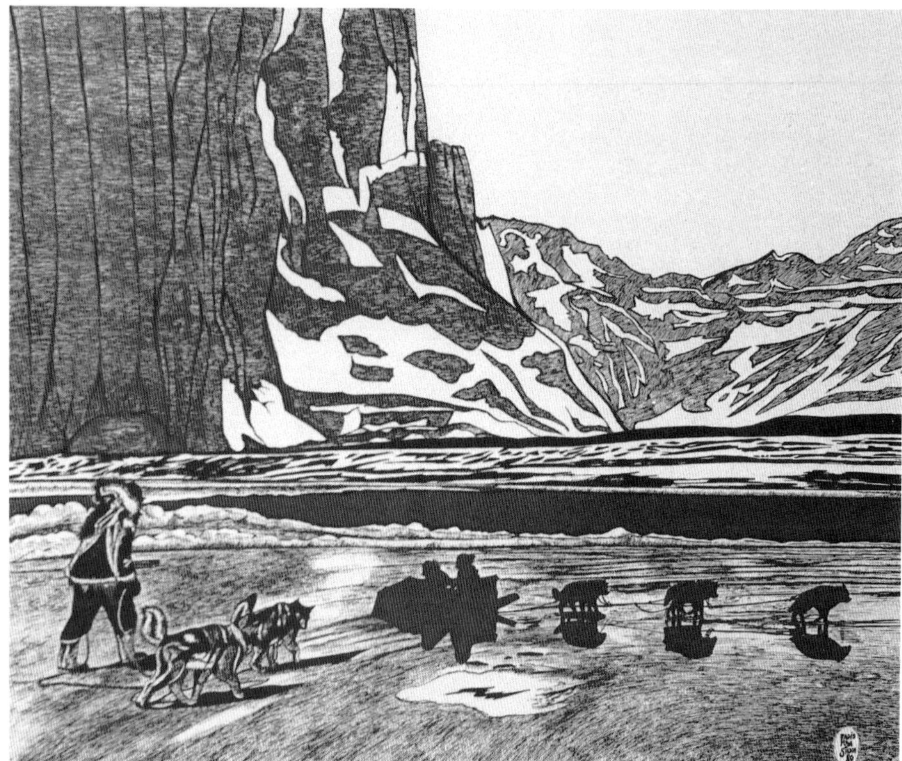

Interviewer: Have you ever submitted any of these magnificent paintings to any local paper?

Ladis: Yes, my pen and ink sketches have been featured on a regular basis in the TORONTO NATIVE TIMES.

Interviewer: That homage speaks for itself.

Your Canadian native paintings do more than merely depict the natural setting. They clearly reflect a lifestyle. I would even go so far as to maintain that they vibrate with the love and concern you feel for the people.

Ladis: I made their concerns my concerns. My heart is with them and I am so happy about their sudden spiritual revival movement.

Interviewer: The gigantic bison predominating an entire scene, has a symbolic meaning, doesn't it?

Ladis: Yes, the bison is a good omen, and this particular painting depicts a brave youth leaning against a rock. He has just heeded the words of wisdom spoken by his elders, was initiated by them and subjected himself to three days of rigourous fasting. Full of inspiration, he then withdrew to the rock where he had his vision — away from his familiar settlement bustling with activity where life goes on as usual.

Most of the native people are still in touch with nature and not yet blind to the beauty so lavishly bestowed by our Creator.

Another painting with special appeal shows a chieftain leaving his settlement in the valley, accompanied by his lovely young wife who carries their baby on her back on a cradleboard, her horse pulling a travois as was customary in the Plains quite some time ago.

The courage of the chief who is on the lookout for herds moving northward, is externalized in the eagle soaring in the air.

Interviewer: I see your interest in Canada's native peoples also covers the brave Inuit.

Ladis: My special admiration for the Inuit made me attend centres for discussion sessions where I had the opportunity to watch them at work on their soapstone carvings. Their folklore strongly appeals to me.

Interviewer: In this picture, the grandiose setting of the Inuit approaching the sea is so real that one immediately feels transported to the northern milieu with its bone-chilling cold. It brings out the challenge shown by man pitted against nature which knows no mercy — nature that is indifferent — with man courageously fighting the obstacles for sheer survival.

Could you ever paint another scene just like that?

Ladis: No, because I do not believe in the reproduction of artwork. To me, art holds an intrinsic value. Besides, a lot of effort and pain goes into every piece of work.

In my opinion, commercialization would cheapen artwork.

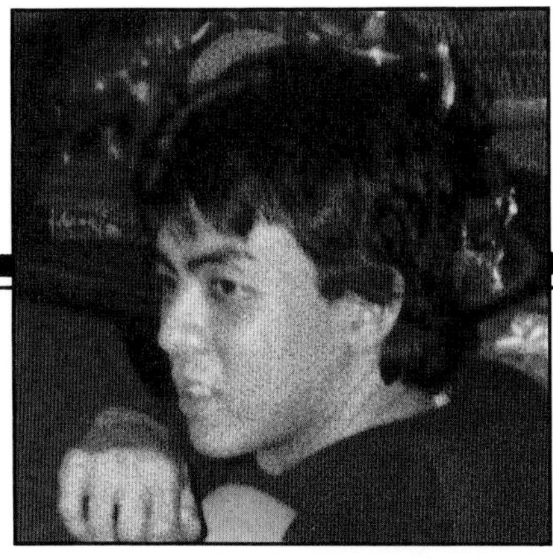

ANDRE ELIAS

painter of explosively vibrant colours, painstaking miniaturist, innovative sculptor and ceramist

(previously published in RIKKA, *Summer 81 issue, vol. 8 #2.)*

This versatile artist is a strong exponent of intercultural art — Native Canadian, Asian, and European. Born on January 4th, 1952, in Banyuwangi, Indonesia, of Chinese origin, Andre studied in the Federal Republic of Germany before his arrival in Canada. Although reserved by inclination, Andre radiates a spontaneous warmth which draws one to him immediately.

Andre: "You may have to draw some of the information out of me" says Andre. "Please don't think that I am reticent to answer — not at all! I just feel that a painter should let his hands do all the talking."

On that note the interview begins…

Interviewer: "I see you let your plants grow wild."

Andre: "But of course…because that uncontrollable growth reminds me of my painting which arises out of the subconscious and, so-to-speak, dictates the outlines of form and inspires the brilliance of colour."

Interviewer: "And yet I sense an underlying discipline, even though I know that your painting borders almost on compulsion. "I guess it must initially have come as a real shock to your family when you told them about your decision to dedicate yourself wholeheartedly to painting, sculpting, and fabric design."

Andre: "Yes, it did. According to Chinese tradition, my parents insisted on a 'solid profession' for their son so that he may some day become a good provider for a hopefully large family. Mind you, I did finish my general business course in order to please my parents. Fortunately, however, they did not realize that I stole as much time from my studies as I could in order to paint or experiment with sculpting. I did most of my assignments as fast as possbile to have ample time for indulging in work after my own heart, at my own leisure, in my own style."

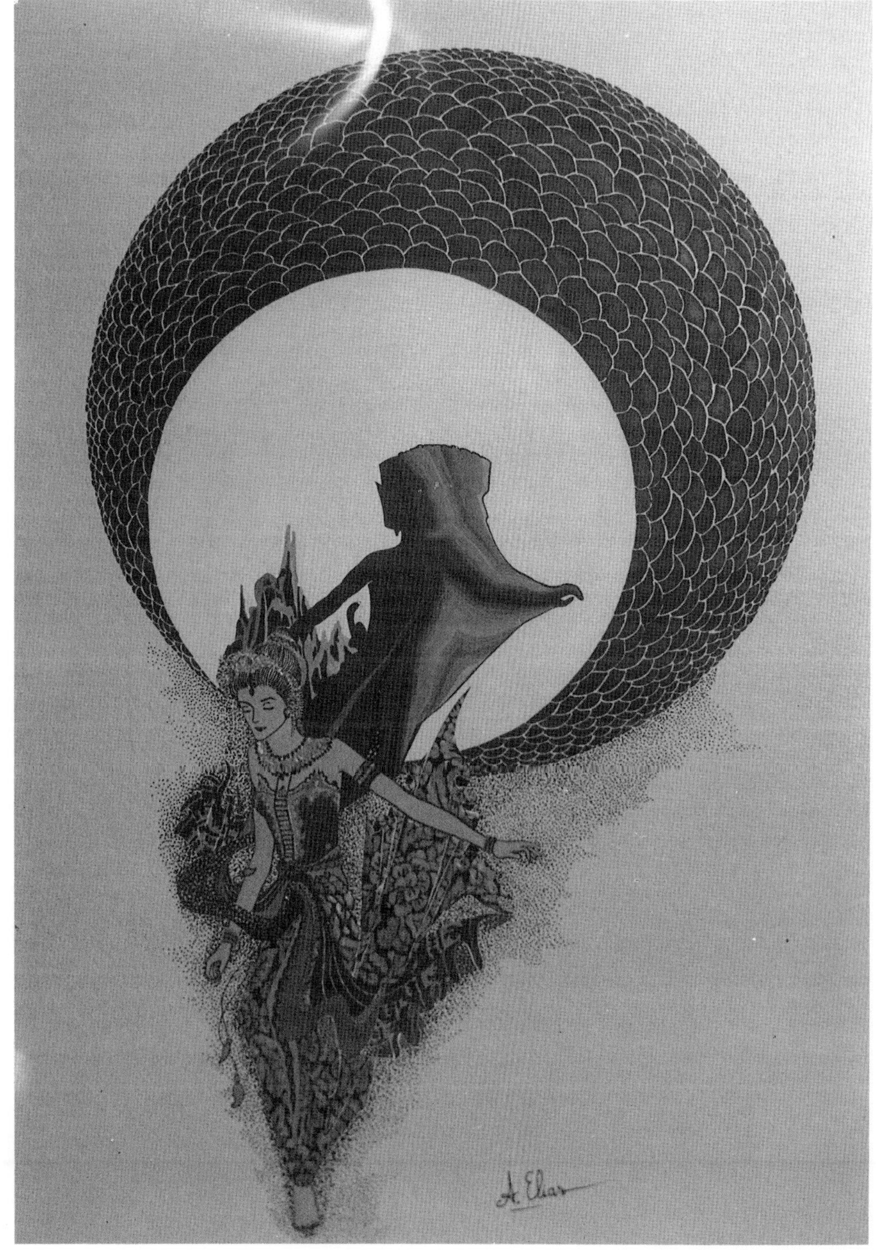

ANDRE ELIAS

Admiring his painting of a Balinese sunset, I ask Andre: "Do you ever get homesick?"

Andre: "At times…and whenever I think of my parents…old familiar scenes such as these (pointing to a group of paintings) surge to my mind.

"I remember the excitement building up to almost a boiling point amongst a group of men anxiously awaiting the outcome of a cockfight."

Andre illustrates with a painting that is a true chromatic experience showing a simple duck shepherd depicted in irridescent shades set against an anthracite grey background, the central figure painted in luminous colours that create an explosive effect.

"You can still see the duck shepherds back in Indonesia today. Back home I never dreamt of painting one…but I guess distance causes us to see things in a nostalgic light."

Interviewer' "Any underlying symbolism in your colours?"

Andre: "I am not quite sure…since they flow from my subconscious. All I know is that there are stages when I am almost in love with bright explosive colours. However, I could not accurately time the duration of any such spells."

"I experimented in using phosphorescent colours. I must admit that I have a certain hesitancy to apply too sharply contrasting colours, but once I have put the initial strokes on paper, those explosive, vibrant colours take shape almost by themselves.

"I am seized, lately, by an ecstasy of colours — colours very much in fluid motion, depicting waves, swirling seashell designs, peacock feathers and such…all painted on the spur of the moment. They reflect my particular feelings and mood at the time of painting and reveal certain affinities.

"And what more ideal figure is there than a woman to carry the movement —get caught up in it, rising to unknown heights — woman finally coming into her element. Jubilant! Passionate! Triumphant!

"Women of Africa, of Asia, Native Canadian women who are depicted in my paintings blend with my own oriental design…women from any part of the world — all different and yet simultaneously so much alike.

Interviewer: "But looking at your paintings I can see that you obviously also believe in the liberation of men."

Andre: "Actually there exists only one liberation — people liberation.

"Take this painting, for instance. Man is shedding his earthbound fetters. By dint of knowledge he reaches out into the spiritual realm. Man is going through a phase of revival, and back to nature, because he realizes that automation — although enriching him momentarily, in financial

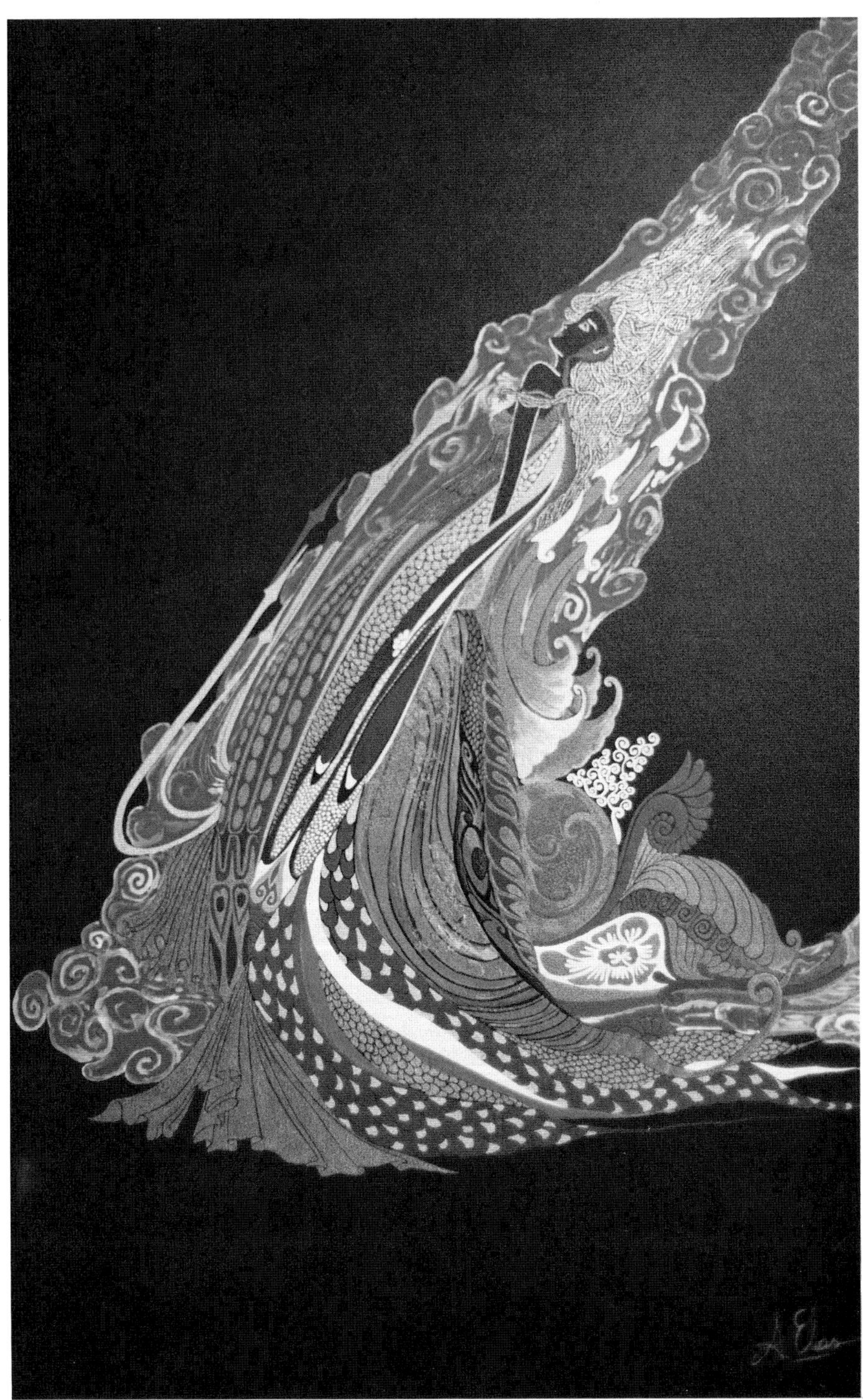

terms — is perhaps deadly crippling in spiritual terms. Therefore, I depicted man. so-to-speak, breaking through the crust of his earthly existence; reaching out to the stars; crying out for spiritual communion with the Higher Being.

"The branches symbolize his getting back into touch with nature, his age-old habitat. The deer stands for beauty and dignity, which one may interpret in different ways…an element of which — at least a trace — should be preserved in the life of everyone, an inalienable component.

"But coming back to women…so intriguingly mysterious and vulnerable at the same time."

Interviewer: "Is that why all your females have such an ethereal, almost virginal touch? Is that why you depict them so often in such an inconspicuous manner that they seem woven into spatial tapestry, blending so perfectly with their surroundings?

You depict women of rare beauty as if you revealed them unwillingly, afraid that stares and gazes defile them."

Andre: "What can I say? I am shy when it comes to the fair sex."

(He casts his eyes down).

"And yet, I have been painting women ever since I was a child…in restaurants and most unusual places.

"Whenever I would accompany my father, I would get hold of the place mat and give free reign to my imagination. Look at these piles of sketches, all done when I was a boy."

Interviewer: "But you are not a slave of the so-called cult of youth-worship by any means."

Andre: "How could I be? There is beauty to every age, just as there is special charm to every season. I find special beauty in well-endowed as well as emaciated bodies with a clearly demarked rib cage, because the pronounced furrows and wrinkles add so much character. Nor does old age detract from beauty, at least not in my mind, but rather adds perspective of intriguing depth and wonder about the type of life the individual has lived."

Interviewer: "Are you particular with your tools?"

Andre: "I work exclusively with brushes. I never use pens. However, I am extremely sensitive when it comes to material. If there is anything wrong with the texture, for instance, even a tiny flaw, it throws me totally off balance. I can't go on with the painting and so wilfully destroy it.

"You may call that idiosyncracy, but it's the way I am. Isn't everybody entitled to his peculiarities?

"When it comes to sculptures, I like them heavy. Light weight conjures a feeling of plastic material which I thoroughly detest. Anyway, I am cutting down on my sculpting due to lack of space."

Interviewer: "I have known you now for

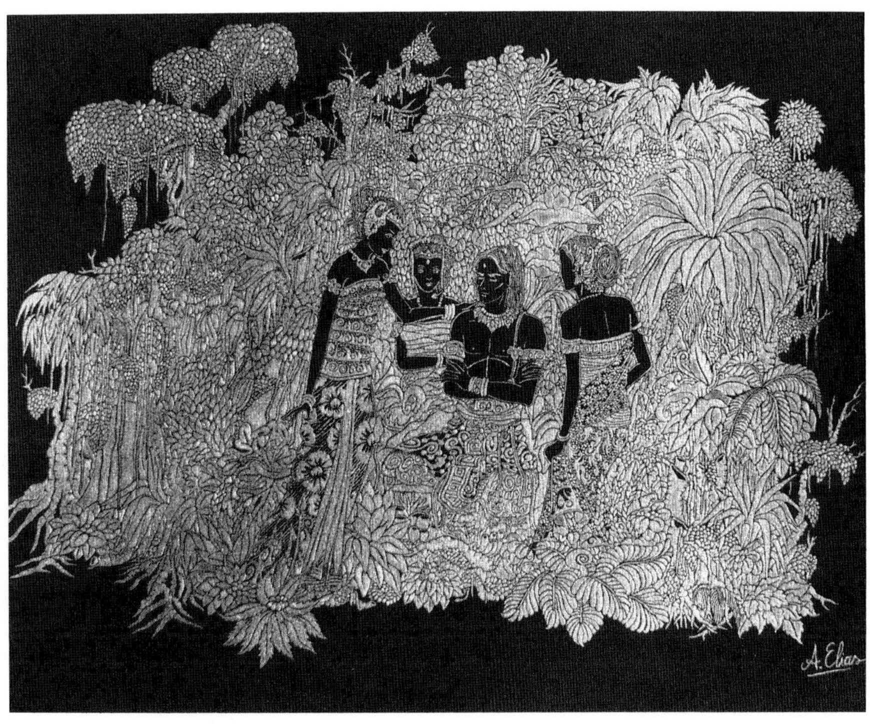

some years but somehow can't relate sculpting to you. Do you really enjoy it?"

Andre: "I actually dislike abstract forms but enjoy them once created, and I get the feeling of the abstract. Then I let my hands glide over their smooth surface and derive almost sensuous pleasure. I have one sculpture, for instance, that I touch every morning prior to starting any new work, irrespective of whether I paint, sculpt, or do ceramics. It's the old man with the long beard. Don't hesitate to walk up to him and touch his beard…but you must close your eyes.

"Lately. I have also done ceramics, although I never actually took any classes. However, I sneaked in on a group of students at work and observed on several occasions. Once back home, I then applied the skills gathered from watching. Mind you, all these vases are strictly for my own use or for close friends."

Interviewer: "Did you enjoy your studies at the Ontario College of Art?"

Andre: "Yes, my years at the College gave me the opportunity to be in constant communication with other art students — inspiring in itself. Besides, I love experimenting with new techniques and exploring new materials."

Interviewer: "Do you adhere to any particular school or style of painting?"

Andre: "Definitely not. Quite the contrary! I follow my inspiration, and my inspiration alone."

Interviewer: "The divine spark of inspiration!"

Andre: "You might call it that. Not that I am religiously inclined, but whenever I reflect upon my Creator I always end up being swamped with a tremendous wealth of ideas. Those ideas suddenly assail me out of nowhere and gradually take form, then just burst into colours.

"As I told you before, I am basically a self-taught man. I started painting when my father presented me with my first oil painting set when I was six years old and I have been driven to paint ever since. — starting out with the faces of girls and women who have always held me under their spell."

Interviewer: "Andre, is it correct to say that your paintings fall mainly into two categories?"

Andre: "I guess you could say that, namely disciplined and free style. When saying disciplined I refer to those paintings of Moorish tradition, gold on a black background. They illustrate mythological tales from the Ramayana, an Indian epic I almost knew by heart since I used to memorize the tales during my childhood.

"Those miniatures demand great discipline, patience, and tremendous dedication for there is not so much variation of form, but great diversification in detail."

Interviewer: "Do you ever duplicate any of your work?"

Andre: "Only by very special request, and I really have to like the person for whom I am doing it. Duplication goes against my grain and interferes with the constant onrush of new ideas, thus interrupting my experimentation with new colours, forms and shapes."

Interviewer: "Once you have completed a painting, do you then totally dismiss it from your mind?"

Andre: "Yes, as of the next morning."

Interviewer: "You make it sound as though it were still alive during the night."

Andre: "Well, this may sound even stranger to you…but as soon as I have completed a painting I know whether it is successful or not. If I feel happy and satisfied, then I get so excited that I can't even sleep but end up staying up the entire night squatting in front of it — just staring at it. However, with the rising dawn I totally disassociate myself and put it away, eagerly starting out on a new canvas."

Interviewer: "Do you suffer from dry spells?"

Andre: "You had to ask me that question, didn't you? Well, let me be totally frank with you. Yes, I do experience dry spells, all the more so since my work is mainly based on inspiration and feelings. When dry spells occur, I feel so despondent that I am driven to depression which finally culminates in despair. But thank God, those dry spells never last long for I am suddenly seized by new ideas gushing forth explosively.

"Lately, I also started experimenting with mainly design-oriented work on fabrics such as silk, and would not mind at all doing that for a side line. Yet, on the other hand, I would also love to teach art to the blind."

Interviewer: "Why do you say that?"

Andre: "The blind have a special sense that the sighted lack. I am truly fascinated with their other highly developed senses and the great beauty created by some blind sculptors I have come to know here."

"Who can foretell what the future holds in store for me?", Andre asks.

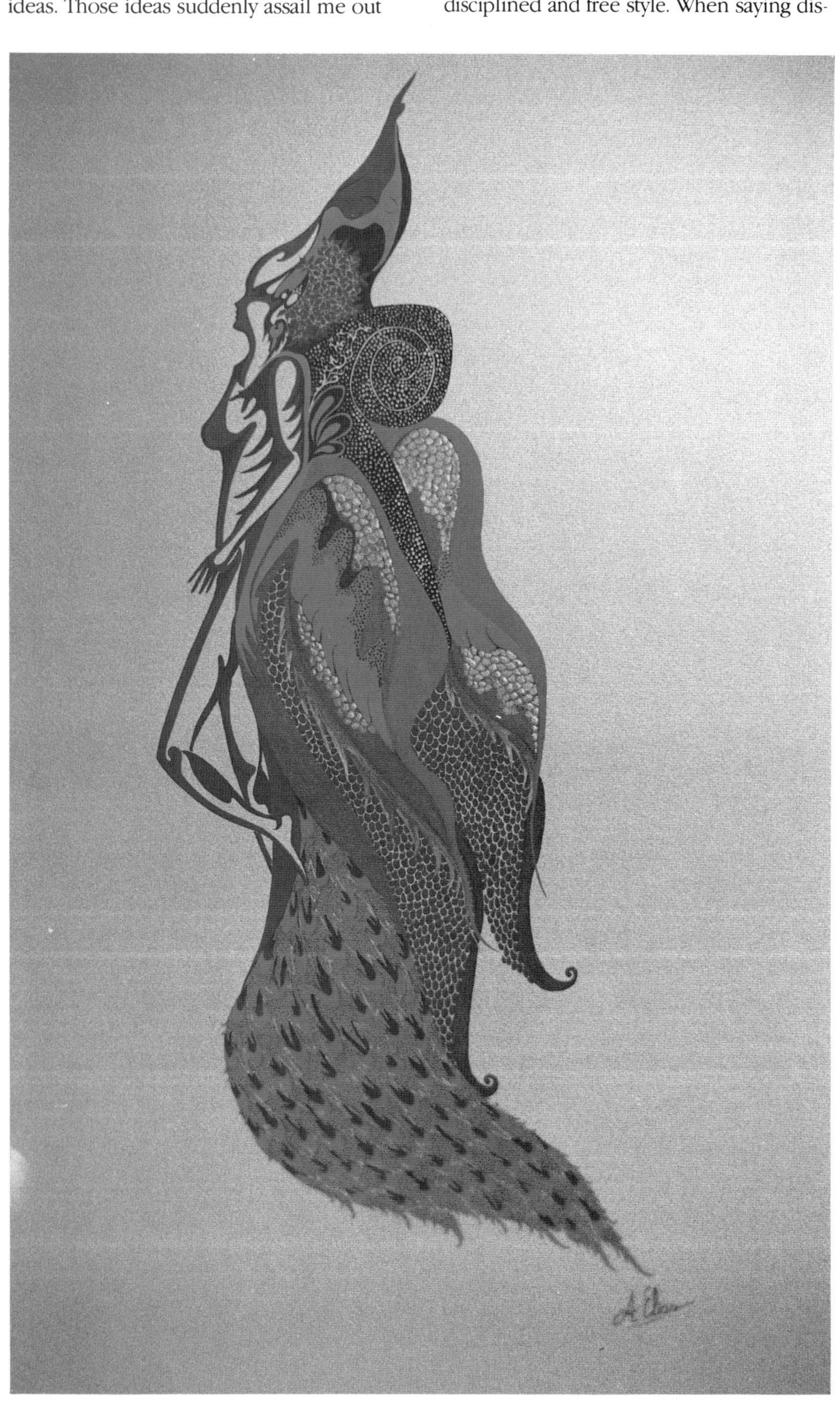

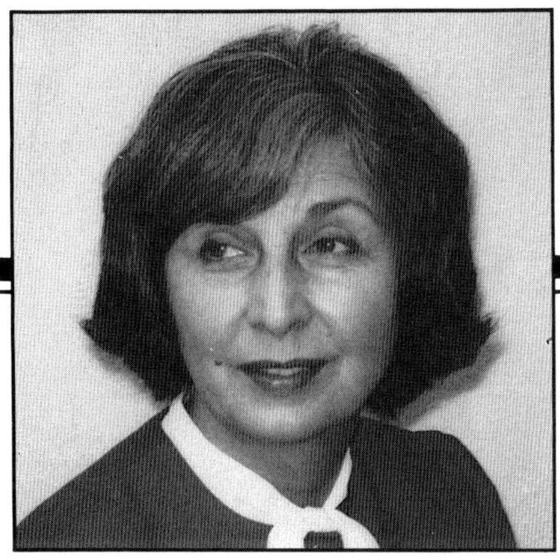

KATHERINE HARRIS

fortunate combination of painter and writer

(previously published in the 1983 Summer issue of THE SPIRES *Cultural Community Focus)*

Katherine Harris became interested in painting at the age of seventeen when she studied for one year under a man named Tom Cummings who was well known in North Bay and throughout the North. However, she then left if for several years as she pursued other interests.

When she moved to Toronto, her creativity was rekindled and she took a ten-week course at the Ontario Art Gallery but unfortunately had to drop it because work hours interfered with her lessons.

Now that Katherine stays at home, she is once again able to work at art and dedicate much more time to it.

She really likes superrealism and is particularly fond of Robert Bateman's and John Leonard's works — a style of painting which has become very popular in recent years. She is, herself, a talented exponent of this form of art and her nature paintings are so realistic that the viewer feels transported into the very setting.

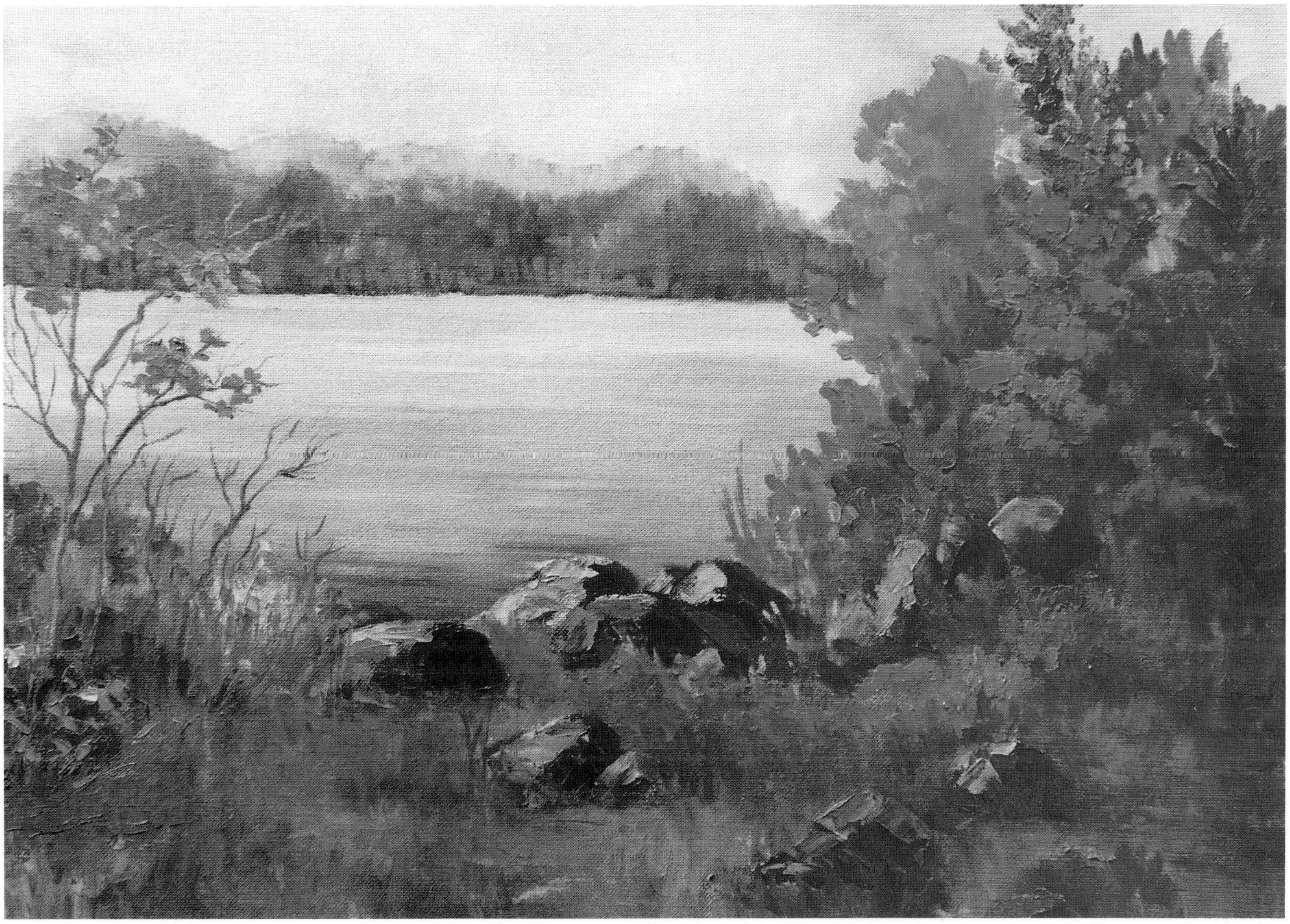

KATHERINE HARRIS

No wonder, then, that visitors who attended one of her exhibitions, presented by V. Joan Pearson, showing four of Katherine's paintings, just could not take their eyes off her work. AUTUMN HAZE is an extremely well-balanced painting of great depth, depicting trees, predominantly in tones of orange and reddish-brown, very realistically reflecting the autumn mood with the ebbing-out of the colour orgy and with a touch of an onset of slight sadness. STEPPING STONES presents the powerful movement of a stream amidst luscious greens of different vibrating colours and shades.

This painter, who is highly diversified, also does mood paintings and still life, the still life on display having featured a vase and pear with the focus mainly on shape, colour, composition, and texture.

At this particular moment her work focuses on flowers which are done in oil — her favourite medium which she finishes in great detail. Being a great nature

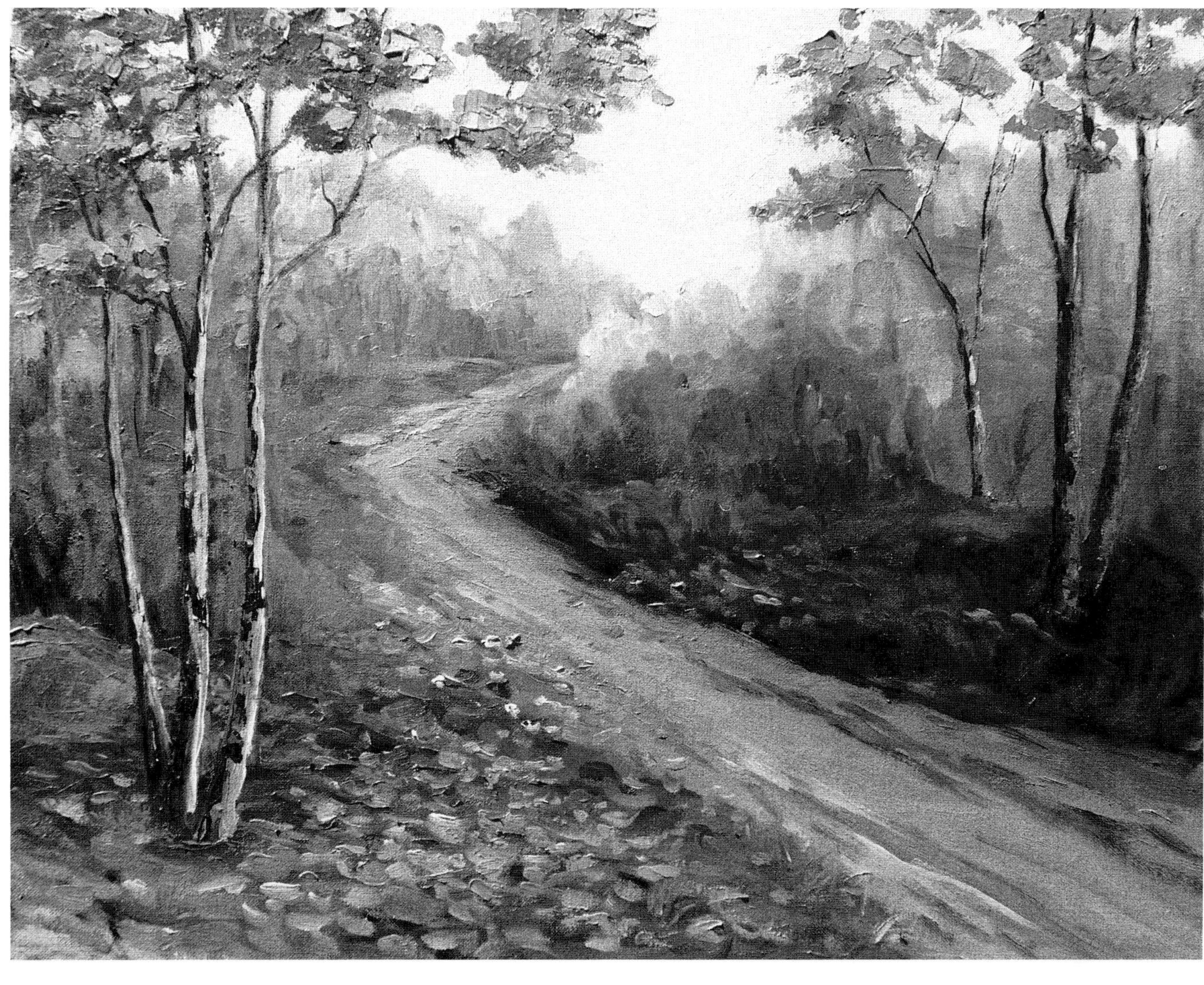

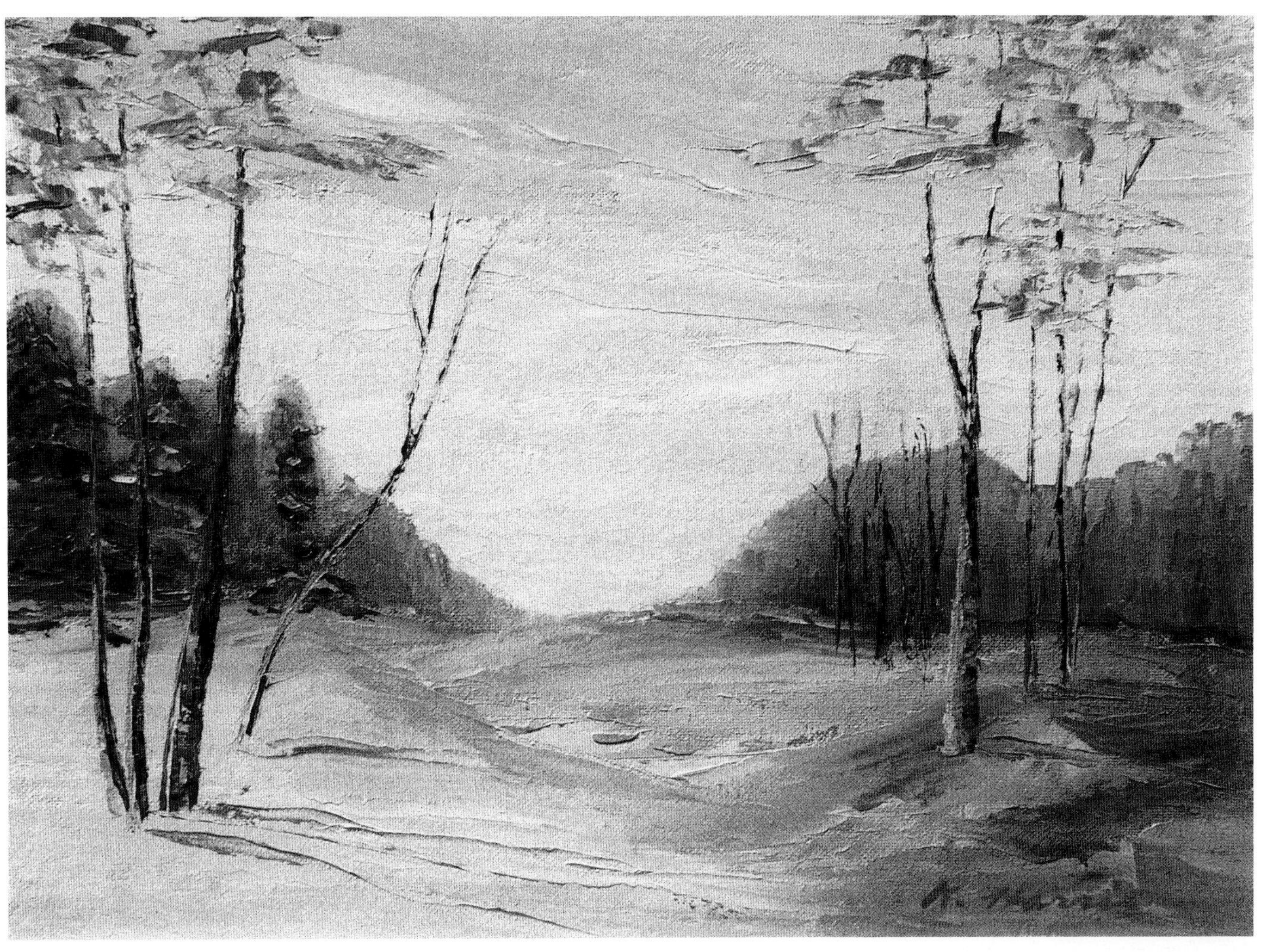

lover, Katherine likes to convey the feeling of open spaces — sea and sky studies being definitely her forté. Scenes like city streets certainly wouldn't be her genre now, yet an area she might perhaps explore at some later stage.

This artist holds the unique gift of awe and wonder so beautifully depicted in the ENCHANTED FOREST painting, capturing its magic in soft pastels with the main emphasis on the movement of the children much more than on colour intensity and composition. Two little girls are held under the spell of the forest, intensely gazing and listening — a moment of wonder skilfully caught on canvas.

For Katherine, painting is a form of relaxation. Painting takes her mind off any problems, since she has to concentrate deeply on what she is doing.

She generally paints from mid-morning until mid-afternoon when the lighting conditions are optimal and her work is clearly affected by the frame of mind prevailing at that time. When she feels a strong urge, she is simply compelled to paint.

KATHERINE HARRIS

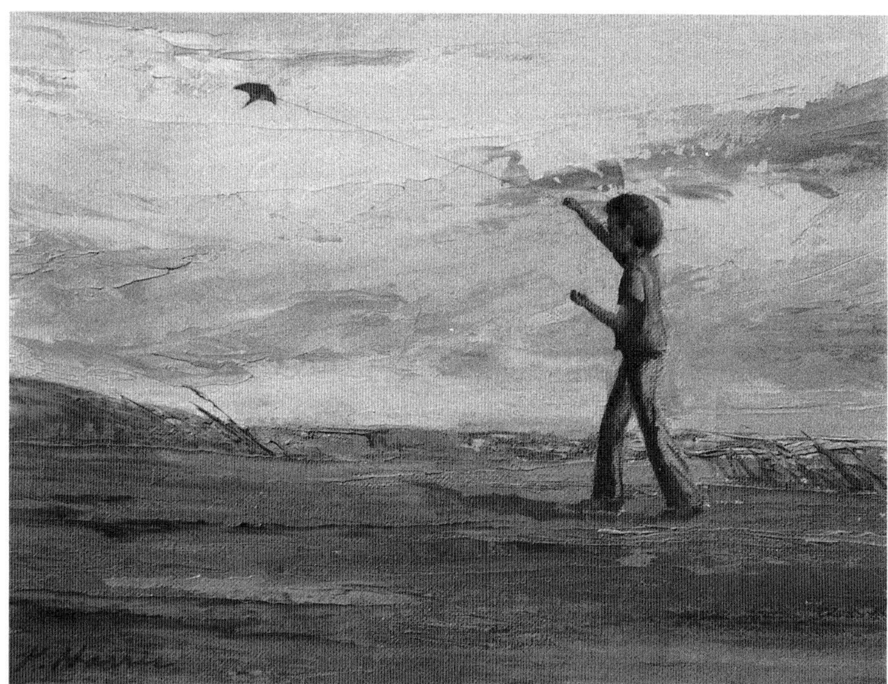

Katherine Harris' teacher, V.J. Pearson, commented as follows:

"Katherine was a little conventional in the beginning but with time she got freer, broke down traditional barriers and now her work has become so much more interesting with that newly acquired freedom. Whereas she initially tied into the subject rather than the mood, she has become confident, putting some of herself into the work."

Teacher Pearson considers Katherine a very dedicated and highly emotional, promising student who — she feels sure — will soon be well known.

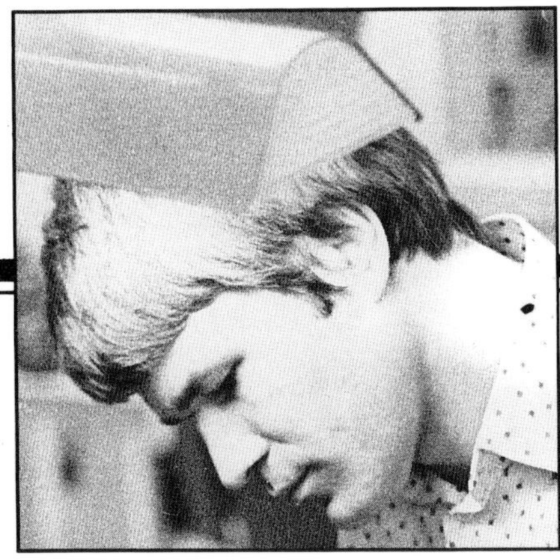

DIETER HUEBNER

ingenious designer, unique gold and silversmith, wood and ivory carver, dedicated metal arts instructor — an Etobian, exponent of artistic talent and skills based on a sound family tradition in the art of jewellery-making

AN IRREPRESSIBLE URGE TO CREATE BEAUTY AND TO DESIGN WITH HIS OWN HANDS — that's how it all started…

(previously published in the Summer 1982 issue of THE SPIRES Cultural Community Focus.)

Having had the pleasure of practical exposure to this diversified expert craftsman as a part-time student of his in the Metal Arts Division at Humber College, the interviewer can state from first-hand experience that Huebner has four objectives at heart:

THE PROMOTION OF MANUAL SKILLS (as a welcome balancing element for the stress-worn intellectuals, businessmen, etc.)
EMPHASIS ON ENHANCED CREATIVITY (you will be amazed at the abundant outcome once you no longer dam the flow of your self-generating creative juices)
TOTAL FREEDOM OF EXPRESSION (you are your own best judge), and
UNIQUENESS OF DESIGN (always dare to be yourself and do venture into the unknown).

Huebner succeeds in instilling in his students sufficient self-confidence to become enterprising by setting an example regarding innovative design and by helping the students along with infinite patience. Even if you break ten or more sawblades during the first 3-hour session and you are ready to pack it all in, Huebner will patiently and practically demonstrate to you that there is really nothing to it. And then — one day — when you get the drift of it, you become so enthusiastically engrossed in the metal arts you won't even notice time slipping by. You will be making exquisite pill boxes, rings, brooches, pendants, earrings, etc. — items you merely stared at in store windows before.

Huebner, a Canadian citizen, comes to us from a truly multicultural background. He was born on August 14th, 1946, in West Germany, married a Dutch girl and is now happily settled in Canada.

In 1968 Huebner graduated in Jewellery Arts — Canadian Jewellers' Institute — and then returned to Europe to pursue his studies in gold and silversmithing over there. During his 8-year stay

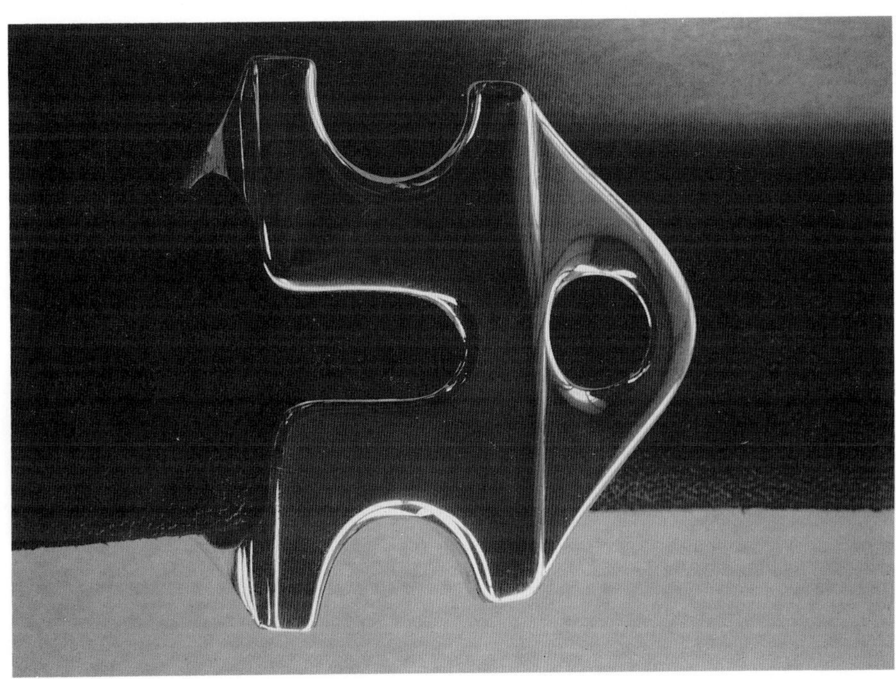

sterling silver "unisex belt buckle"
"honourable mention for design" award

1981 Ontario Crafts Council
central region exhibition

DIETER HUEBNER

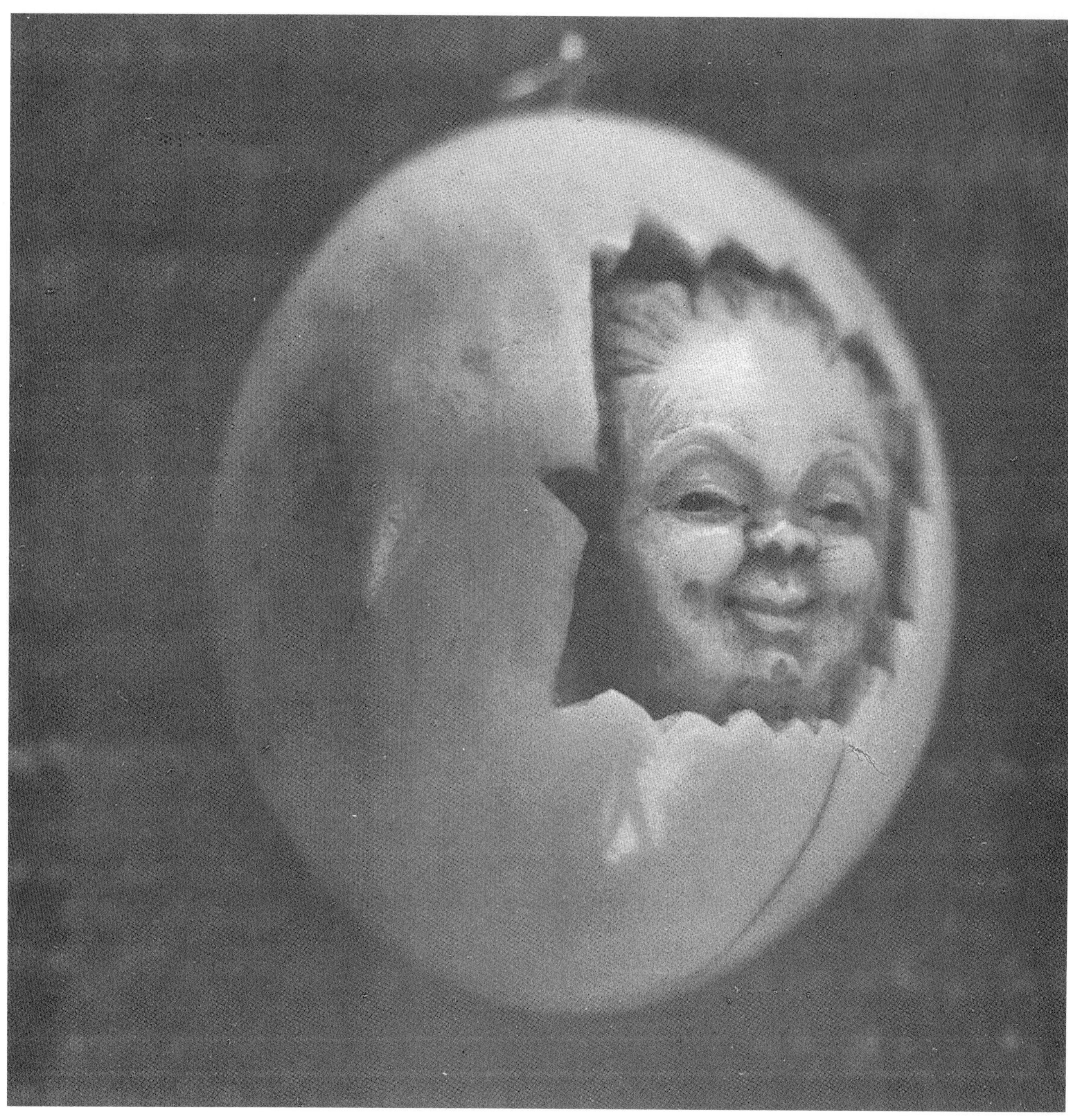

ivory carving

abroad he worked for some of the most prestigious jewellers and diamond merchants, graduated in June 1975 from the Academy of Fine Arts in Hanau (West Germany). During that same year he was awarded his MASTER GOLDSMITH Diploma by the Guild in Wiesbaden.

Huebner, as might be imagined, is a regular participant in both national and international exhibitions, and has received world-wide acclaim and awards for his beautiful and, simultaneously, extremely functional work.

His designs were featured in the EUROPEAN JEWELLER and GOLD & SILVER magazines, 1970, in which he was given recognition for ear jewellery.

In 1975 he was awarded the FIRST PRIZE by the city of Hanau for designing a medallion honouring European partner cities.

He took part in exhibitions of the Oldenburg students; Metal Arts Guild, Toronto; Ontario Crafts Council — and he won an honourable mention for design in the 1981 Ontario Crafts Council central region exhibition.

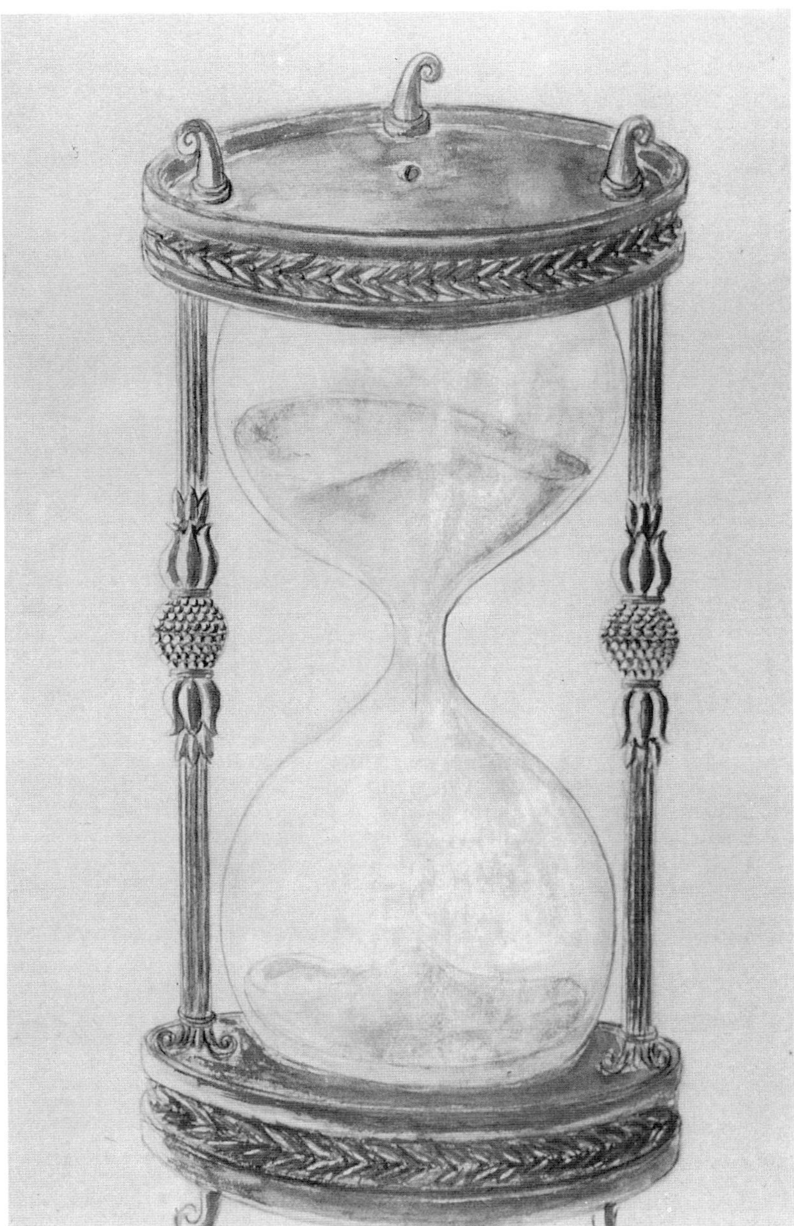

MAGNAVOX hourglass — summer of 1981 Commissioned for MAGNAVOX Communications

DIETER HUEBNER

Dieter Huebner is quite a versatile artist in that he is involved with several materials and techniques. In addition to gold and silversmithing, he also does ivory and wood carving and is presently working in space age metals such as titantium. He is also engaged in anodizing aluminum and working in other experimental metal techniques.

His two 'hour-glasses' for MAGNAVOX COMMUNICATIONS were featured in PLAYBOY and NEWSWEEK and shown on the Leonard Nimoy television commercial.

Huebner served on the executive of the Metal Arts Guild of Ontario for three years.

Since September, 1976, he has been a member of the Creative Arts Faculty of Humber College, teaching design; perspective; rendering; metals and materials; gemology, metal arts studio technology and, lately, CAT, i.e. computer-aided design, and drafting.

He has professional membership in:

The German Gemological Association; Gemological Institute of America; Metal Arts Guild; Ontario Crafts Council; Art Gallery of Ontario.

He is also a member of the Ontario Woodcarvers' Association and of the Port Credit Gem & Minerals Club.

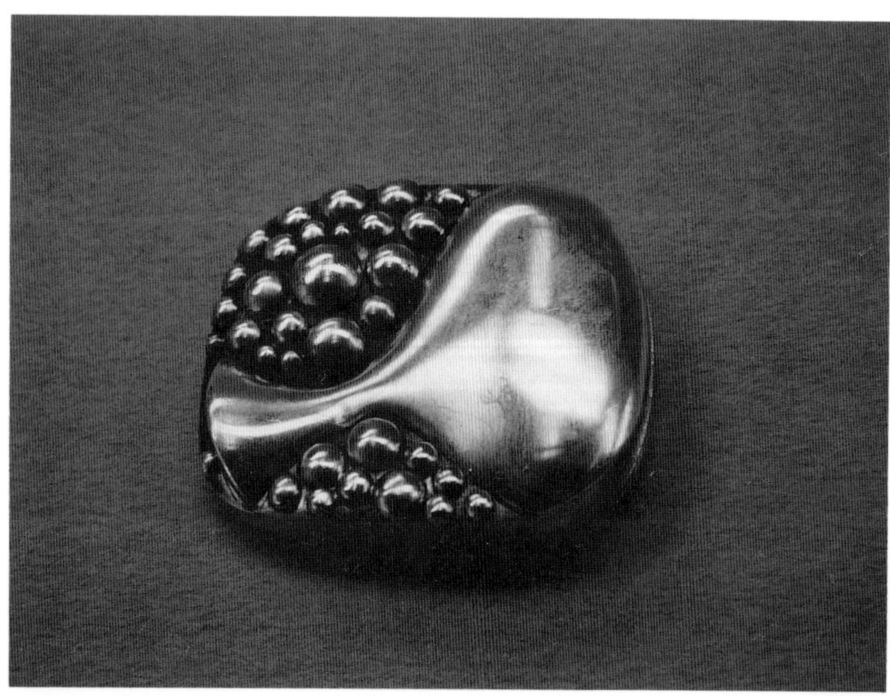

"BUBBLES" sterling silver belt buckle (can also be worn as brooch)

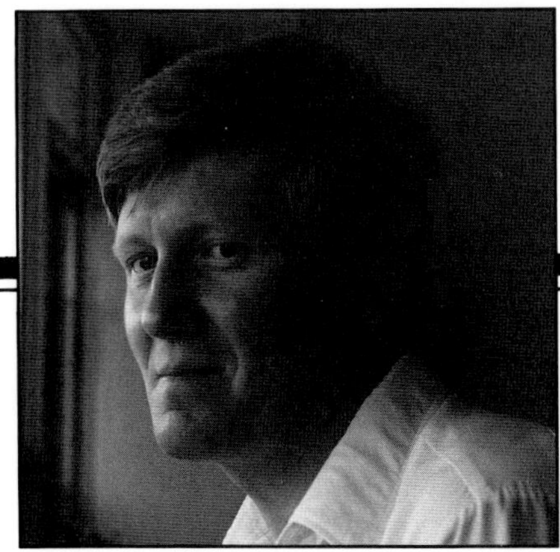

JAROSLAV F. HUTA

internationally acclaimed coin and medal designer, sculptor, painter, illustrator and ceramist

(excerpt published in the Fall 1982 issue of THE SPIRES Cultural Community Focus)

an impressively tall man with a thick shock of golden-reddish hair and kind pale blue eyes that convey a pleasant feeling of serenity and tranquillity — an extraordinarily talented linear artist and illustrator, a superb painter and renowned medal and coin designer

This artist started painting at the age of four, influenced by fairytale illustrations. His work has been featured in group exhibitions in Canada, Czechoslovakia, Italy, and West Germany, and some of his paintings, graphic work and sculptures are part of collections in Austria, Canada, Czechoslovakia, West Germany, and South Africa.

Q: "Did you draw inspiration from any particular sources?"

A: "I was very impressed by old magazines on art décoratif. Then, around 1950, I was strongly influenced by the realist tendencies existing at that time.

"I also drew inspiration from architecture in general. Naturally I was interested in the pseudo-Gothic structures such as those built by the Liechtenstein nobility close to the Austrian border, in the area where I used to live.

"And I have, of course, always been particularly fond of old churches — all the more so when there was nobody else around to disturb me in my contemplation. I used to resent outside distraction and was happy to be alone."

In 1971, Huta won the Prize Of The Friends of Fine Arts in Munich and, in 1974, was awarded the title of MEISTERSCHÜLER (exceptionally gifted student with outstanding artistic achievement) by the Munich Academy of Fine Arts.

He attended the School of Ceramics in Znojmo, CSSR, from 1954 to 1957.

Q: "Was it a good experience?"

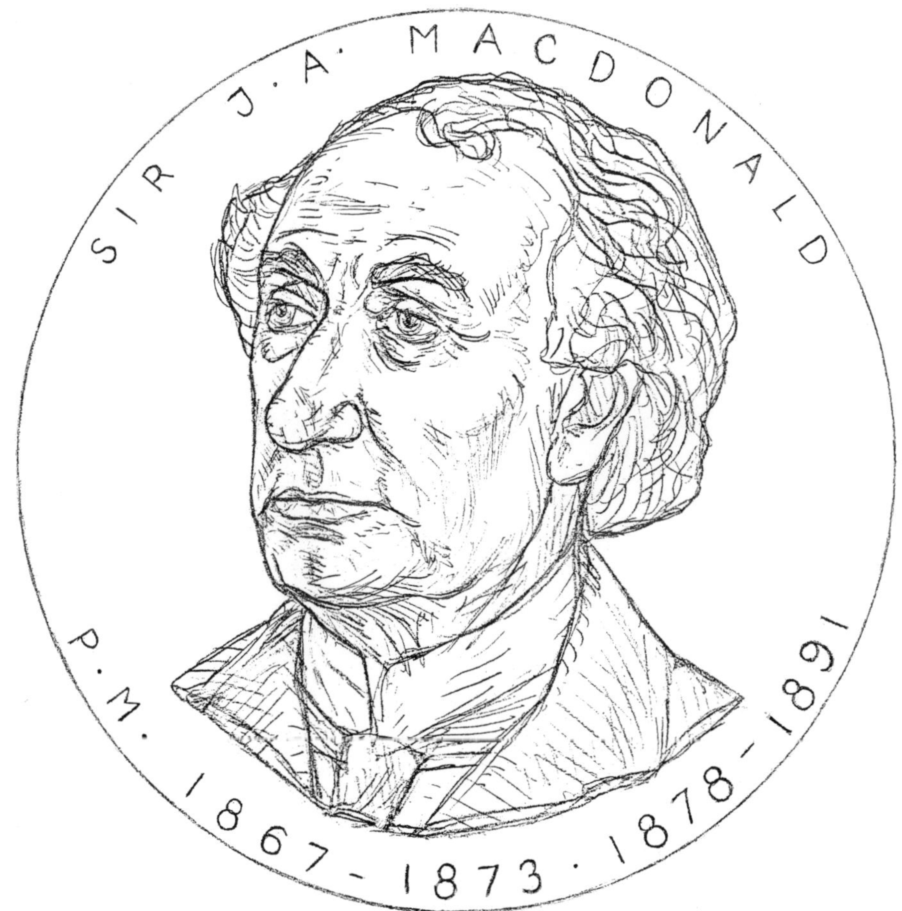

JAROSLAV F. HUTA

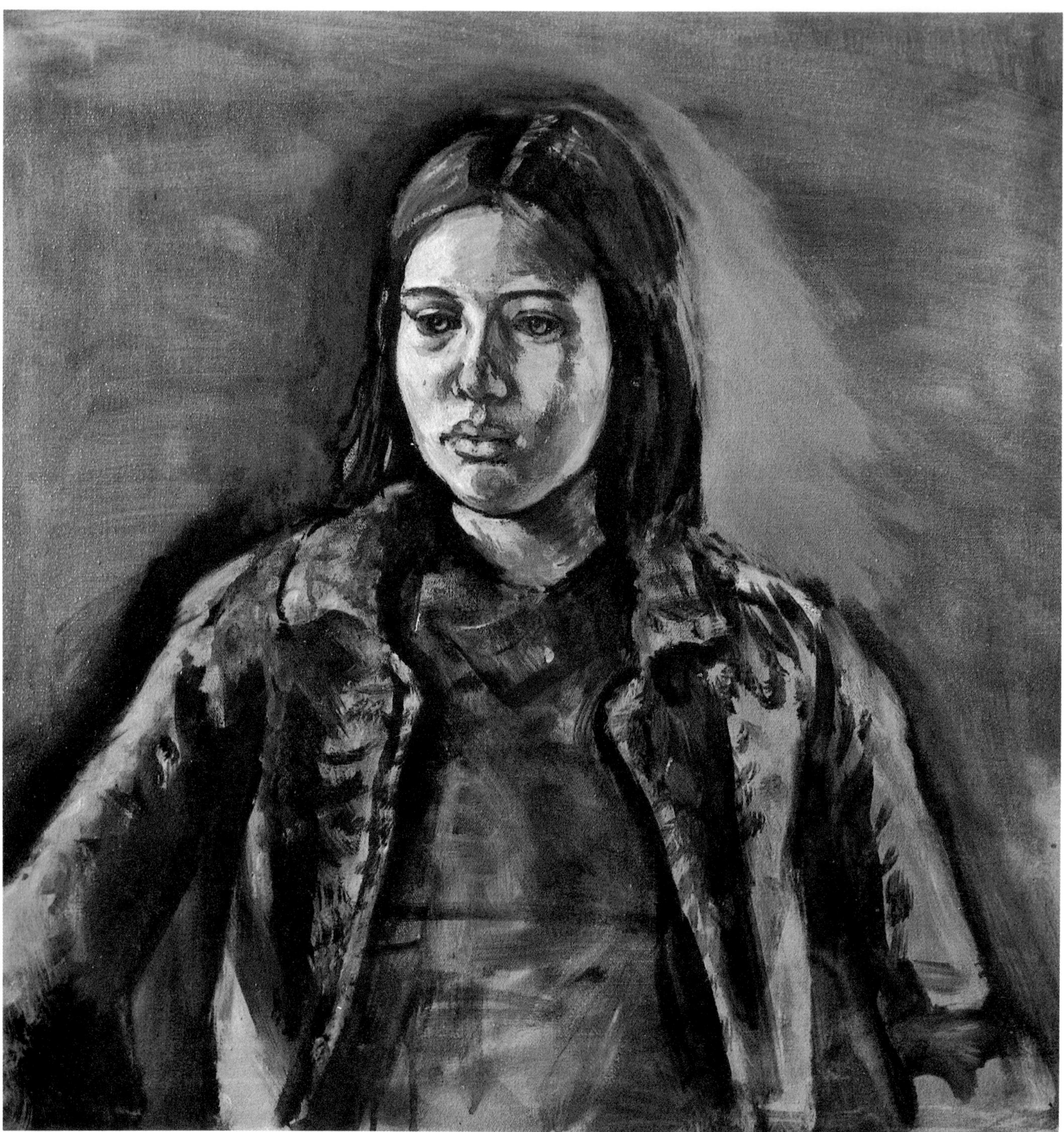

the artist's daugher VERONIKA

A: "Definitely so because, apart from the skills of the craft, we learned new concepts of translating design ideas into practical products.

"From 1957 to 1961 I attended the High School of Applied Arts with emphasis on commercial graphics. Yet, on the whole, the studies were well balanced with liberal arts. I did a lot of black and white drawings during those days as well."

Q: "Did you cherish any special dream then?"

A: "Of course, I wanted to be a student of the Academy of Fine Arts in Pargue. But, unfortunately, I had no parental support whatsoever, as they were worried about my future. They wanted me to take on a "solid profession" since they feared that most artists die of hunger."

Q: "Did you give up in your pursuits?"

A: "On the contary, I put up more resistance and luckily I qualified in the selection examination and attended the Academy from 1961 to 1965, studying painting and graphics.

"During that time I also visited the National Gallery almost daily, and drew from the work of the great masters of the 14th and 15th centuries."

Q: "Is there any special reason why you have such great admiration for classical art?"

A: "It comes to us from very strong universal sources. It is also based on unity and harmony — contrary to some contemporary newfangled works. It is different from the presently "in" works of art that startle modern man's tortured mind, for products with a touch of irony or perversion are naturally more effective in terms of shocking. I feel that it is more difficult to create works of art that convey an immediate sense of contentment, radiating hope and having a healingly, soothing effect on man's mind."

Q: "The Academy must have been a great source of inspiration and a strong influence?"

A: "Yes, I had excellent teachers but some of them were at times rather formal or placed too much emphasis on their own subjective craft. Artists must always be open to new beginnings. I am totally against any pseudo-style or artificial novelties, for I consider them a crippling factor."

Q: "Who do you consider to be a real artist?"

A: "A person whose work reflects strength and depth; a person who is never afraid of final effects; a person whose work is real from the beginning and shows a personal, timeless style. I detest the stealing of ideas that are then slightly changed, adapted to a contemporary vogue and passed off as one's own work.

"The artist must have a deeper reason than merely working on instruction. One could almost say that there is a hidden mechanism at work, a creative force that simply drives the artist. Besides, the genuine artist strongly believes in his work.

"He is not eager to commercialize for the sake of pleasing the crowds and reaping a fast buck. Instead, he lives his art and does not produce a certain type of work just to be "with it"; just to be "in".

Q: "While at the Academy, did you also commercially get a chance for practical exposure to professional work?"

Q: Yes, I worked, for instance, on the documentation for an archaeological excavation in Mara, CSSR."

In 1968 Huta began his studies at the Munich Academy of Fine Arts (West Germany) from which he graduated in graphic and monumental painting in 1974.

During his stay in Munich, he was commissioned to do fairytale illustrations

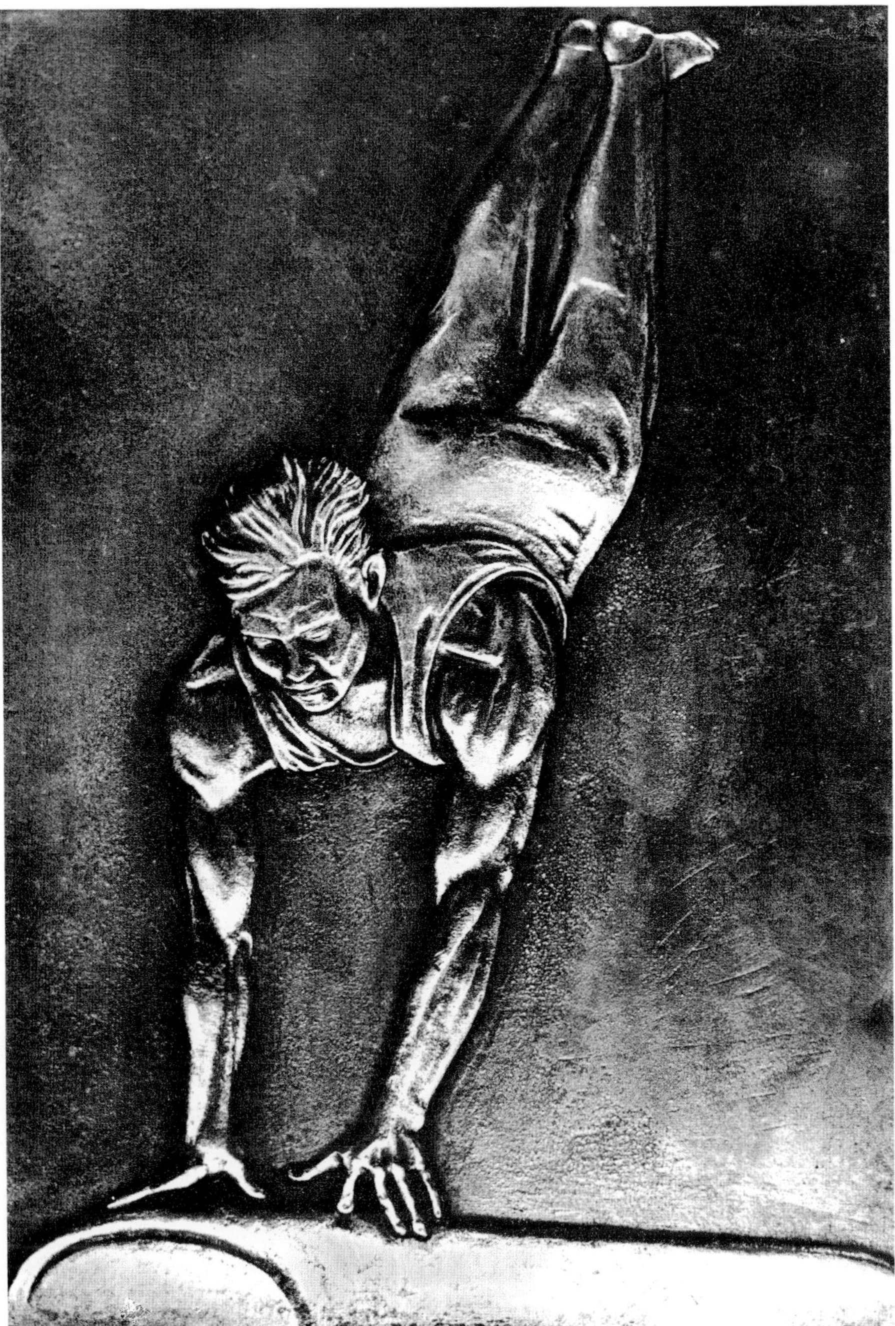

model for METAL OLYMIC STAMP SCULPTURES
Series IV

because of his penetrating characterization despite economy of lines.

His involvement in coin and medallion designing was purely accidental, although he had always been somehow, impressed by profile portraits with emphasis on silhouette rather than three-dimensional effects.

In 1971, when the Franklin Mint Co. opened a branch in Munich, Huta submitted some work samples and, based on his strikingly clear presentation, (simple yet dynamic lines), was hired on the spot to immediately produce a large series.

Of all the geometrical forms, the circle — the oldest magic symbol — is his favourite since he best relates to it. According to Huta, circles can make one aware of the depth in space. No wonder, then, that most of his coin and medallion work is done within the confines of a circle.

He sculpted the coins for the 1972 Olympic Games in Munich and designed 12 OLYMPIA ANTIQUA and 52 medals from a 60-piece German history series.

Based on his accurate, clear rendition and powerful contours, he was also commissioned to do the SCHILLER-series and the portraits of the members of the Opera of Vienna in Austria.

Huta's luck strain in that specialty continued, for when he emmigrated to Canada, he qualified immediately in a design-transfer competition. Canada Post gave him an order for the 4-piece Olympic metal stamp sets in bronze, silver, and gold for the 1976 Olympic Games in Montreal. Huta had to transfer the already existing stamp painting into a relief (series IV and V), a total of 100 pieces of models for minted medals.

His lines on the metal surface remind one of the well-aimed slashes of a superb fencer. They reflect the strength of his energetic and vigorous nature and of his superbly controlled mind. They are clear-cut lines devoid of any superfluous embellishment.

Q: "Did you get any other commissions?"

A: "Yes, during the very same year I also did two designs and models for embossing. These were maple leaves for commemorative folders and government stationery as well as numerous other orders.

"Besides, in the same year I did the portrait of Her Majesty, Queen Elizabeth II, in bronze. The size of the casting was 190 mm.

"That relief was chosen, in 1976, in a Canada Post competition, the design having been approved by Buckingham Palace and by the Prime Minister's Office. Once transferred, a photograph of the plaster relief was then used for the 12, 14, 17, and 32 cent stamps. The original model is being preserved in the Postal Museum in Ottawa.

"There was also a short television movie made about the Queen's stamp followed by several write-ups, as well as BBC interviews in May 1976 and March 1977.

"Besides, I sculpted a relief for a medal which was struck only in one piece for the visit of Pope John Paul II.

"I also did a portrait medal of A.J. CASSON, the last surviving member of THE GROUP OF SEVEN, for the Yaneff International Gallery.

"I created models for the celebration of the birth of Prince Henry, for Birkdale Coin.

"Furthermore, I sculpted the portrait of Countess Mountbatten for the Monarchist League of Canada."

Q: "Do you belong to any professional associations?"

A: "Yes, I am a member of several academies and select societies."

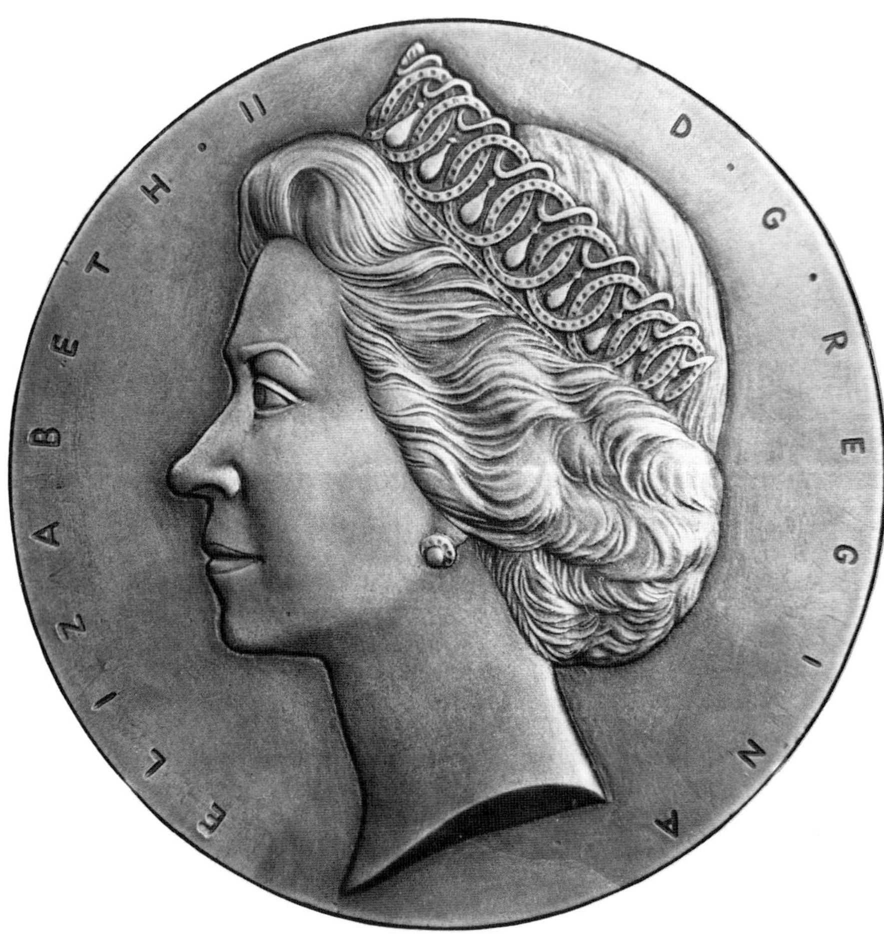

portrait of HER MAJESTY QUEEN ELIZABETH II Day of issue: I - III - 1977 Ottawa, Canada

This relief was used for the 12, 14, 17, and 32 cent Canadian stamps.

MANY FACES~MANY SPACES

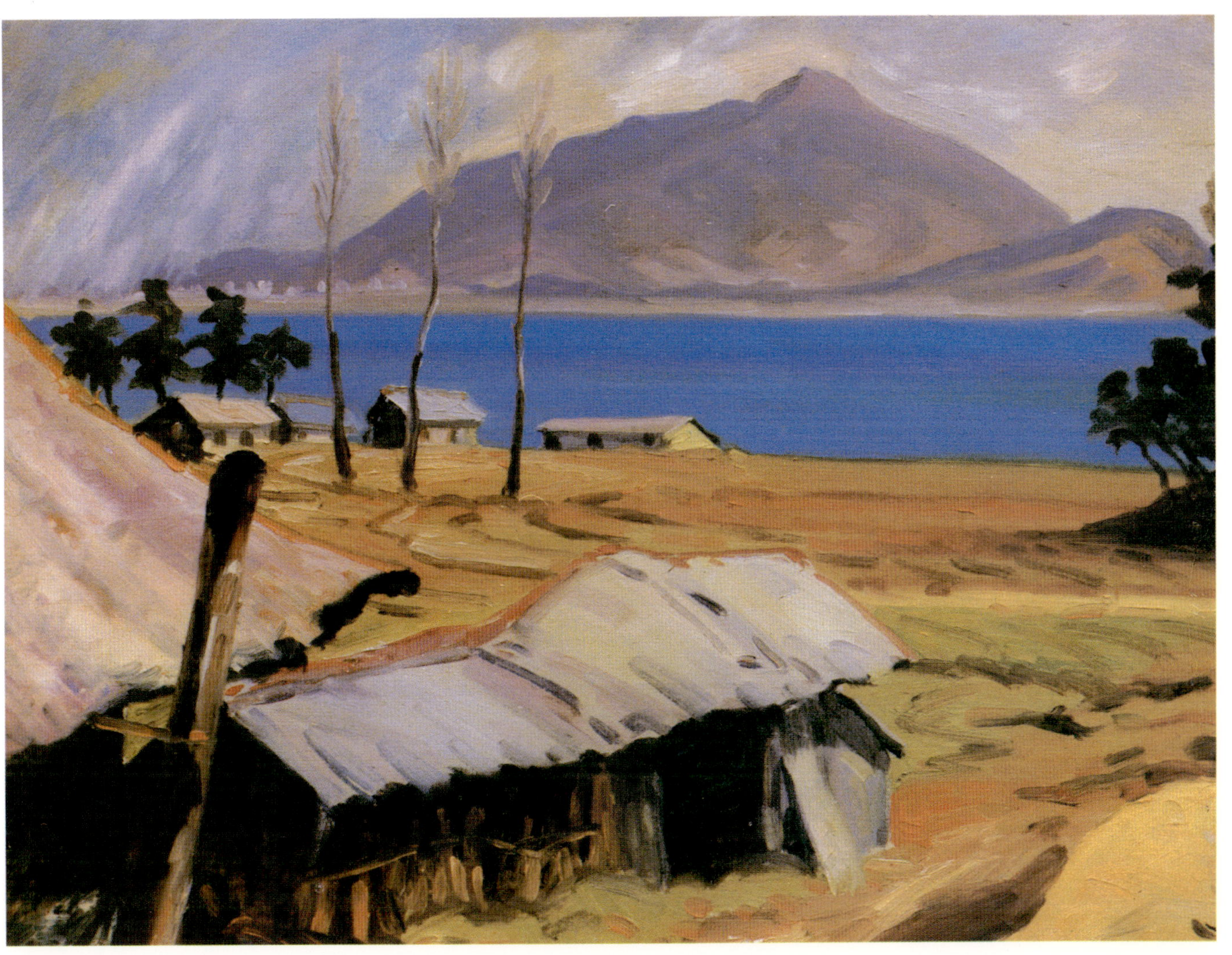

KEN BELL

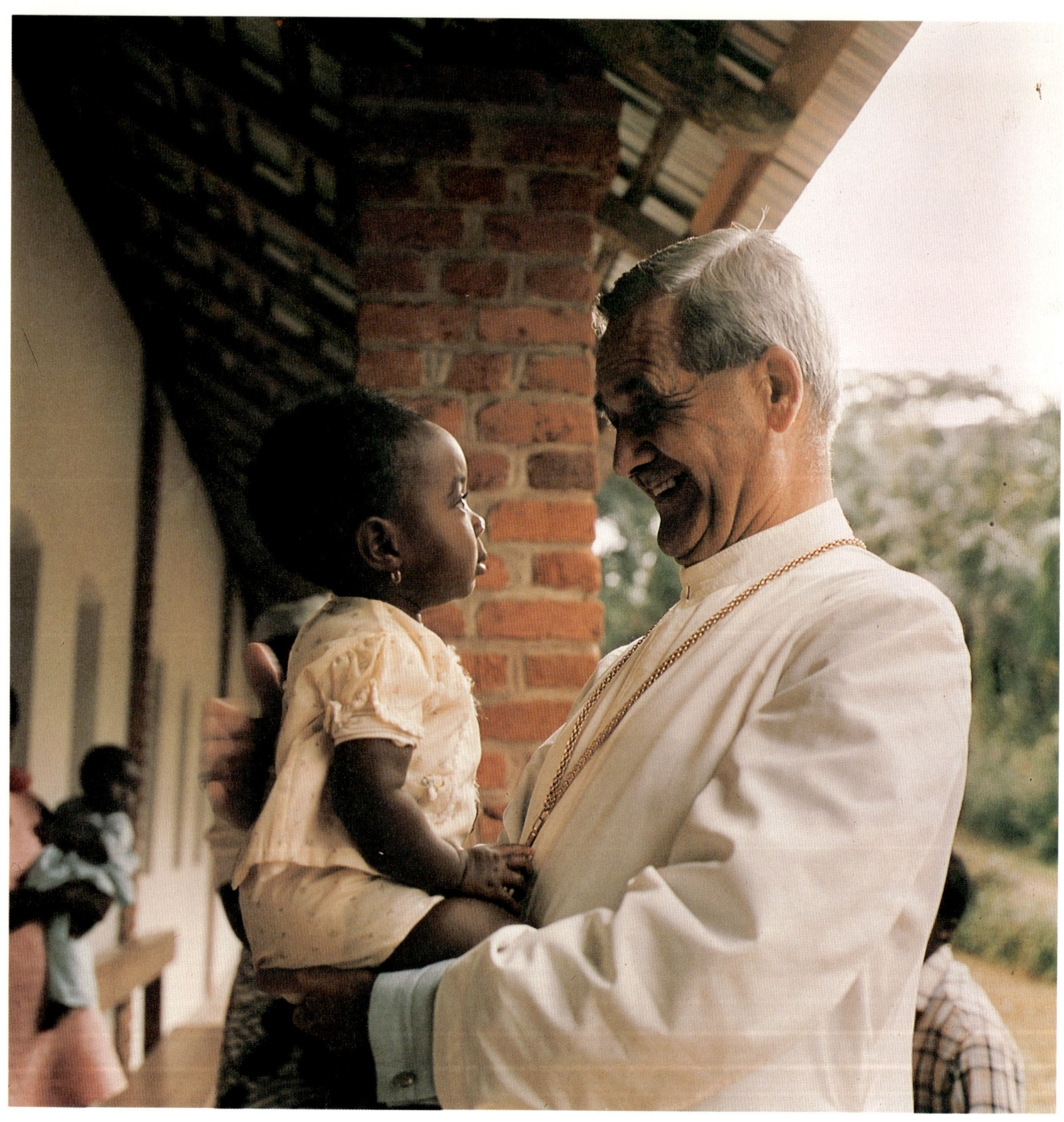

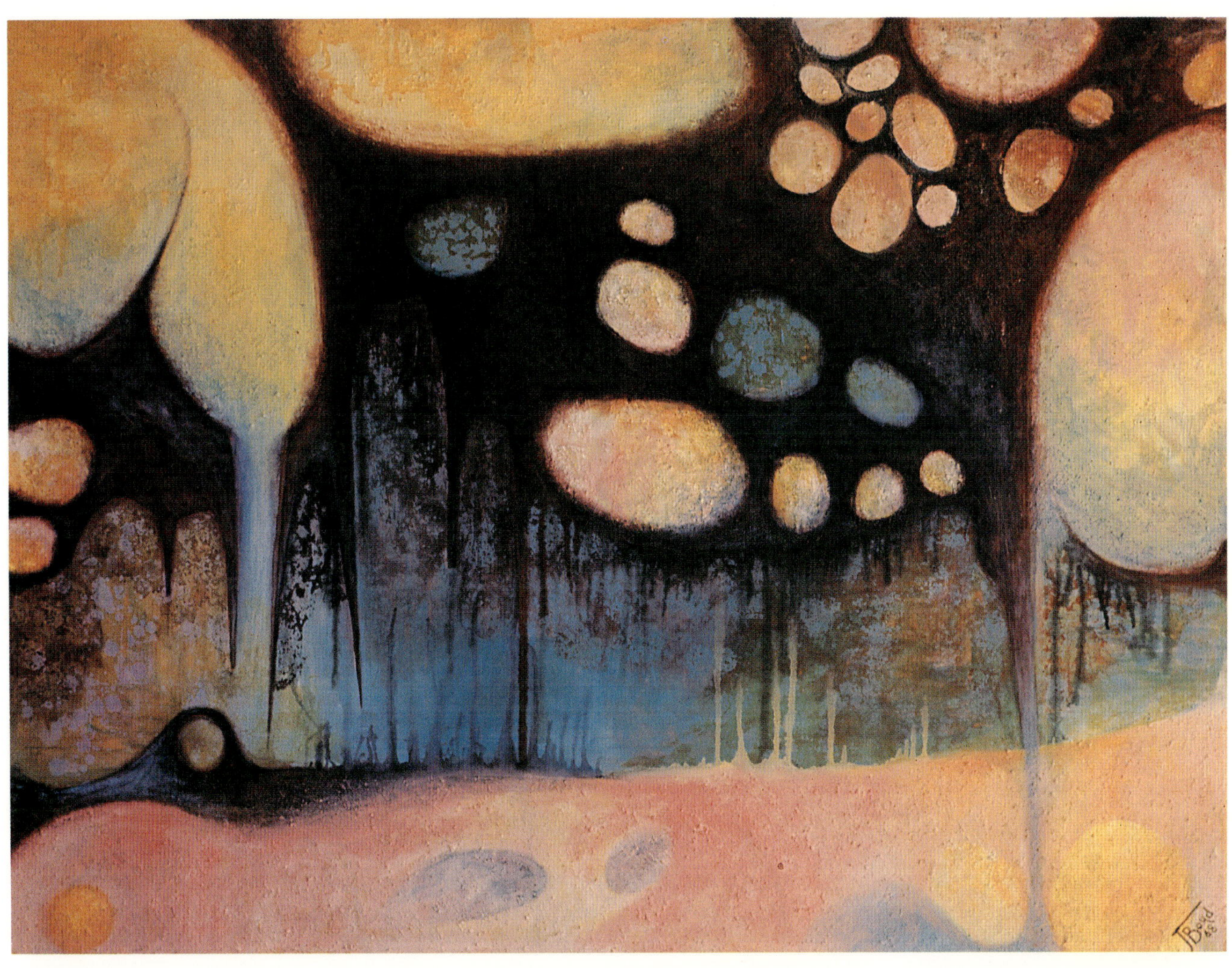

ALEXANDER BULZAN

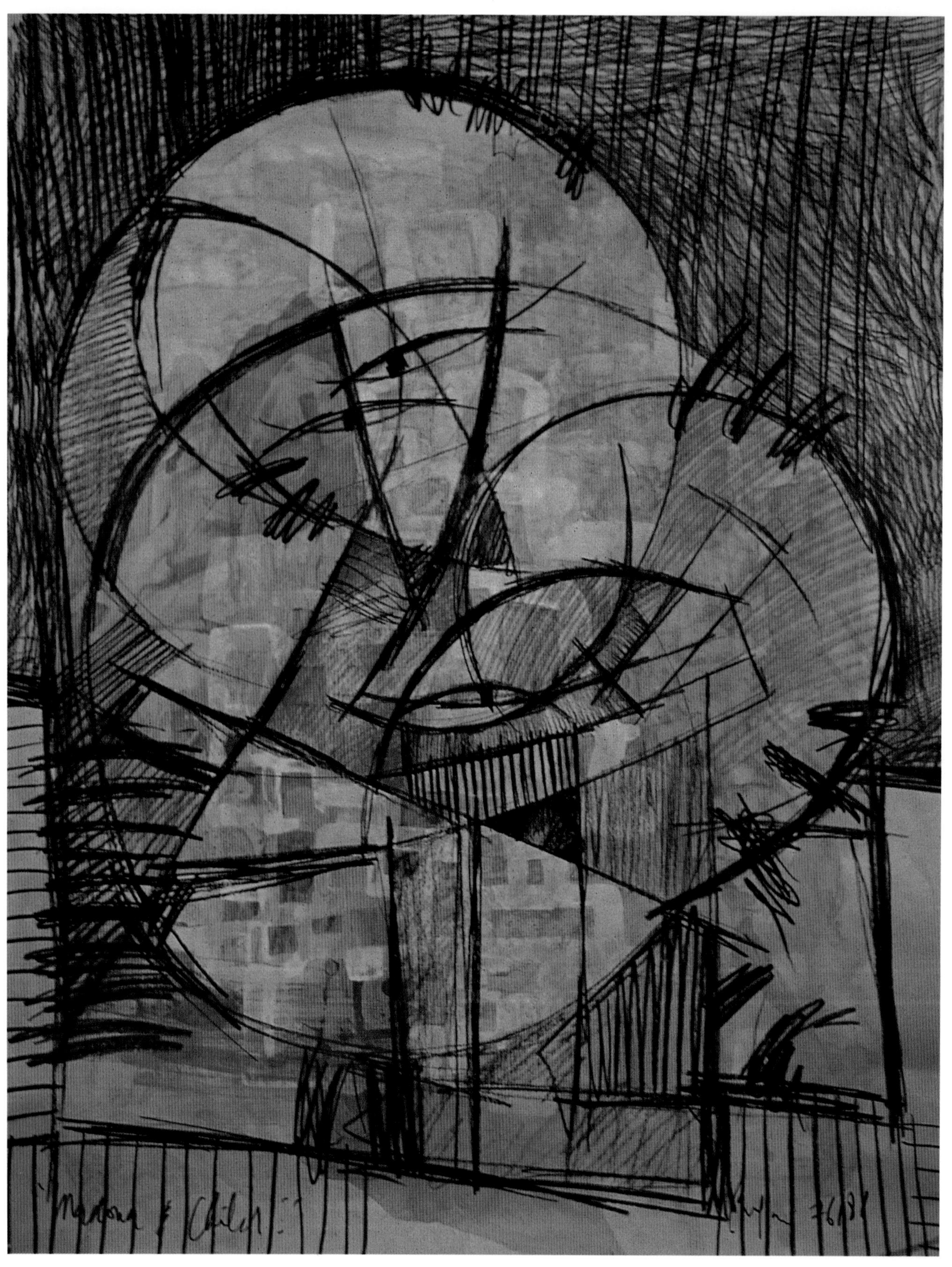

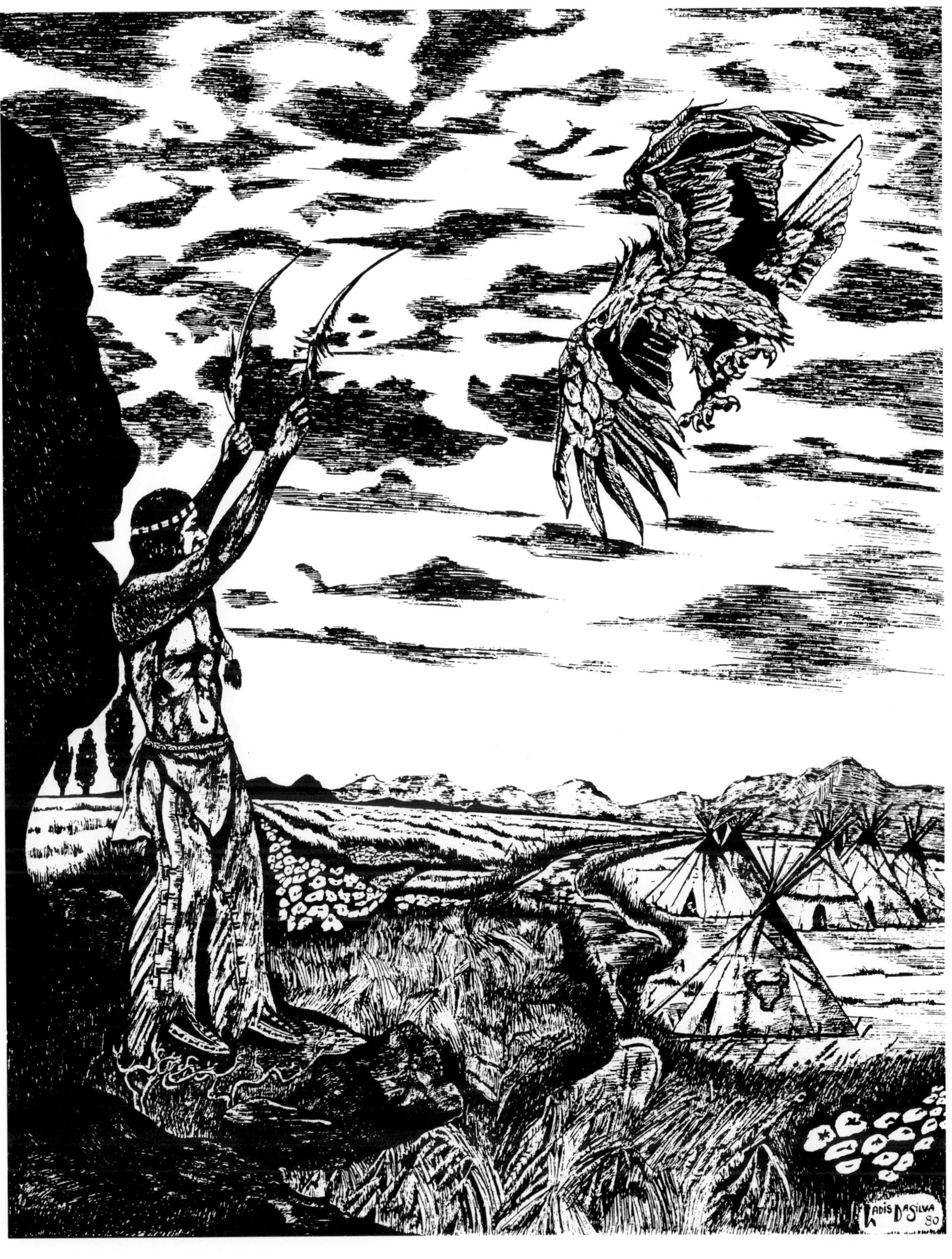

ANDRE ELIAS

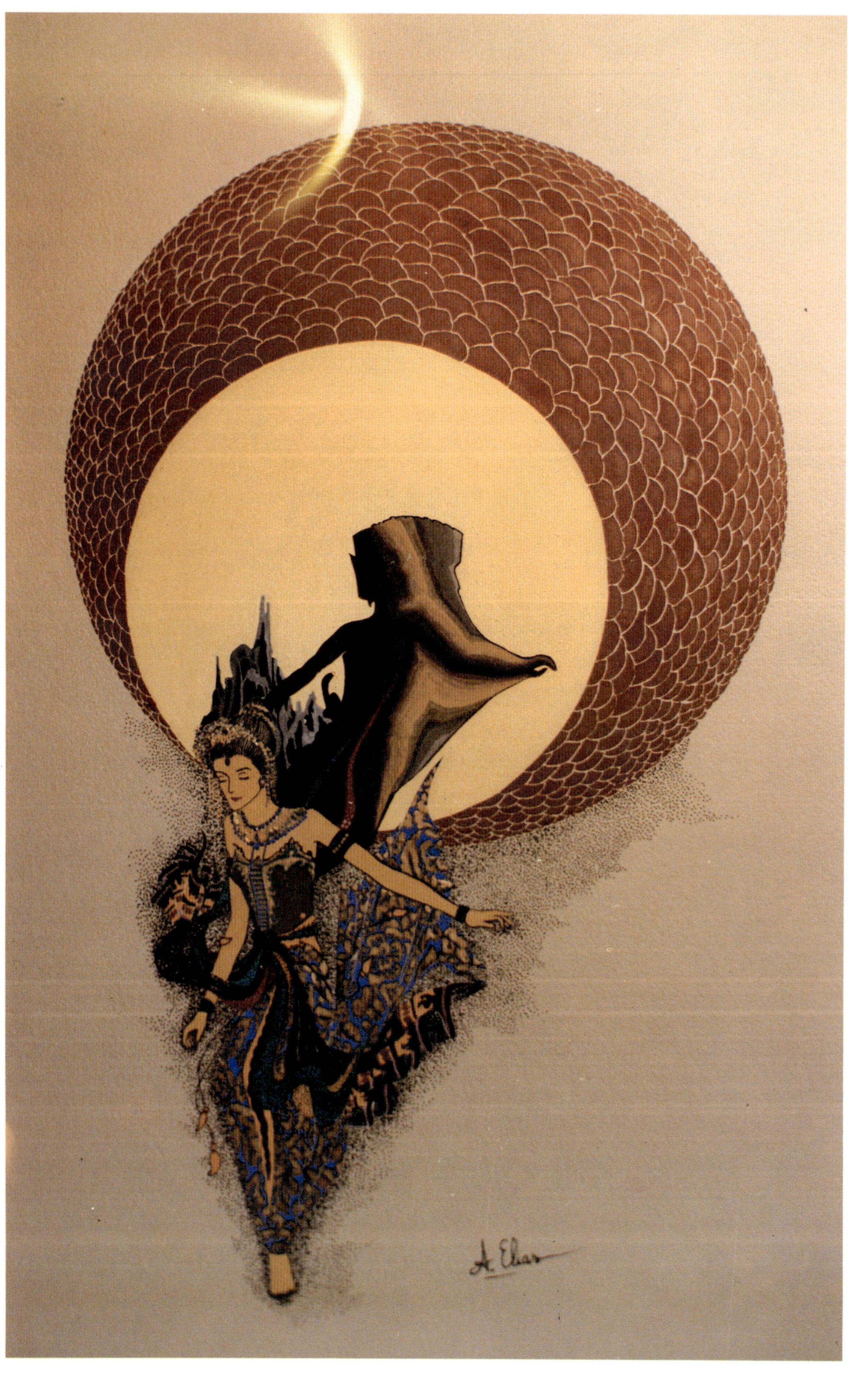

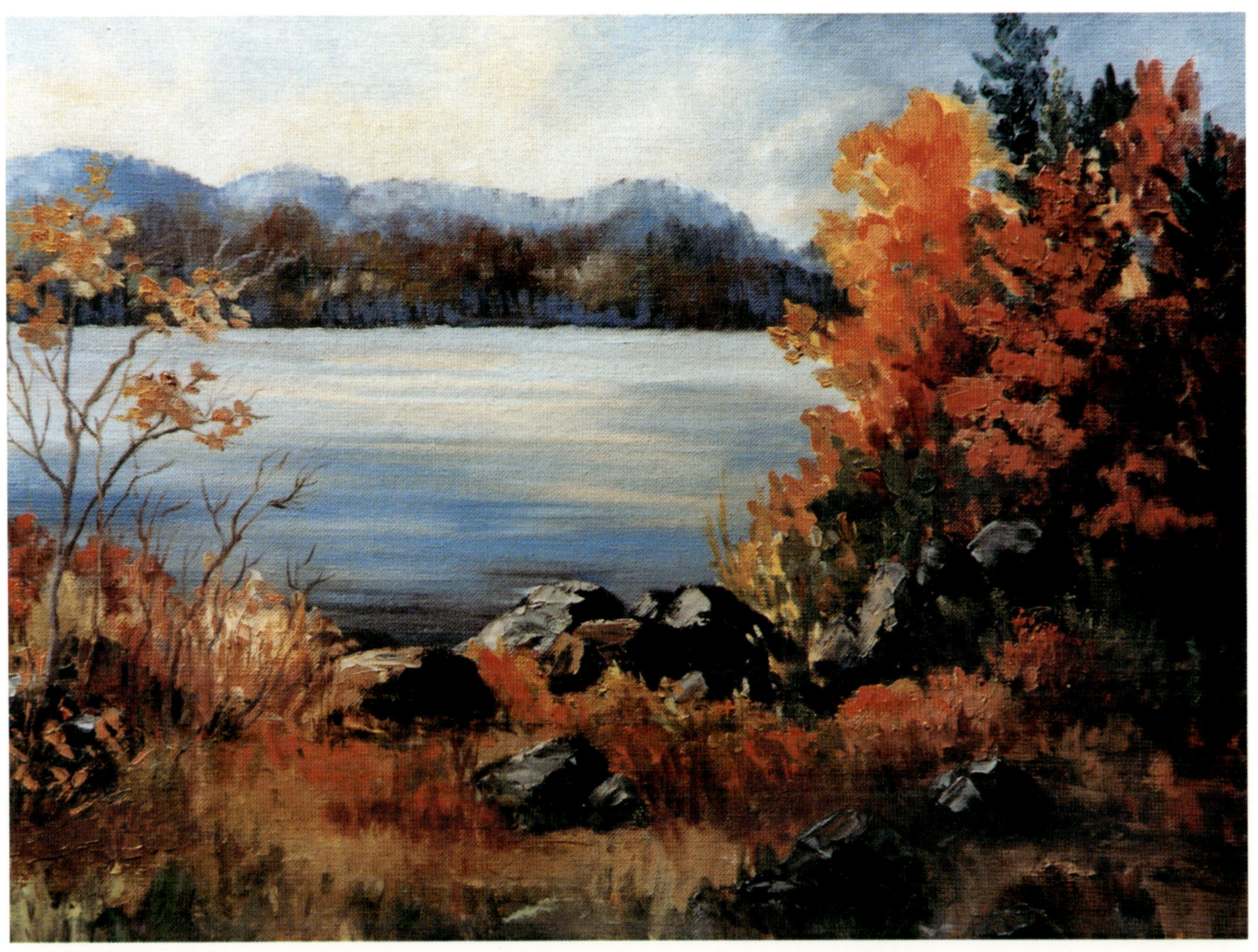

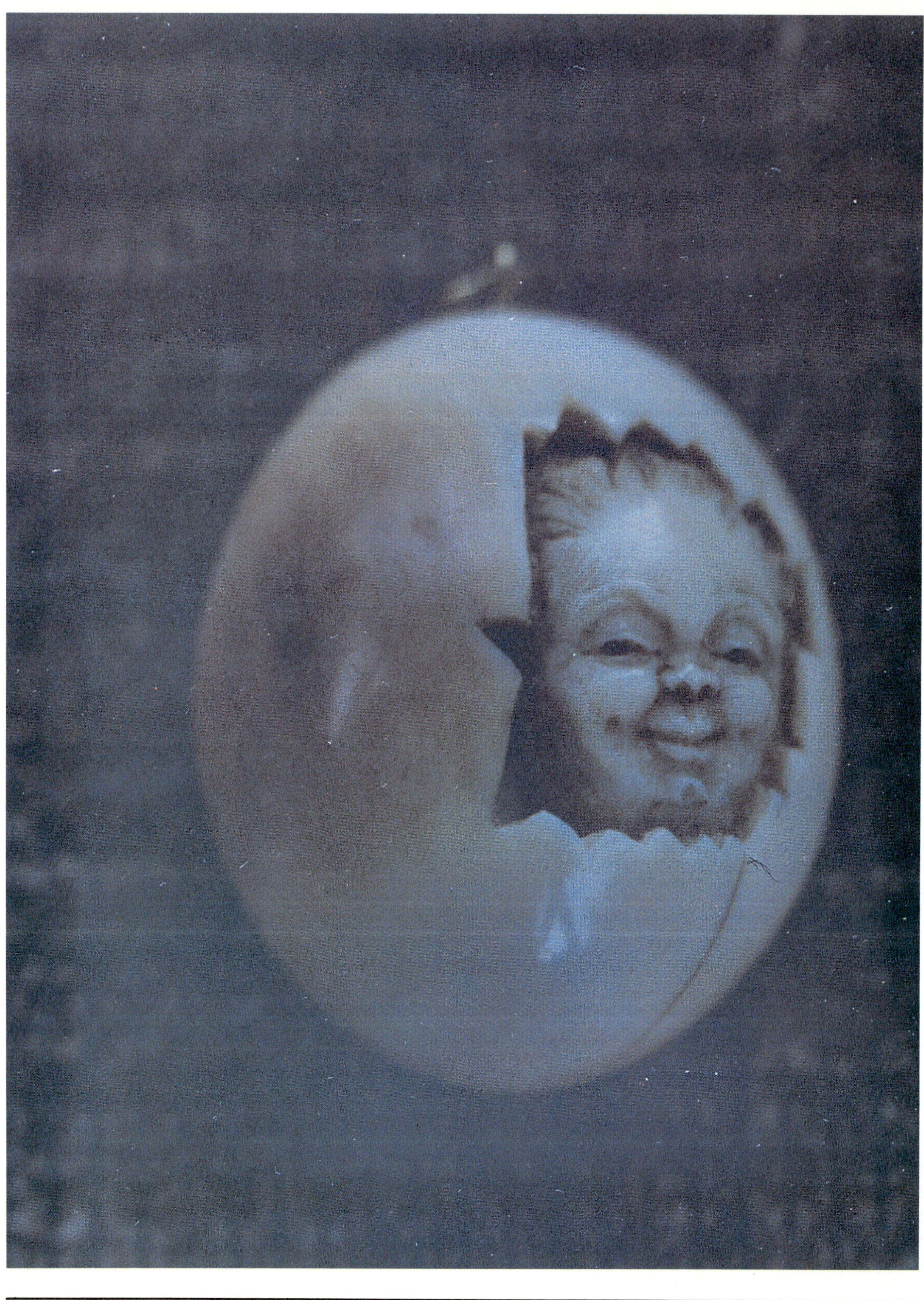

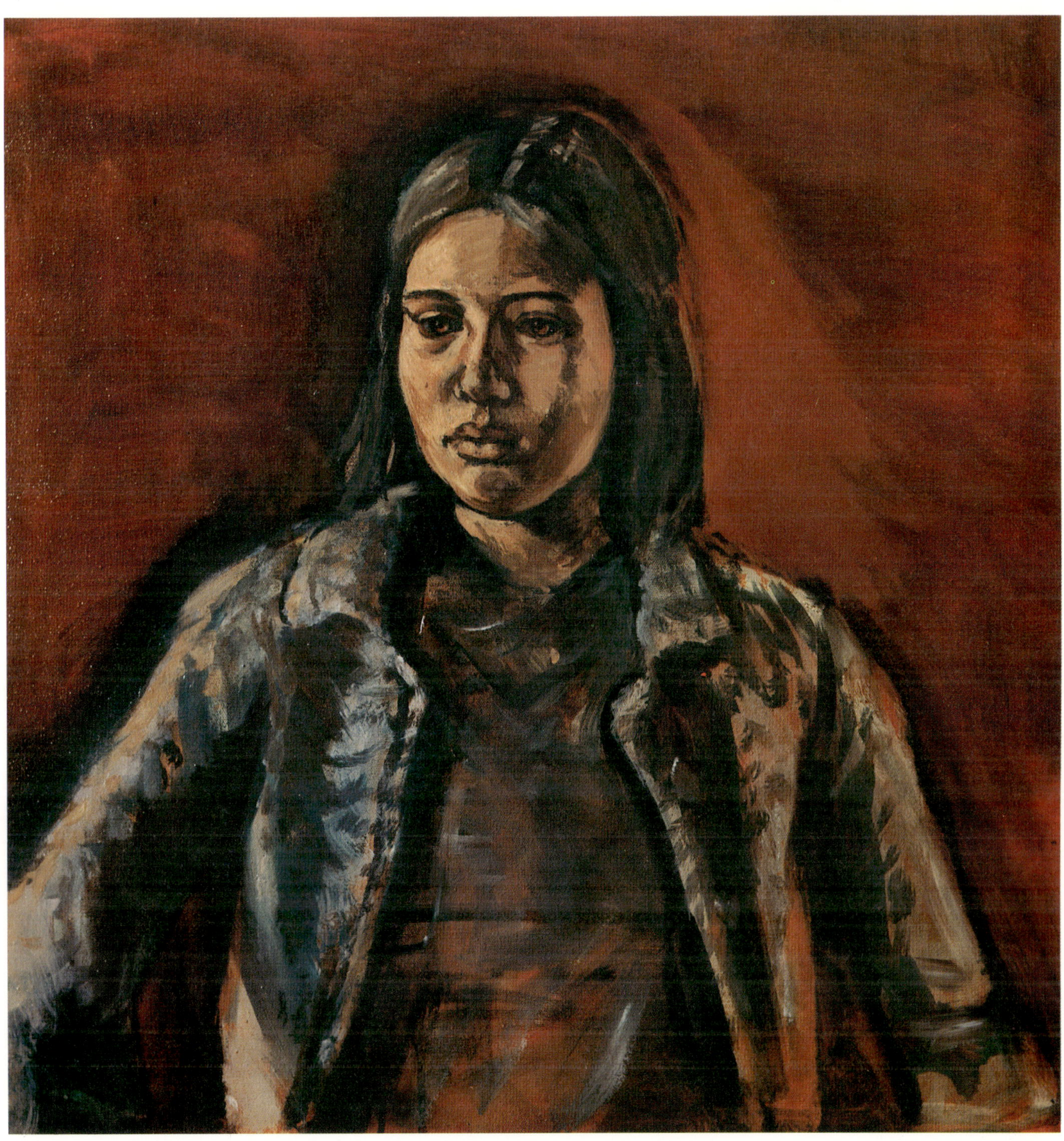

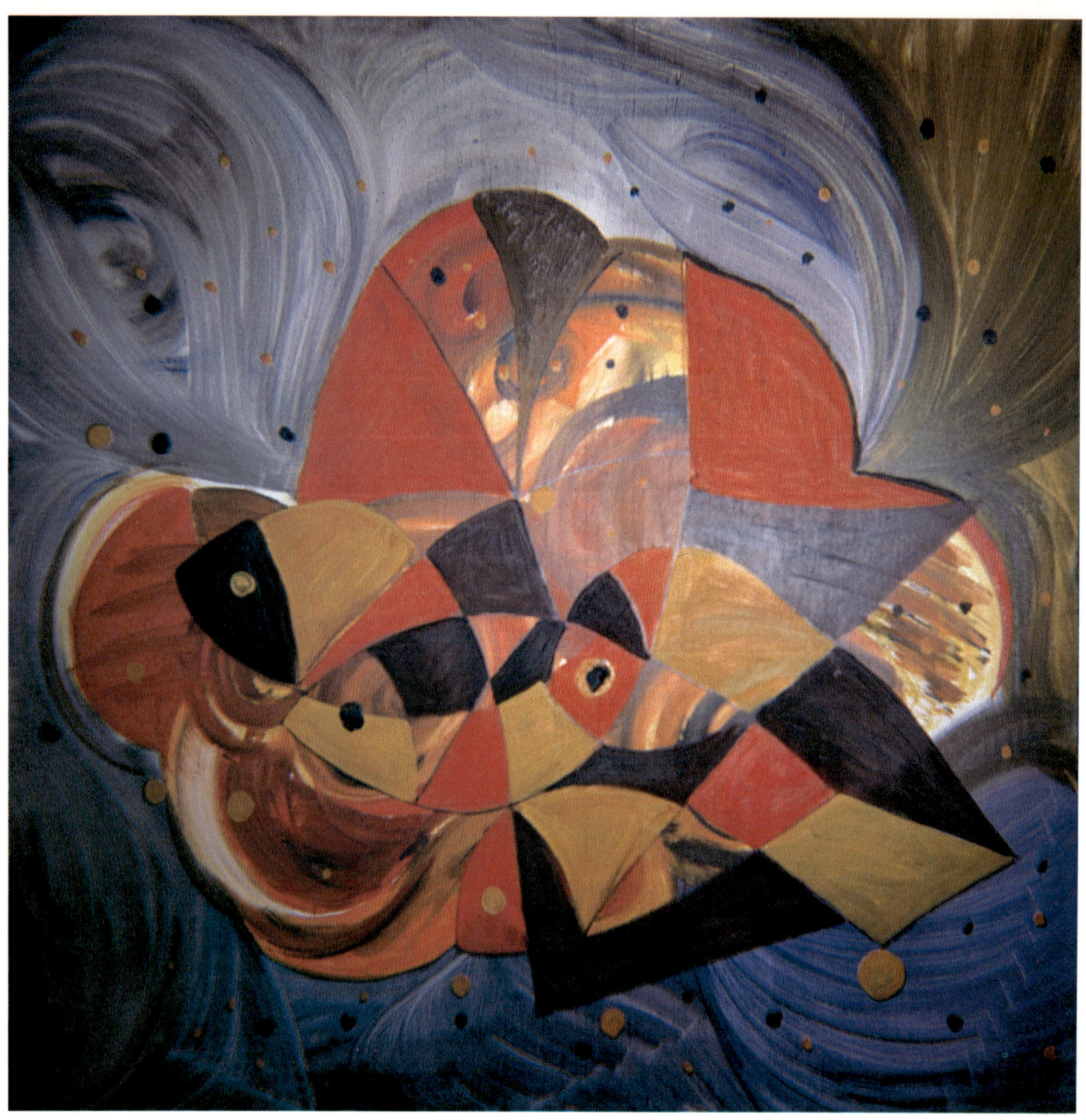

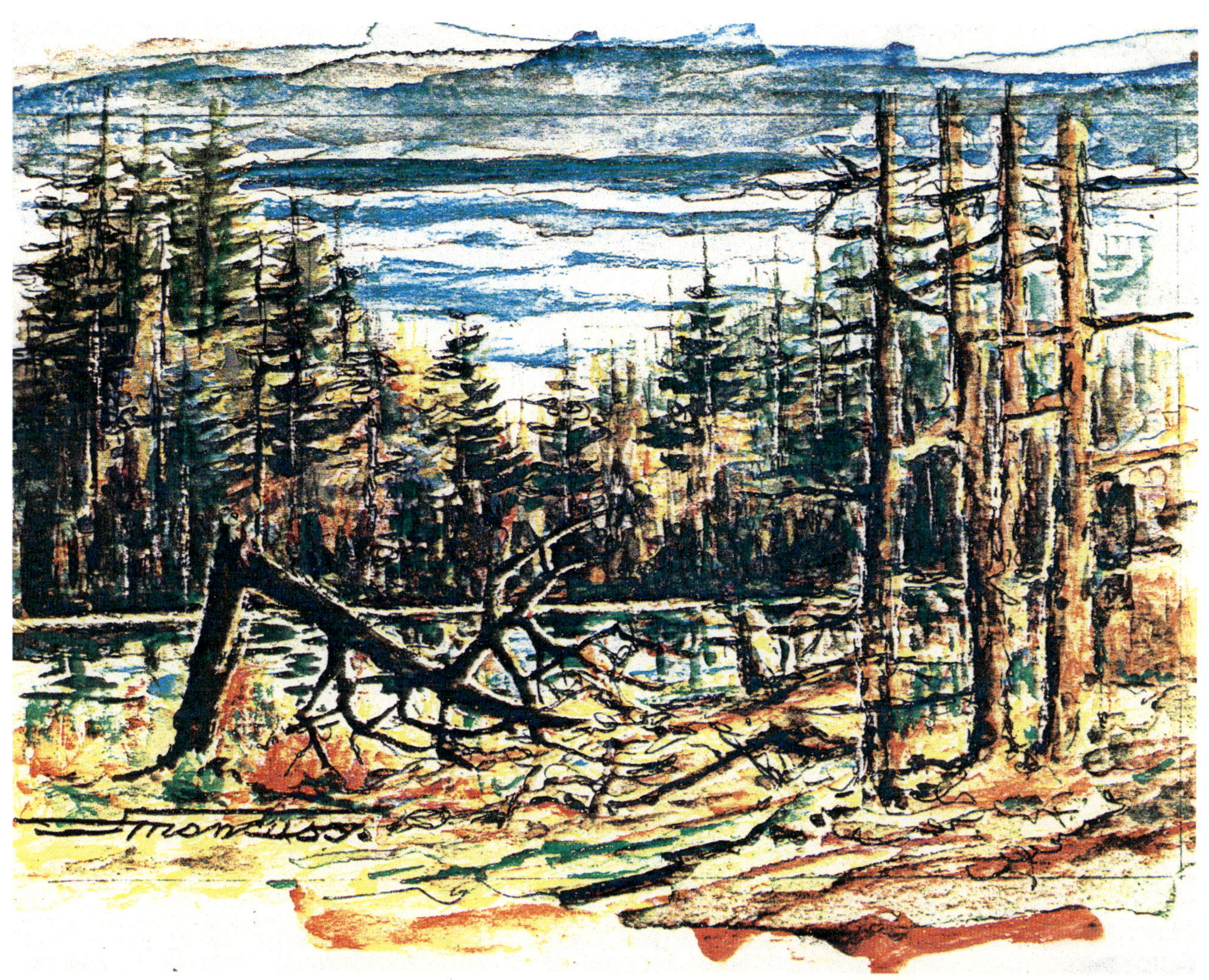

JOHN NEWMAN

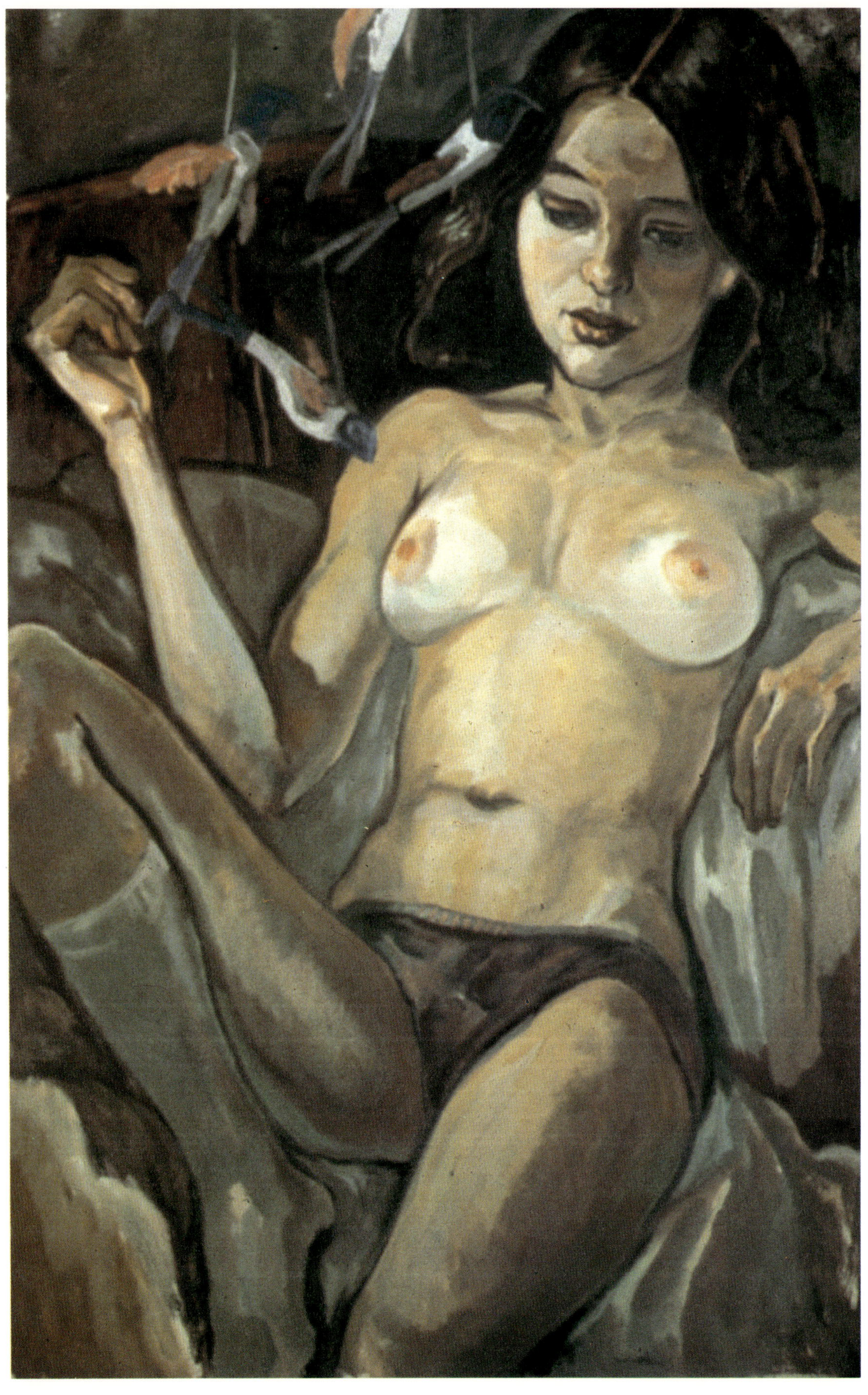

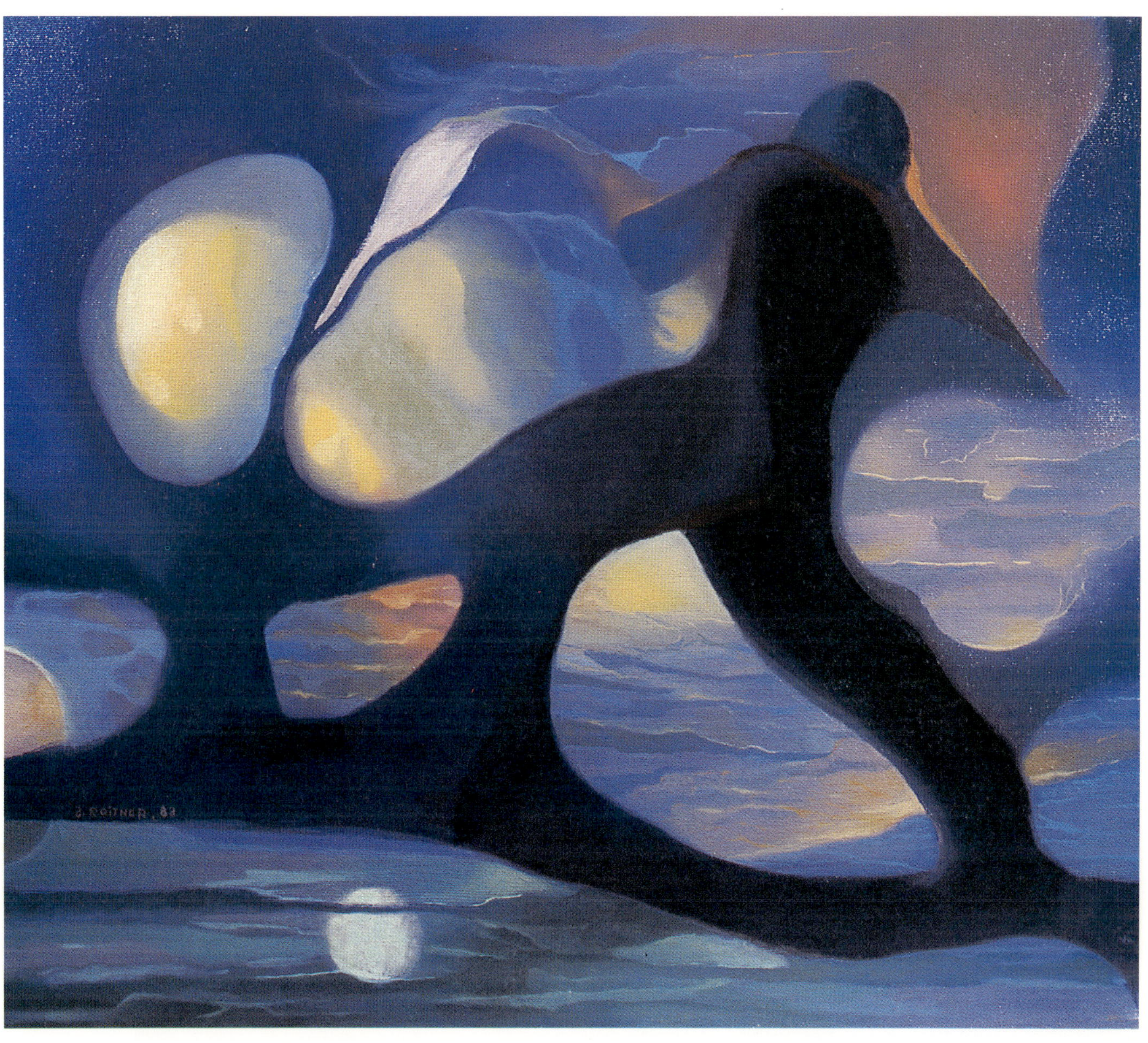

NELSON SEGURO

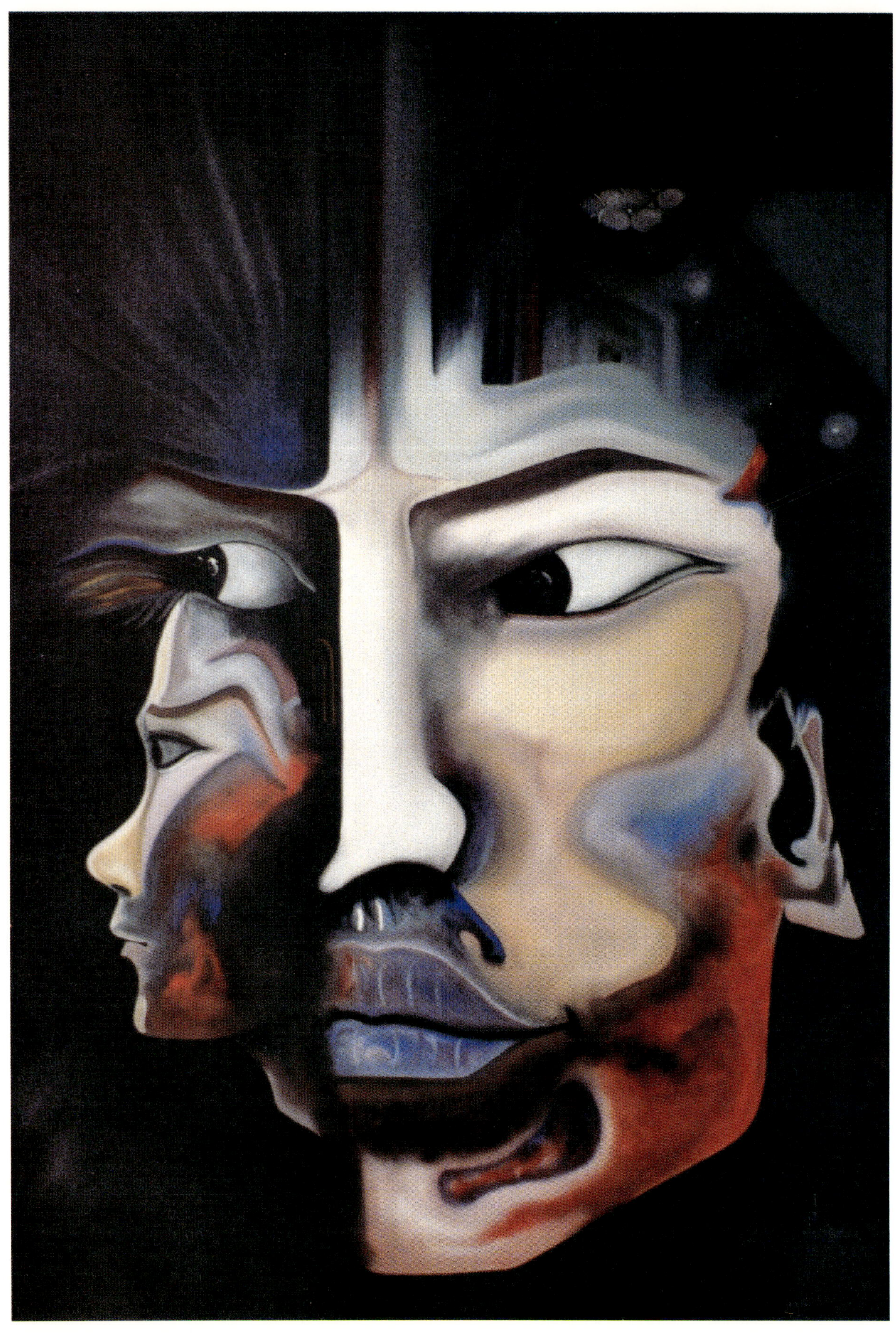

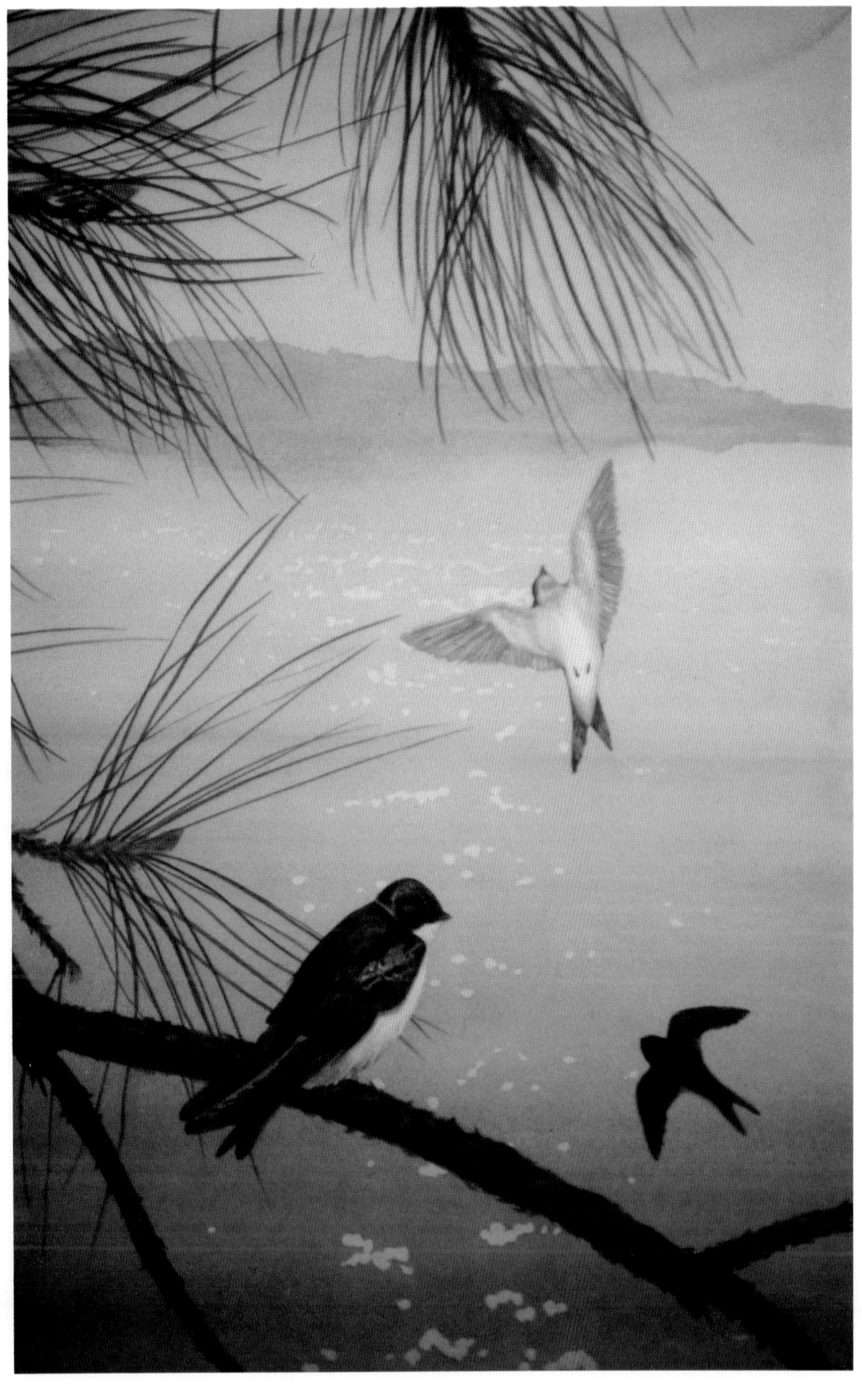

FREDERIC STEIGER

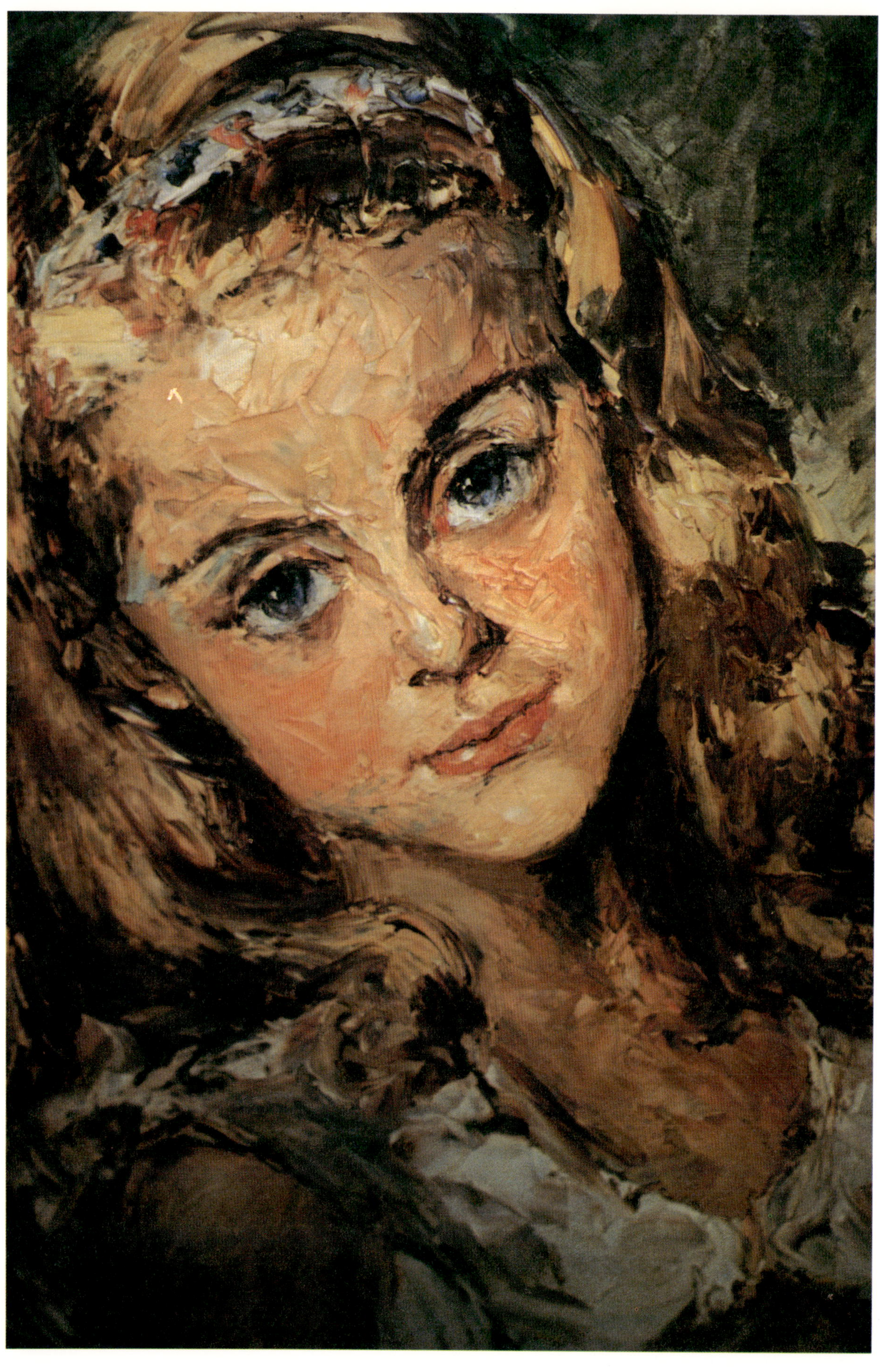

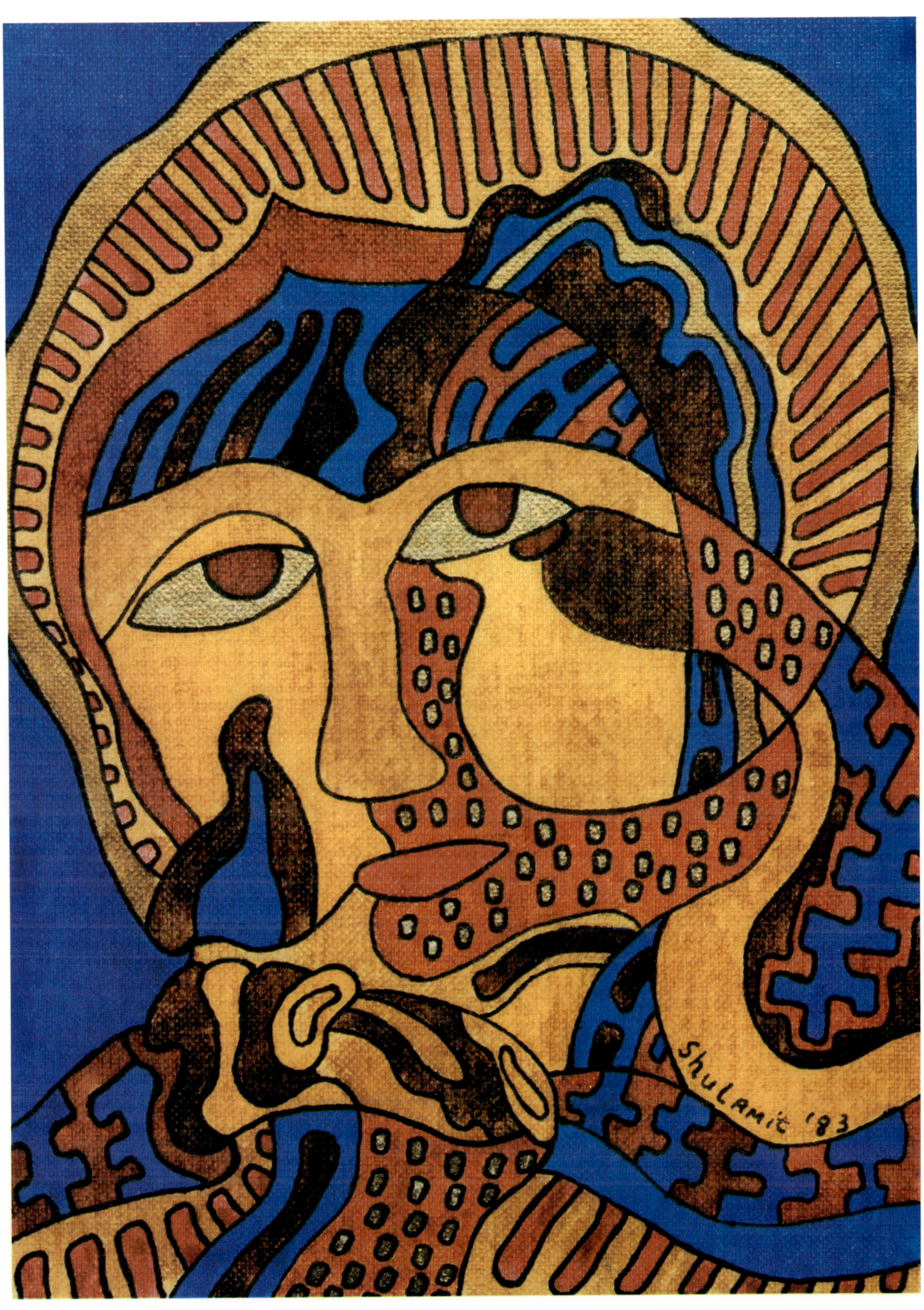

IGOR P. SUHACVEV

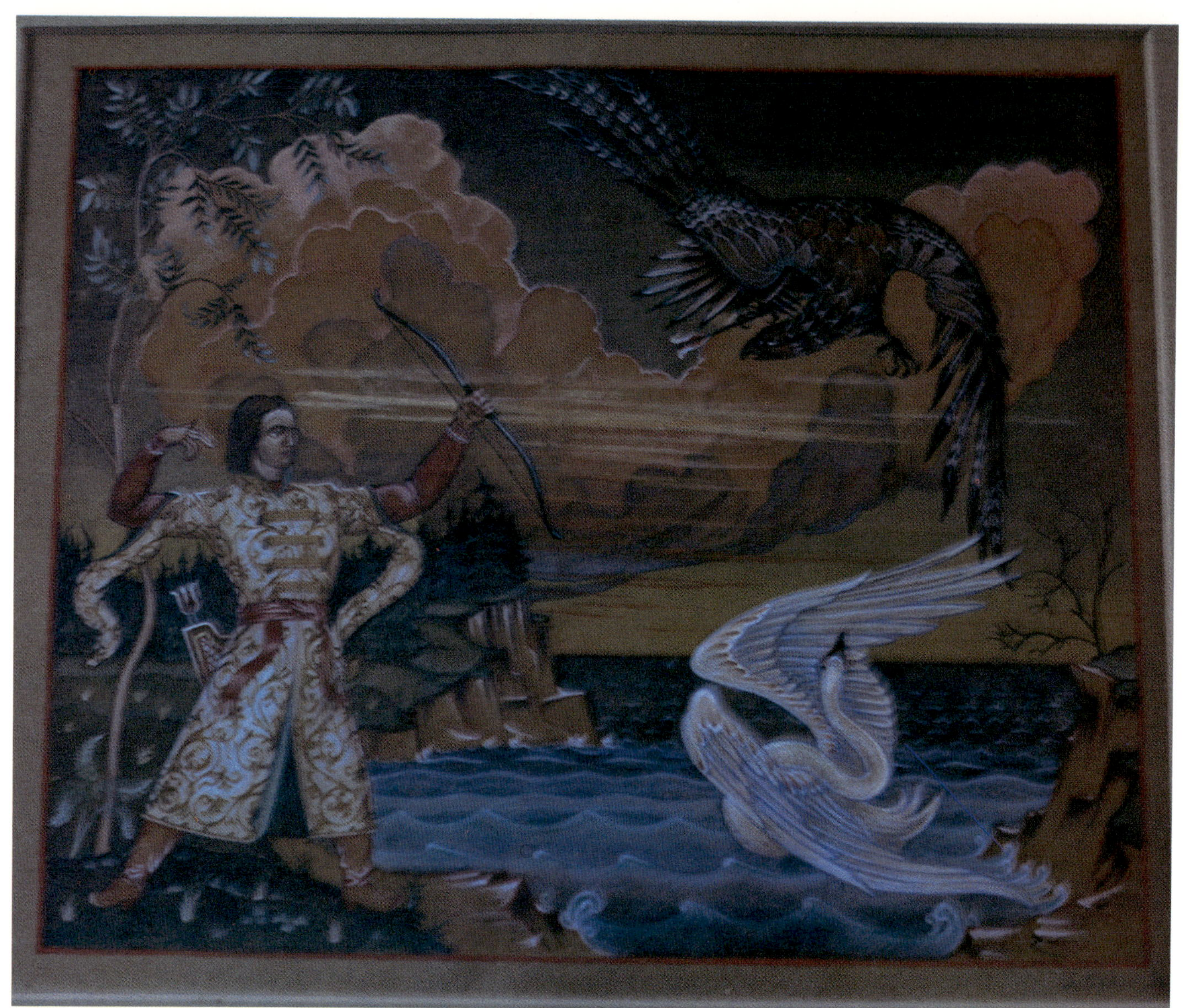

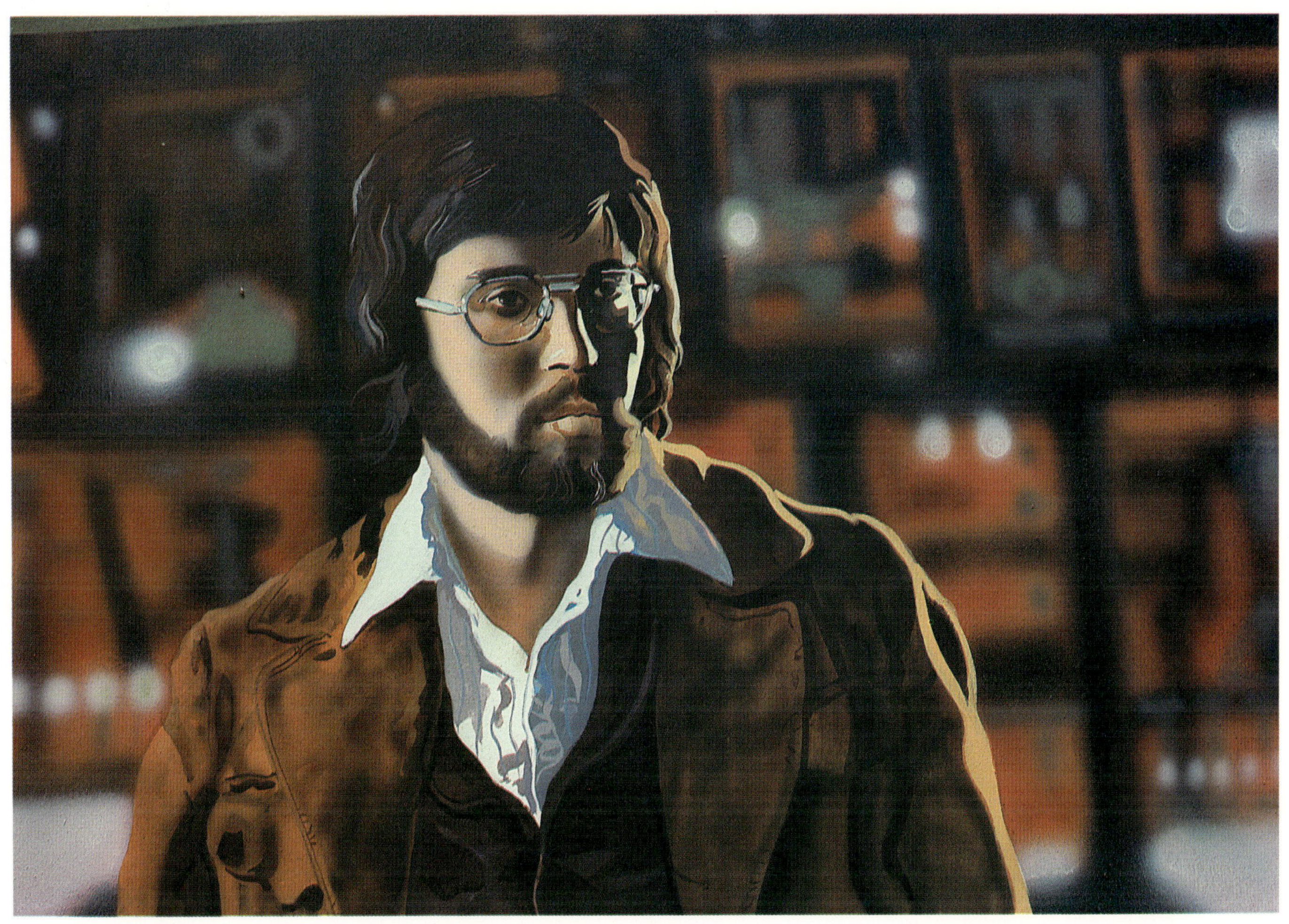

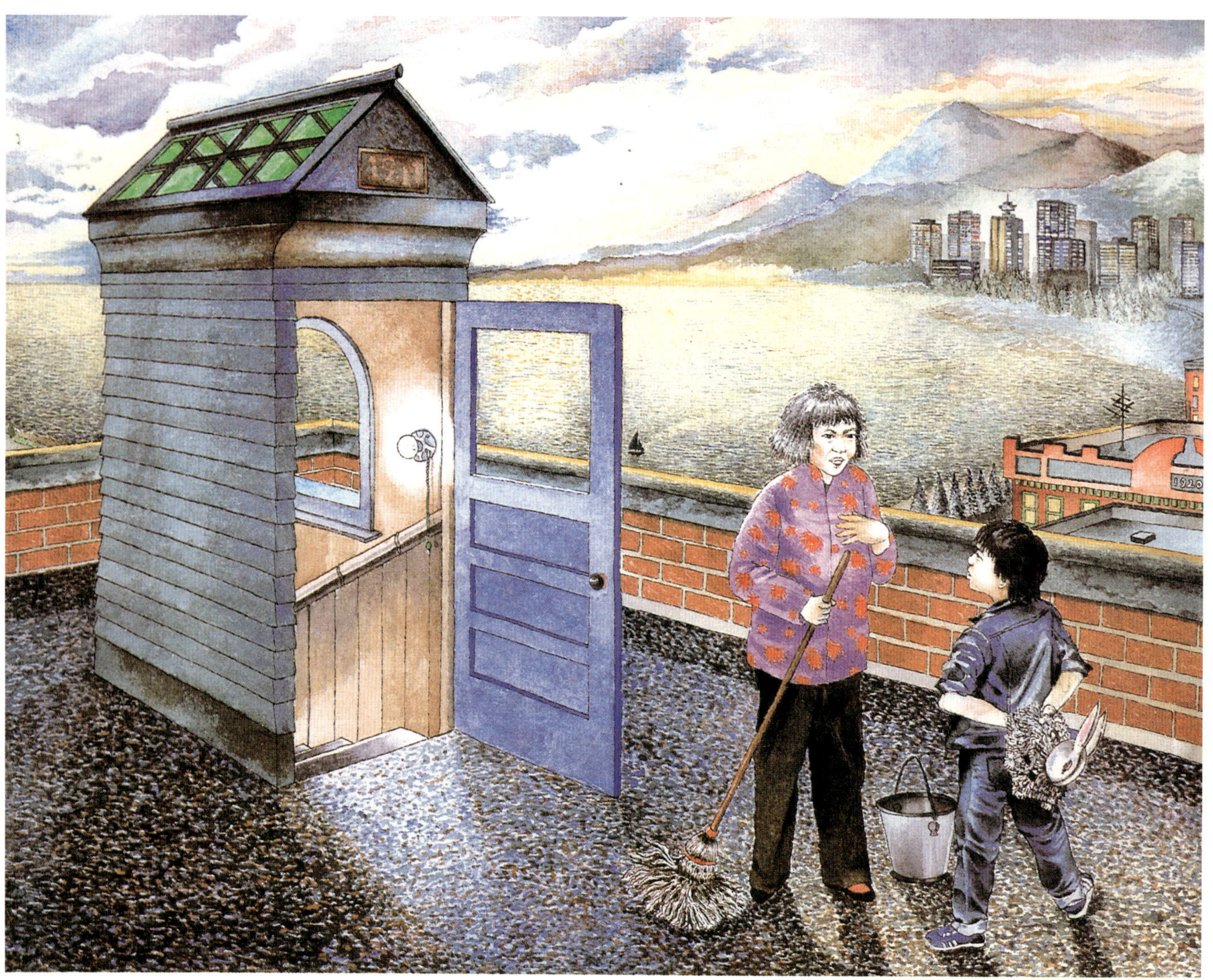

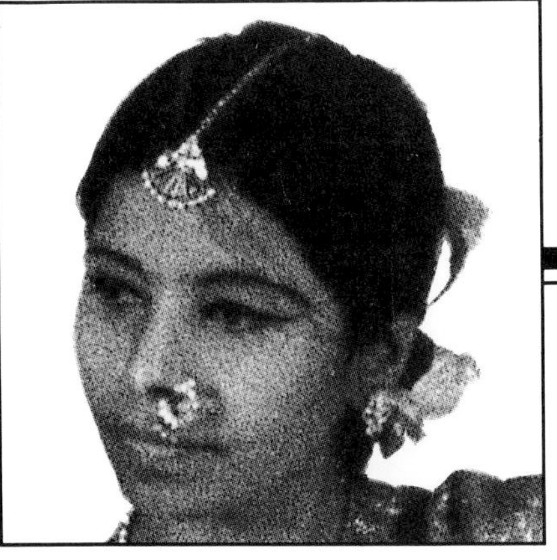

KHALETUN MAJUMDER

an accomplished painter, costume designer, illustrator, teacher, choreographer and singer

(excerpt previously published in THE SPIRES *Cultural Community Focus)*

Khaletun Majumder, was born on December 25 in Bangladesh, in the city of Rajshahi, on the banks of the river Padma.

During her childhood she would write verses and put them to music as well. She was equally fond of painting, an art to which she is still whole-heartedly dedicated and which she teaches at the Ontario College of Art, her sphere covering:

COSTUME ILLUSTRATION: in the Communications and Design Department.
EAST INDIAN DESIGN: in the Fine Arts Department, and
EAST INDIAN DANCES: in the Liberal Arts Studies Department.

During recess the interviewer had the opportunity to observe Khaletun in the midst of her students, a group with whom she blends in perfectly although she is authoritative in class and extremely demanding.

Intrigued, the interviewer asked a student of hers:

"What do you consider outstanding in your teacher?"
Student: "The way she encourages us to let our minds take the most daring flights of fancy and then convert our ideas into practically applied concepts, her dream being to see her students as successfully established artists."
Interviewer: "Is she accessible to students beyond class hours?"
Student: "Khaletun! She is approachable at all times — be it with new ideas and questions as to how to put these down on paper, or with personal problems. Her always open line for teacher-student communication, is an asset I highly value."
Interviewer: "I saw you doing an Indian folk dance on stage, and to judge by your dedicated concentration, you were quite obviously enjoying it."
Student: "But, of course. Otherwise, you would not have seen me there. After all, it

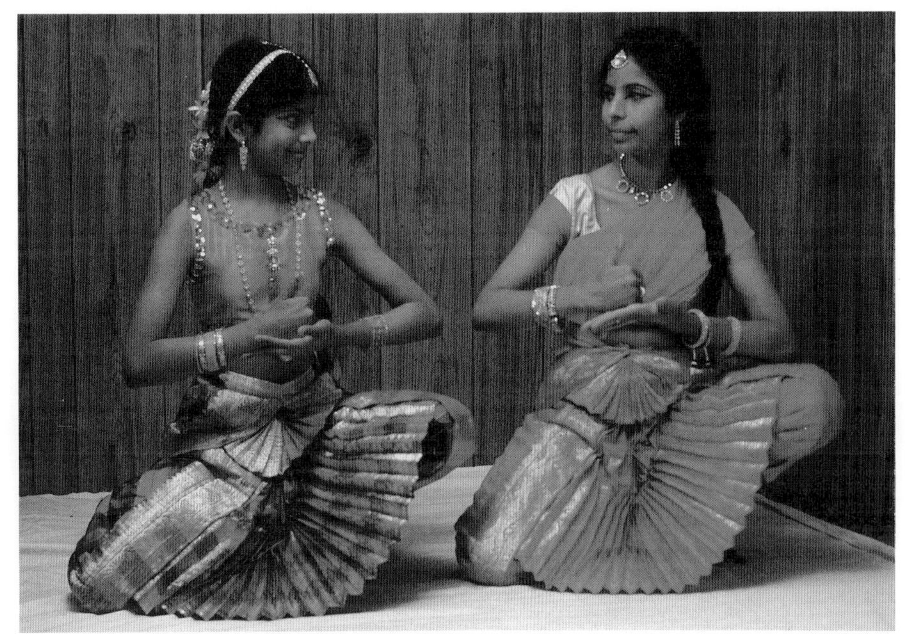

took months of hard work to get the meanings, acquire the facial and manual skills (especially the difficult neck rolling) and to finally graciously and rhythmically combine interpretation and movement. Yet Khaletun imbued us with such an awareness and love for oriental art and culture that it has become part of us."

No wonder the Indian dances performed by Khaletun's predominantly western students, leave such a strong, favourable echo in the hearts of even the most severe Oriental critics.

The interviewer asked Khaletun how she went about her teaching.

Khaletun: "I combine theory and practice. Having enjoyed folk dance as well as classical dance since childhood, it's not a chore, but a great pleasure for me to pass it on to others."

Interviewer: "Those dances are so intricate with every eye, facial, and hand movement having a separate meaning."

Khaletun: "The students caught on amazingly fast. Look at this pile of dance illustrations. (She draws out approximately 200 of them). I did these to help to clarify difficult poses. Don't forget that my students are all artists who have no difficulty in correlating the illustrations with the actual movements.

"I really enjoy doing illustrations and preferably in ink, as you can see from all those illustrations in UNDER THE SPELL OF INDIA. Every one of those sketches was done in free-hand without any rough draft, or correction. I perceive the image in my mind and simply try to recapture the very scene on paper."

Interviewer: "You seem to be influenced by the Moghul miniatures."

Khaletun: "Yes, I underwent training in that field. I am also familiar with the Kangara School of Painting that evolved from the former. It brought about a shifting from the Muslim influence of the Moghul style to the Hindu philosophy reflected by the Kangara style, the result being a harmonious blending of both."

Interviewer: "Have you illustrated any other books and, if so, did you change the medium or apply new techniques?"

Khaletun: "I did illustrations for the bilingual Bengali-English children's book, THE TWO SISTERS, a transcultural undertaking for the preservation of the Indian heritage (published by Kids Canada Press).

"No, I did not change the medium, since I actually execute all small-scale illustrations in ink. However, lately I do prefer ink mixed with water colours, a combina-

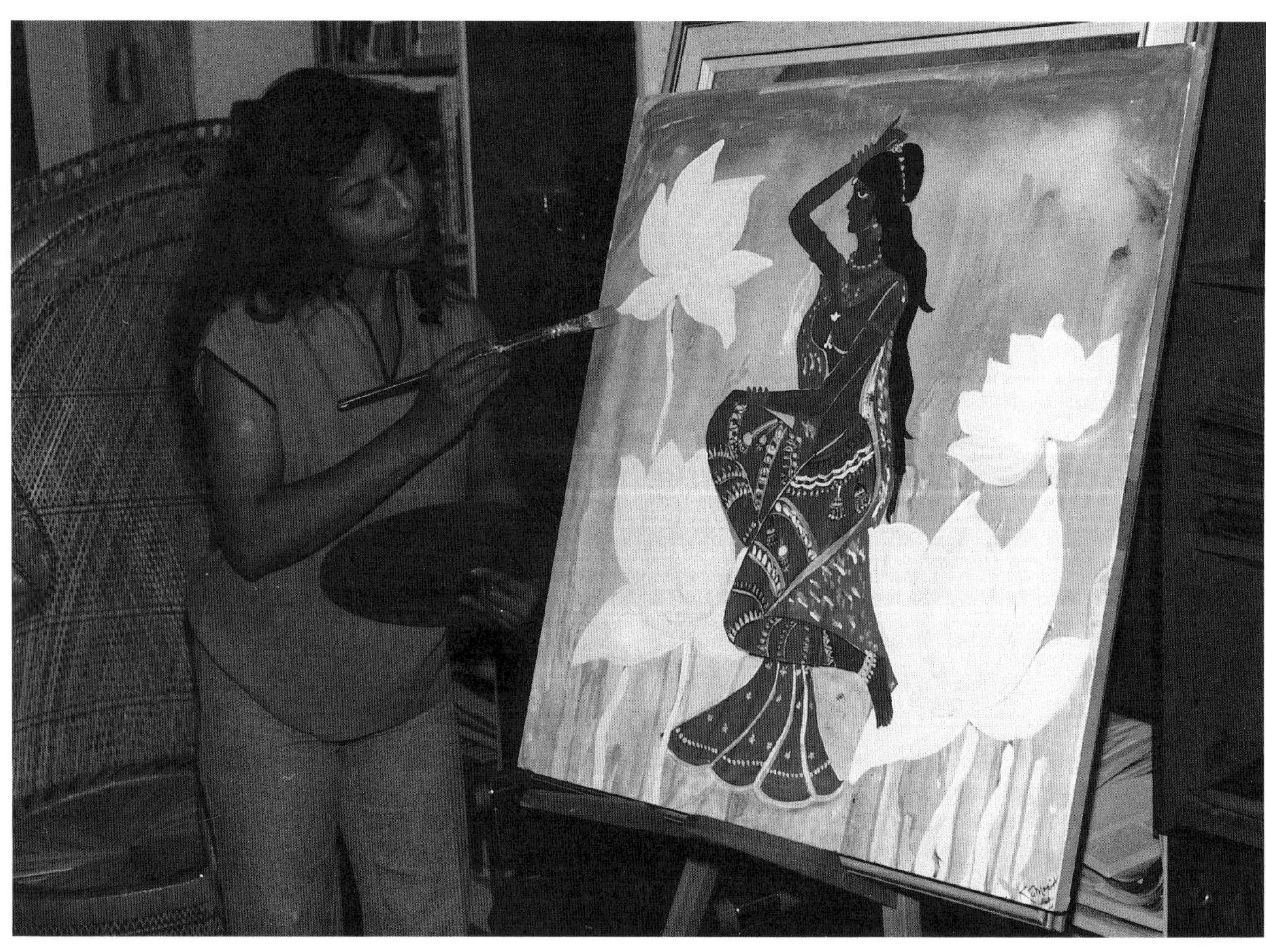

SOLITUDE photo by Mohammed (Mitu) Khaledul Haq

tion that creates a certain warmth on account of the liquid 'wash' effect."

Interviewer: "Is there any reason why you never depict your lovers in an embrace?"

Khaletun: "Although love is the recurring theme in practically all my sketches, drawings and paintings, it is a love on the highest level, a love never physically consumated but rather spiritually consuming the person.

"To me, there is nothing greater than love. I believe in human growth exclusively through love. The concept of punishment and reward is something totally alien to my philosophy. And although Muslim by birth, I hold a pantheistic belief."

Interviewer: "You seem to draw strength from your faith."

Khaletun: "I draw all my inspiration and strength from the love of my Creator and my faith in HIM, fusion of God and Allah all at once.."

Interviewer: "I see you changed to oils and your style reminds me somewhat of Dali."

Khaletun:" As of late, I do all large-scale paintings in oils. And, once again, the theme is platonic love — the woman floating in space (ethereal aspect) with the clouds serving her as garb. The adolescent, the god of love, kneels down out of respect for the purity of her love, making his offering to her on his knees."

Interviewer: "Yet, no matter how lofty your theme may be, you never seem to totally lose touch with reality. This is clearly evident from the solid lines encasing the painting, framing, so-to-speak, every single one of your pieces of work. They are well-balanced compositions in which objects are interconnected, yet preserve their distinct form retaining a beautiful perspective."

Khaletun: "Since you mention that, I must admit that I am extremely particular when it comes to spacing, centering, and the balancing of the completed composition.

"And as to the frame, that (at times) detailed ornamental design is the only repetitive pattern I ever use."

Interviewer: "How do you achieve that special graphic quality that gives your paintings a certain three-dimensional depth?"

Khaletun: "Since I work exclusively in freehand, the free flowing lines — some call them dancing or rhythmical lines — arise automatically. But in order to achieve the three-dimensional quality, I usually invent some interesting environment or background that catches the viewer's attention. From there his attention is then guided to the actually intended focus of interest. I generally add a touch of bright, scintillating colour to the main object and accentuate the outer lines to express a sculptured effect. These are the lines that make the female figure."

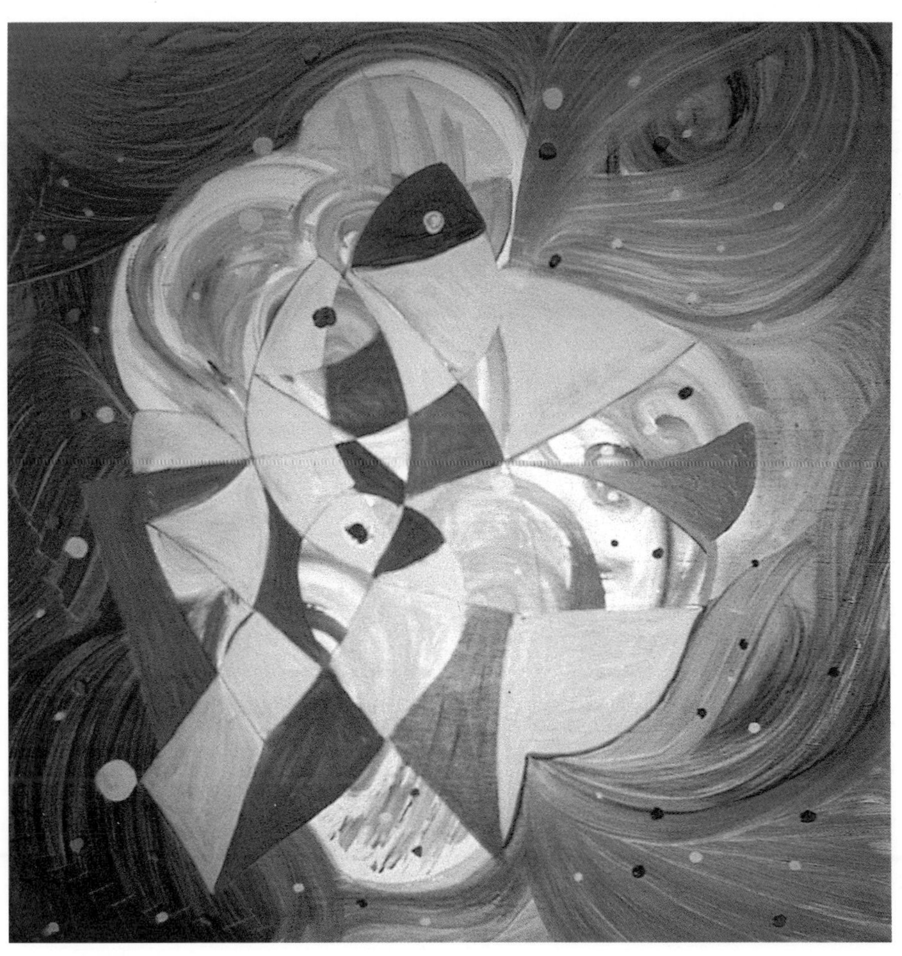

DESERT UNITY   medium: oil
photo by Mohammed (Mitu) Khaledul Haq

KHALETUN MAJUMDER

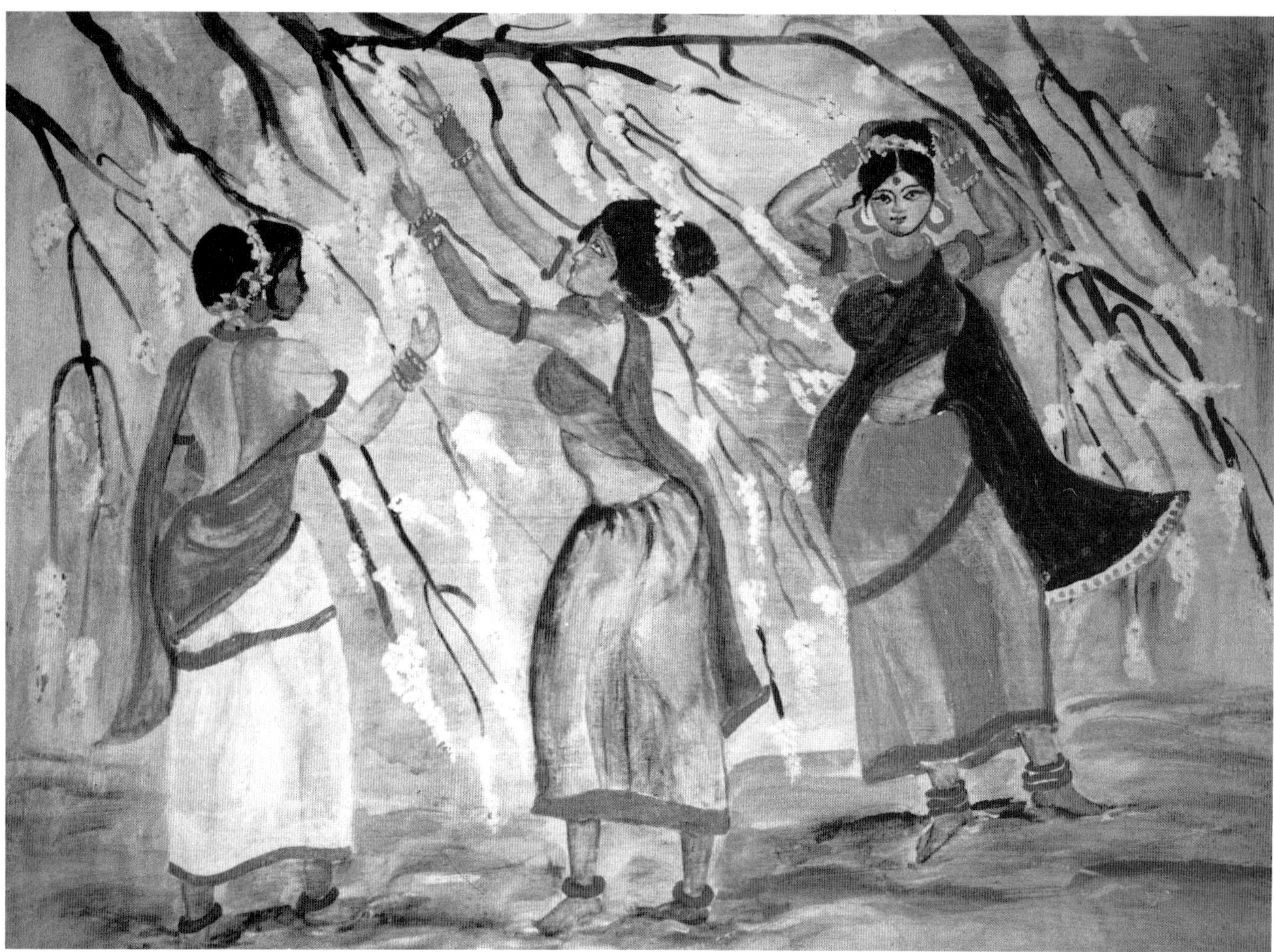

REACHING FOR ESSENCE meidum: oil
photo by Mohammed (Mitu) Khaledul Haq

Interviewer: "No matter how stylized some of your paintings may be, they seem, somehow, to be natural and that applies particularly to the female figure."
Khaletun: "They are natural, modelled on real life situations or drawn from the vivid images clearly stored in my mind. Those women are perfectly happy with the world they live in. They are in their element and exude a strength and serenity all their own.

"Besides, it's so easy to make a person look happy." (Khaletun takes a brush and to an unfinished face merely adds a dot near each end of the lips and there the figure is — all asmile!"

Interviewer: "When do you feel most creative, Khaletun?"
Khaletun: "When I drive along the highway. Then I have an onrush of ideas — perfect compositions in bright colours — which I sort out mentally and arrive home with read images waiting to be put on canvas."
Interviewer: "I heard that you also wrote poetry in your homeland. Is that so?"
Khaletun: "Yes, I used to write poetry and short stories and had several published in BEGHUM, a Bengali Weekly. Besides, I always did my own illustrations (mainly in ink) for everything I wrote."

It is understandable that an artist such as Khaletun attracted a very talented husband. Soumen Majumder, a well-known Bengali singer and instrumentalist. No wonder, then, that through the years they have shared innumerable shows and television programmes. They are often supported by their gifted daughter, Setu, an accomplished dancer — having assimilated western and eastern styles — and their son Mitu, a drummer and piano player who has a band of his own with emphasis on western music.

Their shows are enjoyed by western as well eastern audiences.

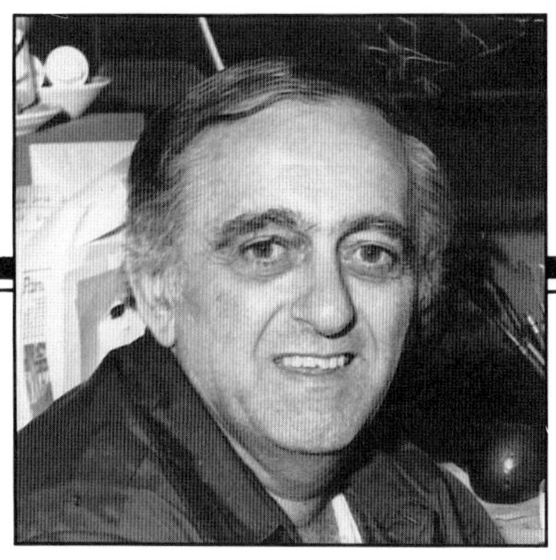

FRED MANCUSO

a fine arts painter resident — West Park Hospital

1984 marked Fred's 47th year as an artist who has so far produced close to 10,000 pieces of artwork.

(excerpt published in the 1982 Spring issue of THE SPIRES Cultural Community Focus.)

This cheerful, outgoing Sagittarian (born on November 23, 1925, in Lachine, Quebec) is of Italian descent and feels at home conversing in English, French, and Italian.

Fred's interest in art was kindled when he was twelve years old and a Russian scenic artist, rather advanced in age, came to decorate his parental home. This interior decorator also happened to be an oil painter. Fred was so intrigued by his style, and the fine arts painter so flattered by the boy's persistent interest, that he offered to

NORTH BUSHLAND — old macazza   Laurentian Mountains, north of Montreal, Quebec   water colour

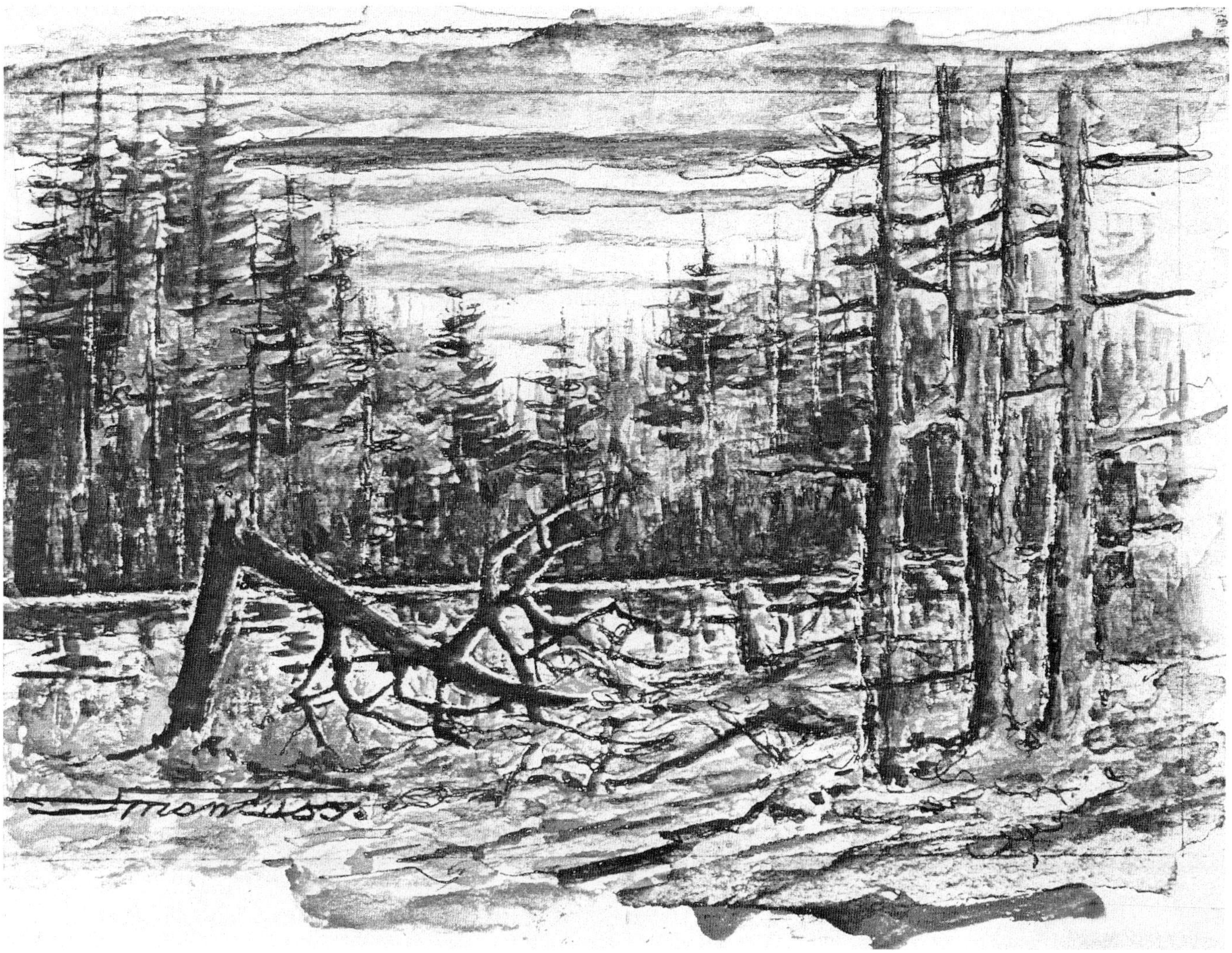

FRED MANCUSO

teach him. Oh, the thrill of painting in oil!

Fred also enjoyed strong support from his elder and only brother who was the guiding light of his childhood. He was the one who enrolled Fred with the Washington School of Art (Washington, D.C.) — a correspondence course programme he successfully completed. Himself a creative artist, he understood his younger brother and fostered a great appreciaton of art in Fred, keeping his interest alive by taking him to art galleries, art shows, art auctions, and antique shows. He was Fred's teacher of a sort and also imbued him with a love of music, and symphonies in particular.

All through school, Fred was the class artist and even qualified for the bronze medal awarded for excellence in art "I could have used it in math", he sighs.

Fred's father — when confronted with his son's wish to become an artist — had a quite different outlook on his son's artistic endeavours. He definetely wanted Fred to choose another — more solid — line because a career in arts was something that seemed rather bleak to him. Being a good Italian boy, Fred listened to parental advice and decided to work for an engineering company.

Suddenly blue-eyed Agnes with long straight blonde hair, (once the runner-up in a Beauty Queen contest at the OCA), lit up his life. She was an artist, too, having graduated from the Ontario College of Art. They met in 1953 when she came to Montreal looking for a job as a textile designer. It was love at first sight — for both of them. They soon got married and have one daughter, Patricia.

Fred had always nourished the dream of having a business of his own and — finally — his dream came true. From 1958 to 1961 he ran his own commercial art studio, covering mainly the production of silkscreen card designs (for souvenir sector), commercial graphics, sign writing and lettering. His wife gave up the position of designer she had found, meanwhile, and helped Fred build up the business. Soon they were able to expand and hire additional staff.

However, in 1961, Fred started feeling ill, and it was probably the onset of MS. Of course, adjustments became necessary in their lifestyle. His wife deferred her painting to weekends, working as an occupational therapist during the week. She is now the Director of Recreational Activity at the Leisure World Nursing Homes. But how did Fred cope? Luckily he has his art to fall

WINTER FARM owned by Mrs. Hagerman, executive director/WEST PARK HOSPITAL

photo by Caren Hendrick

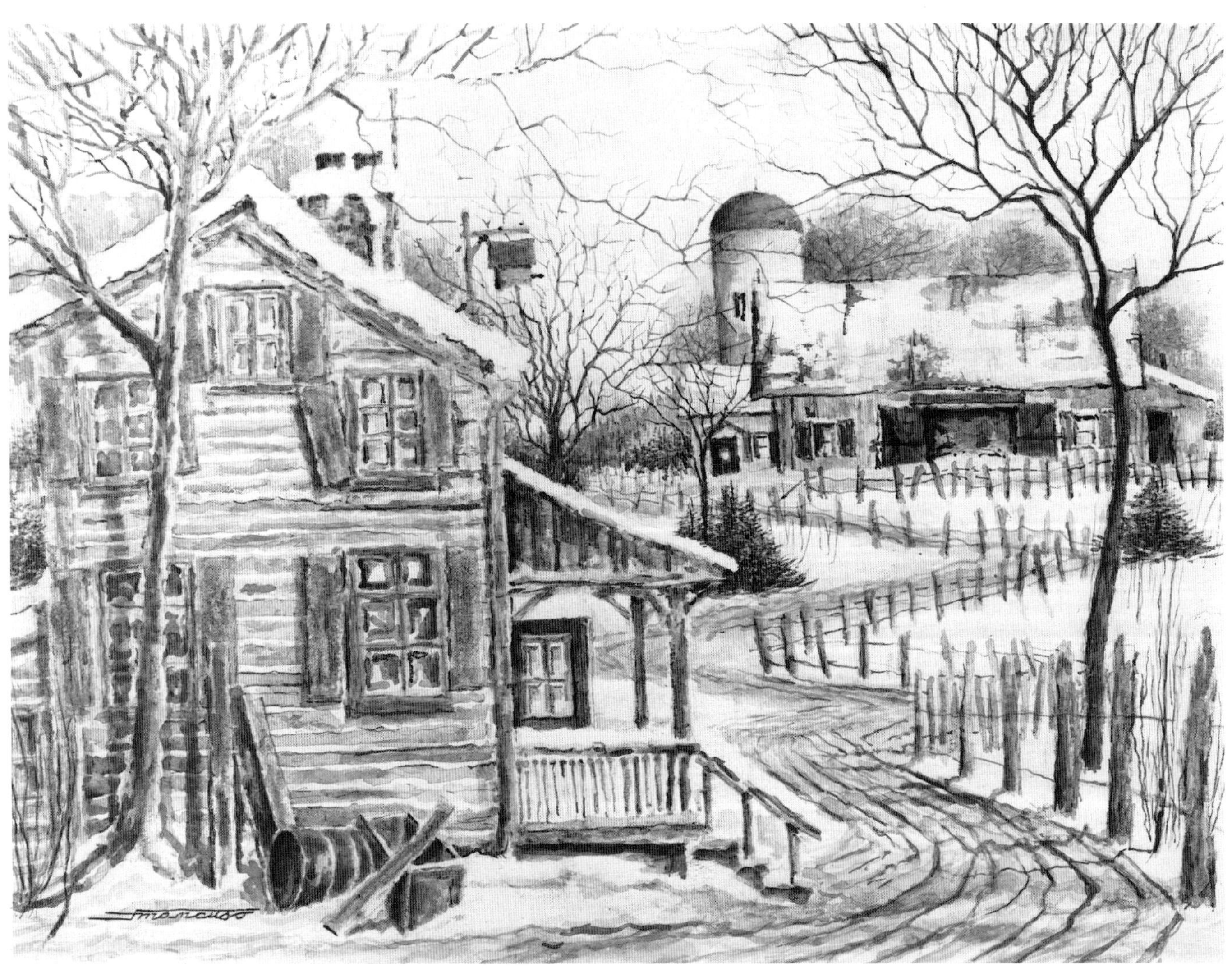

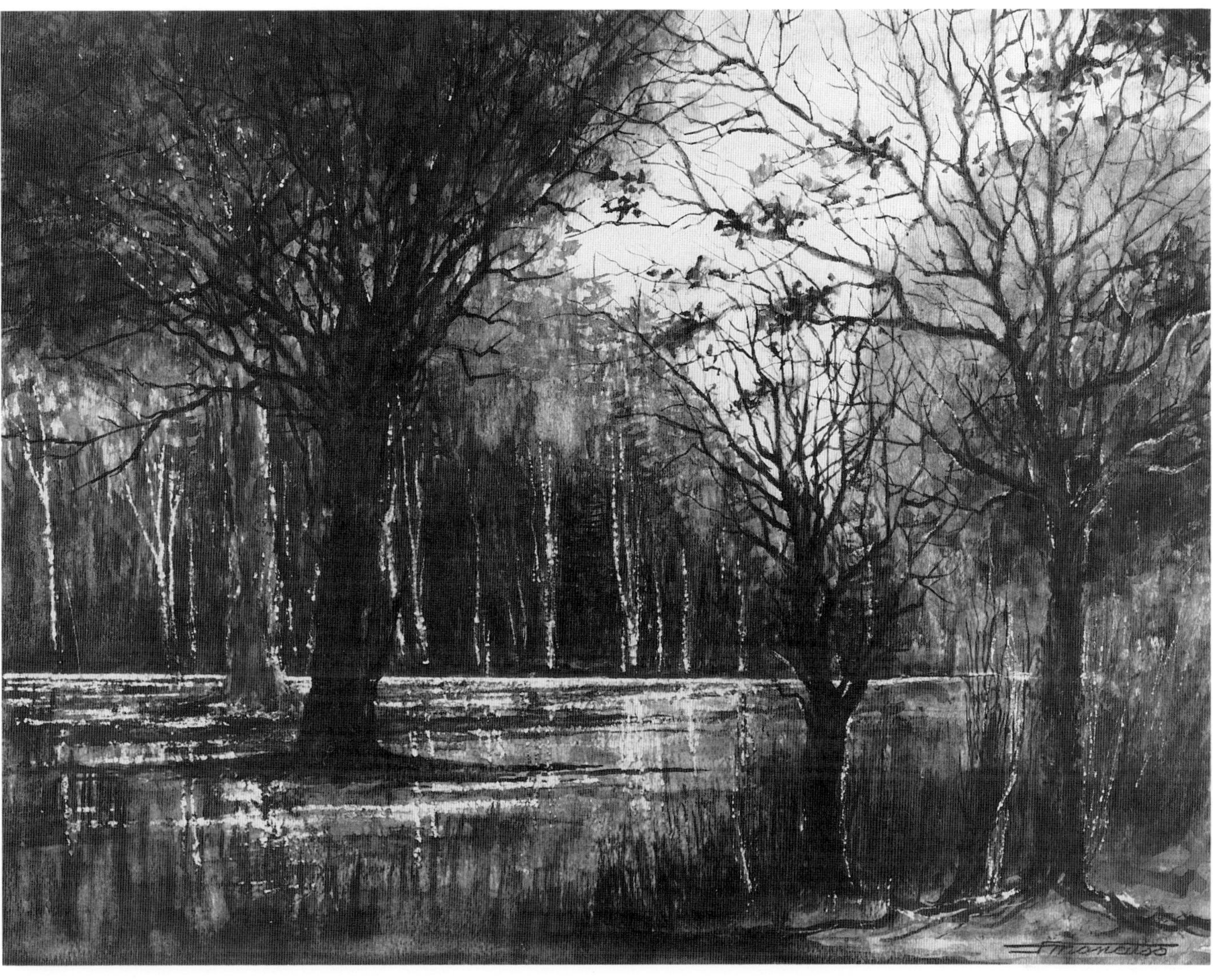

photo by Caren Hendrick

back on. Now a resident of the West Park Hospital, he holds no bitterness. Instead, he finds strength and peace of mind in a positive philosophy.

Nowadays, he usually paints from 7:30 in the morning until 10 in the evening, and does so exclusively for pleasure. He does sell some of his paintings, keeping the prices as low as possible so that his art is available to anyone who appreciates it. Fred believes it's wonderful to be appreciated through one's art. To him, that is a satisfaction no money can buy. It would be painful to Fred to have his paintings sitting around collecting dust when they could be hanging in someone's home where they could bring so much happiness.

With a dreamy look of nostalgia in his eyes, Fred explains: "I had always been an outdoorsman. The bush held a magic" a peace and joy I could never understand. Painting was a way to speak of that tranquillity; those forests of freedom. It's a great thrill to be able to capture a moment in time and nature."

Replaying those golden moments in his mind, Fred adds: "I guess it was the harmony with nature, and the company of friends that was most enjoyable. We would pretend we were going deer hunting but we never ever shot anything. It was the adventure of getting out into the forests; of being able to climb mountains, enduring the cold, sitting on top of a hill on a sunny autumn day, looking at the rolling countryside in its flaming Fall colours, watching the puffy white clouds sail by, and having the wind blow into your face."

He pauses for a while, remembering with a slight touch of sadness.

These days he often sits by the window and dreams of having a little farm with a creek running by and a forest 25 feet away — a forest with birds and an odd wild animal. Fred truly loves nature. Of course, he also enjoys the company of people but needs solitude for painting. He has to be alone in order to be creative. However, he enjoys music at all times.

Fred feels that — no matter how contradictory it may sound — sadness also renders a lot of happiness in that it activates a necessary relief valve, often accompanied by an outburst in creativity.

FRED MANCUSO

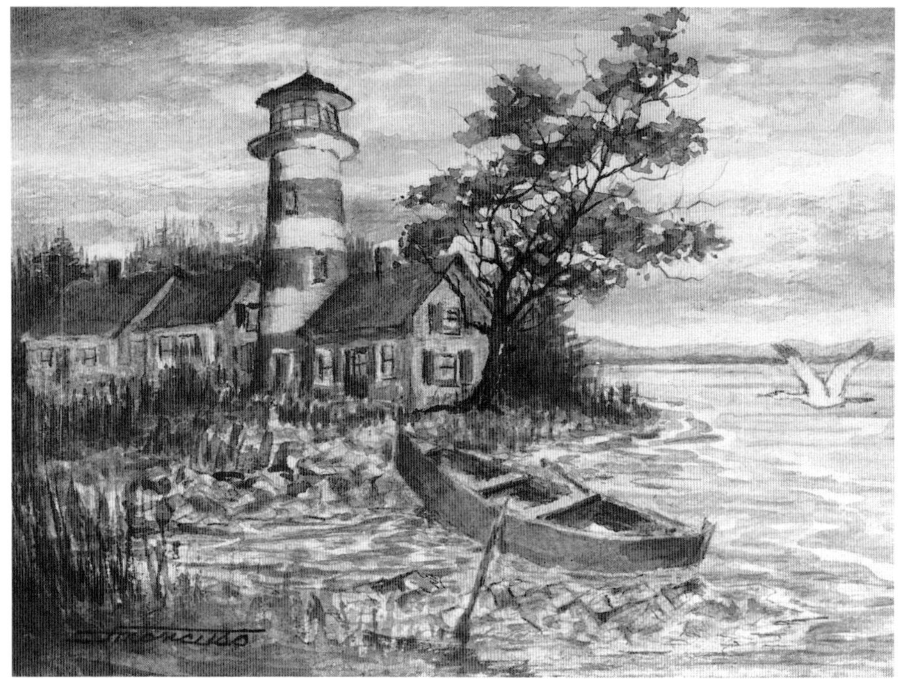

His favourite media are oils, water colours, and acrylics. His artwork is focussed on typically Canadian nature scenes with immediate appeal to the viewer. It is based on superb drawing and an extremely interesting composition with strong emphasis on atmosphere evoked by means of painstaking detail and soft, fluid lines. His great love for Canada, her countryside, and nature in general, shines through in all his work. You can almost feel the fresh and uncontaminated air of the countryside.

Mancuso, who is well known all over Canada and throughout the United States, has had his work featured on calendars published by the Schwab Rehabilitation Hospital of Chicago, Illinois; Handicapped Artists of Canada; calendars put out by the Sister Kenny Institute in Minnepolis, Minnesota; the Toronto-Dominion calendar (for the month of October), and a painting bought by ITT Canada Limited for their official Christmas card.

Besides, he has distinguished himself four times with the Best Choice/Best of Show prizes in 1966, Junior Chamber of Commerce Show in Lachine, Quebec; in 1976, at the International Art Show in St. Catharines and, also in 1977, for his watercolour, 'Country Home', as the Krelitz "Best of Show Award" at the 14th Annual Sister Kenny International Art Show by Disabled Artists, held every Fall in Minneapolis.

As Fred says, his works span places he may never see, ranging from Canada in the north to Chile in the south; from Europe in the west to Japan in the east.

Fred has been designing the cover of the West Park Hospital patient newspaper THE TRUMPETER for the past three years.

Furthermore, Fred has also been written up in A GUIDE FOR THE HANDICAPPED TEENAGER, expounding his philosophy of doing art for the sheer enjoyment of it and having a career that allows you to make a living while doing something you love.

His painting A QUIET LAND was purchased by Bell Canada and a reproduction of the painting, accompanied by information about their Telecomnunication Centre for Special Needs, was featured on the inside back cover of most Bell directories in Ontario during 1985/86.

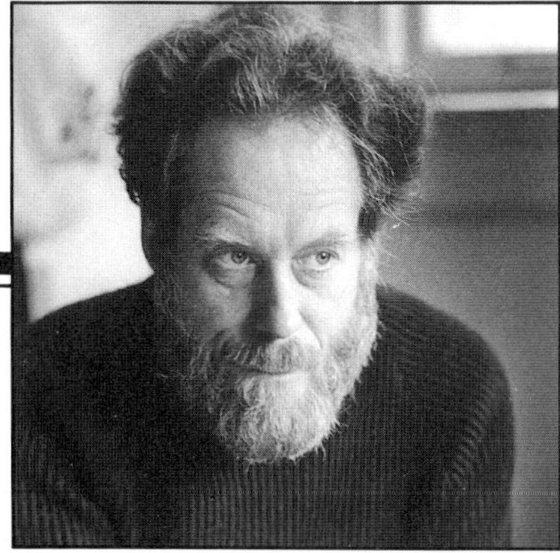

JOHN NEWMAN

One of Canada's outstanding figure painters

I had always wanted to be an artist from the time I was very young. In my first year in kindergarten, the teacher advised my parents that perhaps they should encourage me to be an artist.

My parents were ordinary, working class people. My father had a cartage business. My grandfather had come from London, England, directly to Toronto — I think — and lived in west-end Toronto in what was called the town of Parkdale then, now the Parkdale district. My father was born in the house and lived in it until he was sixty-two. He moved after that so that he grew up in the city.

I was born on April 6, 1933, in the same house as my father and I went to the same public school followed by attendance at Parkdale Collegiate.

My mother was the daughter of Irish immigrants and was quite Irish in her feelings and moods. Her parents, from all I heard, (I never kenw them), were both typically Irish.

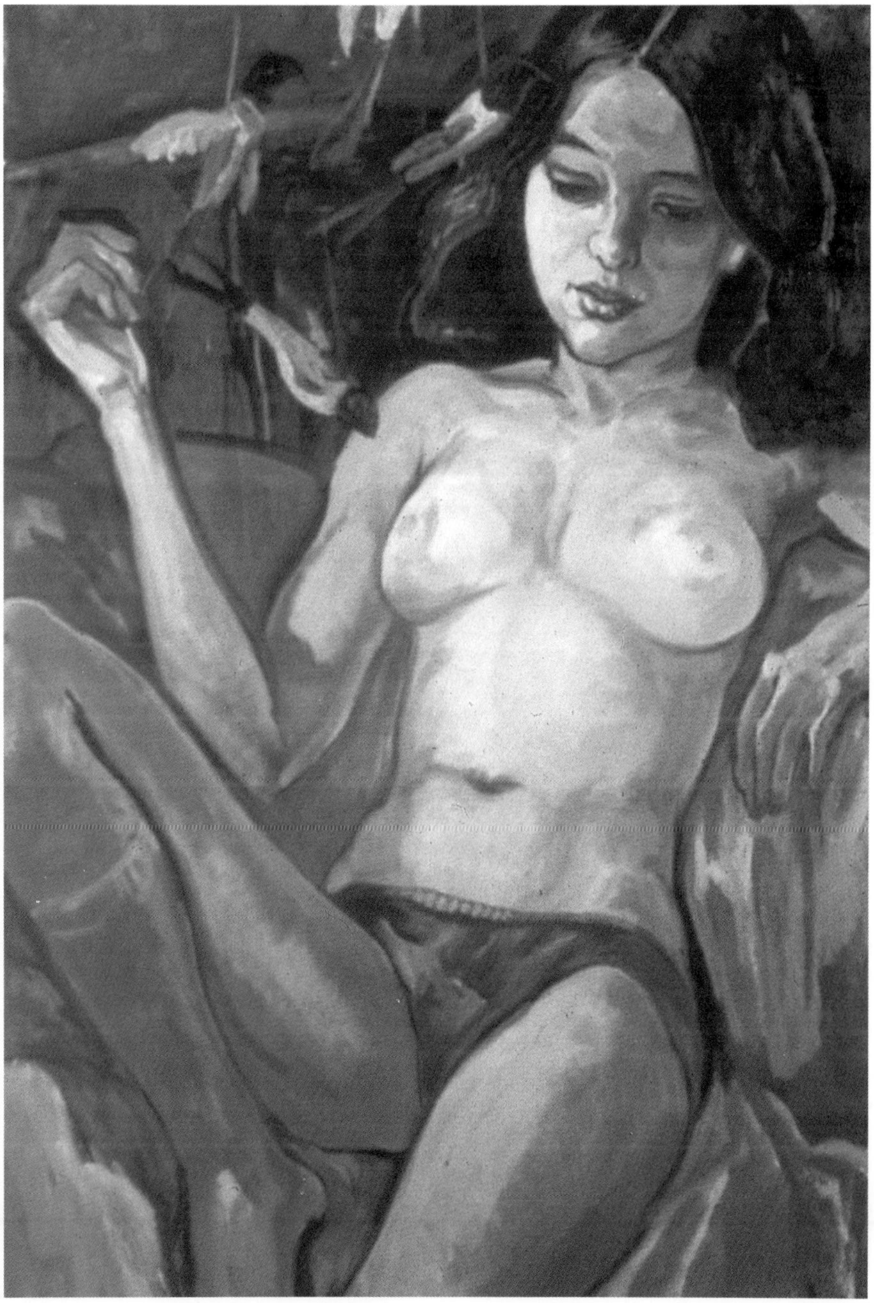

*YOUNG WOMAN
AND THE TOY
BIRDS
1978
(20 x 30)
Art Bank*

young pubescent female on the threshold from fragile beauty and dreamy innocence to womanhood

It's a celebration of life — transition enhanced by soft setting that adds a balancing protective warmth. Colours and tones are most skilfully adapted to this mysterious transitory stage — strong yet simultaneously soft-hued touches lovingly enveloping the budding female figure.

JOHN NEWMAN

One of my sisters studied art, for a couple of years, at Western Technical School. She used to give me materials to work with when she was babysitting me, so I got that kind of encouragement, even though my parents didn't know much about art or didn't actually realize what the implications of becoming an artist were.

When I was in grade five or six, a teacher recommended that I go to the Saturday morning classes at the Art Gallery. So I began to attend those. I remember that, even in those early days, I really wished that they would give me some instruction.

I wanted to take art in high school. However, my father wanted me to get an academic education. He agreed that he would support me, if at the completion of an academic high school course, I still wanted to be an artist.

During my academic years at high school, I did get away from art a little bit because it was very difficult to do. I tried to take art classes at night, but I had to have permission from the principal at the academic school, and he refused to grant it. Then as soon as I reached grade 12, I reminded my father of his bargain and he allowed me to go to the College of Art. There I received some very good instruction. Those were great years. In my first year I worked terribly hard — so hard that my father was worried.

After graduation, I won a scholarship to go to the Art Academy of Cincinnati. I got married that September and went to Cincinnati for a year. My wife and I thought of working and going to live in Europe for a year, but by then we had a son. We came back from Cincinnati and I had a little trouble getting work. The times were tough. I did part-time teaching with children's groups and amateur groups and some display work. I worked for eight months for Eaton's as sort of an independent display artist. Then I joined the exhibit staff at the Royal Ontario Museum (ROM) where I worked with Harley Parker, who was a close associate of Marshall McLuhan's. I worked with Harley and often saw Marshall during that four and half-year period. Around the same time I began teaching evenings in the Art College. When Jock MacDonald had a heart attack or stroke — in the late Fifties or Sixties — and was away from school for some time, he suggested that they get me to replace him. I always thought that was very interesting because Jock and I were good friends but he was never really my mentor. We held diametrically opposed points of view on art.

I should mention who strongly influenced me when I was at the College of Art. John Alfsen was a very strong influence in those days — perhaps the strongest while I was at the College.

Later, Eric Freifeld, Fred Hagen, and Harley Parker were all important influen-

ces. Eric has always been a great supporter of mine. When I was a student, he and John Alfsen gave me a great deal of encouragement. He seemed to believe in me and was a great source of strength in my early, formative years. When I came on staff, I learned a good deal about teaching from him. Over the years he has exerted quite an influence on my work, particularly in the Sixties.

My mother had died and I think that, to some extent, brought a focus to the whole meaning of life. That brought things into question fairly early. However, during my teens and early twenties I went through a tough struggle with myself and finally broke with the idea of traditional church. I think that came through in my art of that period, and later when I was no longer a student.

Yes, quite a bit of my work was tied up with religion and even ten years after (at least ten years or more) I was still wrestling with that question. I did a series, in the mid-Sixties, called "Consider the Angels" which was a kind of autobiographical thing, although not in terms of any literal

happening. I took the symbol of an angel, looked at it and explored religion through the idea of an angel.

In terms of media, I use almost all the media; oil, acrylic, pastels and all different kinds of graphic media, but I always harness my media to my work. Many times I use mixed media to get the effect I want.

My work separates into two general kinds. One is work done directly from the model, and for about at least three or four years I have been doing a lot of work — drawings and paintings directly from the model — kind of interpretative drawings but nevertheless with the model present, with something visual in front of me. I have concentrated on the adolescent. I try to talk about the whole period from the time they first enter into adolescence to when they are a woman. The variations, I find, are just unbelieveable. In each model I have a different way of talking about the same idea. So what I am doing in most of my drawings and paintings, is expressing that idea, not consciously but deeply buried, and it usually comes through in one way or another.

Bride and the rocking horse

- seeing life through a veil
- shedding one veiled existence to move on
                      to another

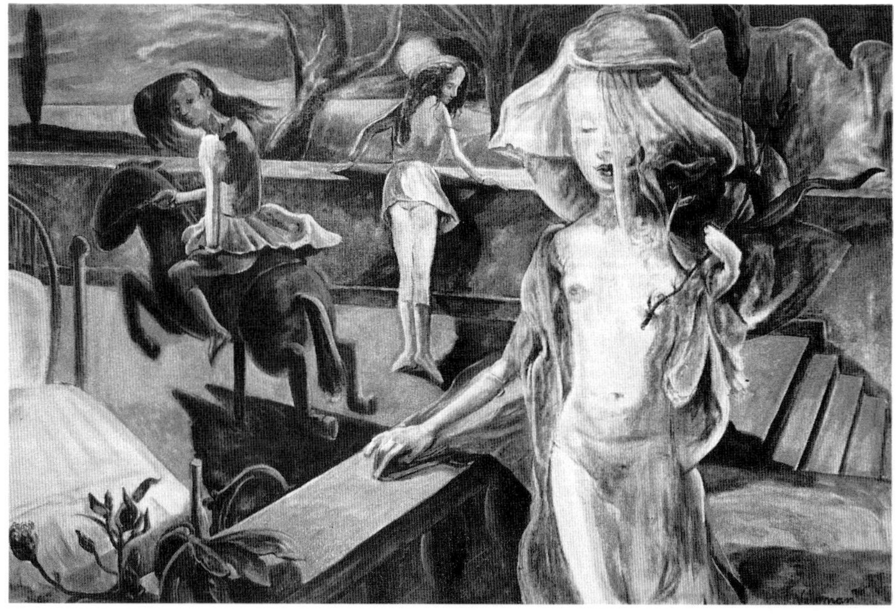

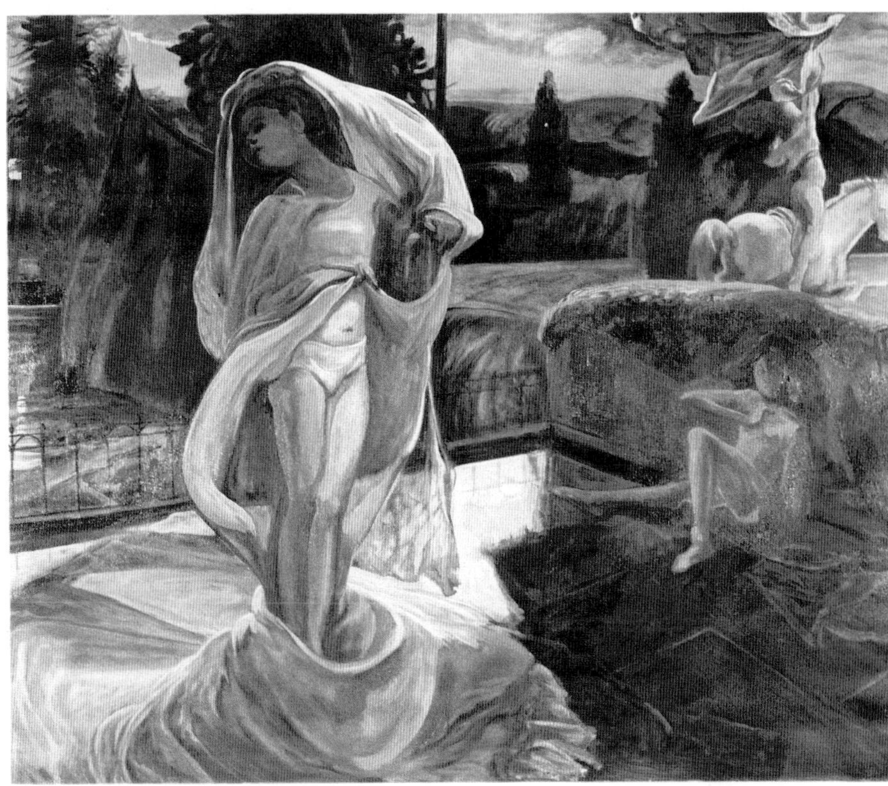

emerging from a cocoon

The other kind of painting I do — or drawings — are imaginary compositions. During the Sixties up to the mid-Seventies I concentrated more on these.

The year I spent in Italy, 1976-77, I did seven compositions just working out of my head without any models posing. Although some years I have concentrated on fantasy compositions, I always do some drawing from the model.

These are ways of expressing myself that I expect to continue with all my life.

Interviewer: "Yet the pubescent female seems to be somehow the focus of your work."

Newman: "Yes, I have always been intrigued and fascinated by that stage the female passed through, for I have never had any younger sisters nor any daughters of my own (I have three sons). My young-est sister is actually eight years my senior. Thus I have never been close to anyone at that crucial period of time in her life."

Interviewer: "I take it, then, that you have always been interested in the life cycle in its entirety as well."

Newman: "Of course. If you study my earlier paintings you can clearly witness the depiction of that cycle from man's emerging from the earth till his return to dust."

Interviewer: "But don't you think that puberty is a rather delicate stage — not meant for everybody's eyes to share?"

Newman: "Yes and no. It is such a pivotal point in a woman's life because it is the transition echoing the childhood of a woman and heralding her potential as a mother.

"It is beautiful, per se, but societal conventions tried to turn this natural mira-cle into something embarrassing. Yet it is something that does not go unnoticed, for there occur many changes in the female — changes that are ovvious to everyone, such as a change in personality, in physique, etc. The changes in the male are much less dramatic."

Interviewer: "Maybe a great majority of people feel threatened by a model in the puberty stage because of the sexual under-tones?"

Newman: "Yes, because it is a powerful force which many people may hesitate to admit.

To be quite frank, in the case of a man being married to a beautiful woman, chances are that he might certainly find that same beauty reflected in his daughter. And what is wrong with that?!

"I sincerely wish anyone could tell me

JOHN NEWMAN

why fathers are suddenly expected to turn
off their affection so lavishly bestowed
upon their daughters prior to puberty.
Some people seem to be making a very
serious mistake here — confusing affection
with eroticism.

"Reverting to my models, what differ-
ence — if any at all — does there exist
between an attractive sixteen- or twenty-
year old female? Yet society — in its hypoc-
risy —still seems to uphold some
artificially created age barrier. I am sure
everyone will agree with me that there are
some sexually attractive teenagers and one
can simply admire their unfolding beauty."
Interviewer:"Are you ever hurt when people read, for instance, all kinds of sex motifs into your painting, THE TOY DUCK?"
Newman: "No. To me, it is merely the
humorous paraphrasing of LEDA AND THE
SWAN. Well, people often see what they
want to see and that actually tells us a lot
more about the people than they might
even realize, or care to admit for that
matter."
Interviewer: "Could it be that we Canadians are bound to a Puritanical asexual
landscape tradition in art? Maybe we are
not overly people-oriented, especially
when the emphasis is focussed on the
human figure?"
Newman: "Yes. I often hear people comment: 'But why should I put up a painting
of a person I don't even know?' Yet, when
facing such people with the counter-
argument: 'What about putting up a
landscpae you have never seen either?'
they remain baffled.

"However, we Canadians have come a
long way and finally realize that it's the art
that is important — not the subject matter."

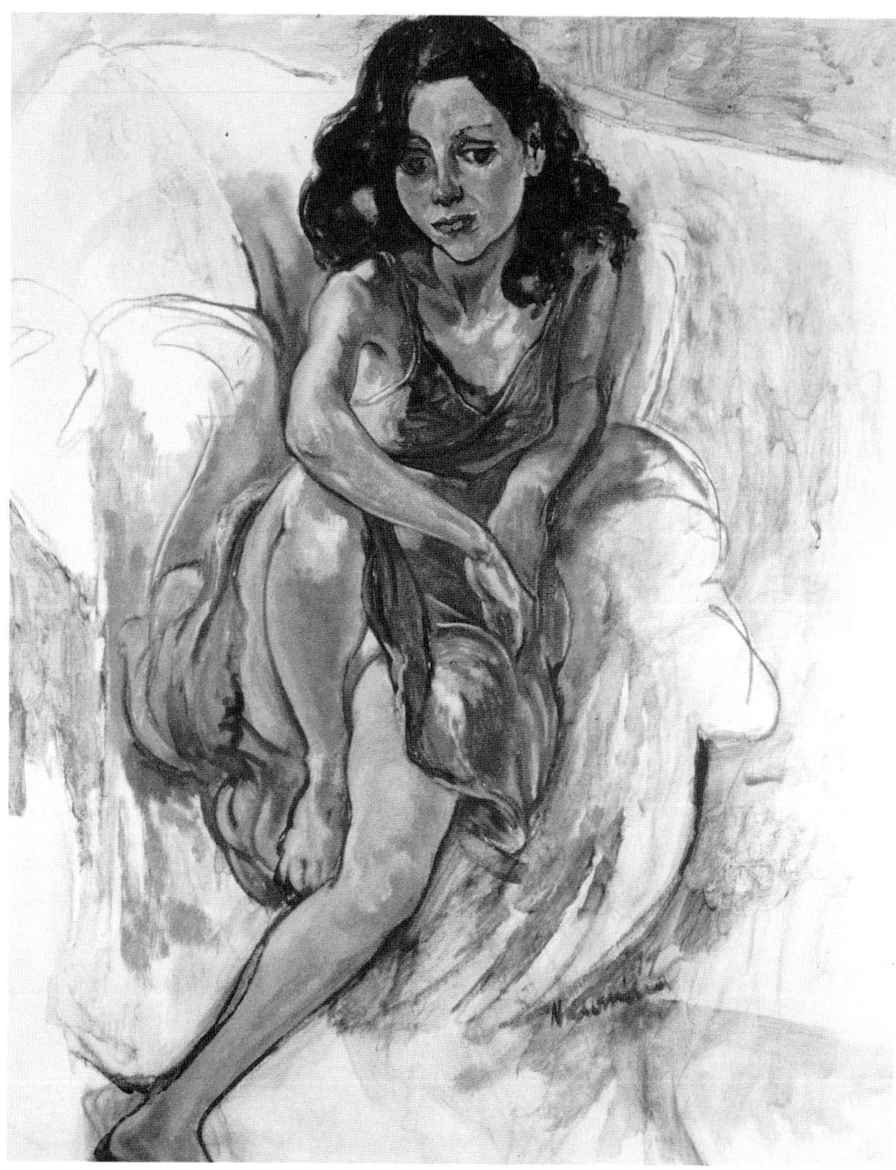

VICTORIA
Regina, 1979
owned by
Dr. Paul
CHAPWICK
(32 x 39½)

by Prince Arthur Galleries
33 Prince Arthur Ave.,
Toronto

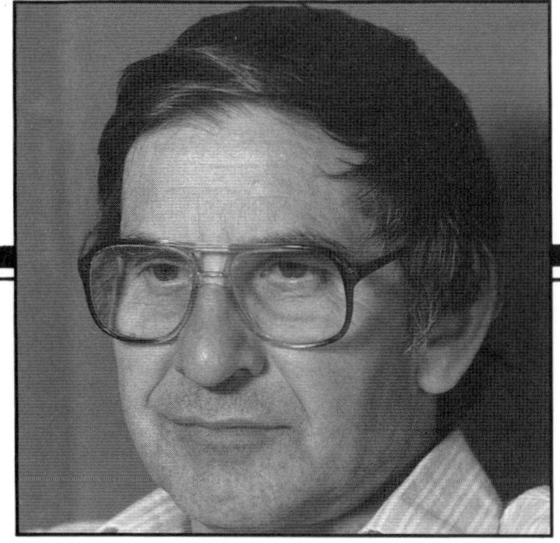

JOSEPH ROITNER

(Master of Fine Arts)
painter, poet, and short story writer

He was born in Austria, in 1929, where he studied at the College of Art in Graz, and at the Academy of Fine Arts in Vienna from which he graduated, in 1953, with an honour prize.

Roitner arrived in Canada in 1958 with no other qualifications than those of an artist. He worked for twenty years, mainly in factories to make a living but, above all, to establish a certain independence while carrying out his creative work.

Since 1980 he has been freelancing as a Scenic Artist for television, films, and commercials. This occupation is somewhat closer to his ability but is still merely a trade — art being something that happens mainly in seclusion.

Painting and writing, as expressions of Roitner's emotions or perception of our and his world, go back to a time prior to his art studies. The two different means of expression rotate or alternate in his development both as an artist and as a human being.

Perhaps it is fair to say that, through his writing, one is able to gain wider access to his paintings. Although the subjects seldom directly relate in one or the other media, they do complement each other.

Many of his short stories (both in English and German) take place within an ethnic environment. And it is not surprising that his themes and topics fully capture the reader's attention. They present the kind of reality to which many immigrants can easily relate as they, too, faced more or less the same problems and hardships when first settling in Canada. His stories tell us about newcomers, torn out of their familiar surroundings, and who feel oddly out of place. They are unable to understand what is going on around them because they can't communicate and are not understood by others, many of whom are struggling for their own survival.

Roitner describes the inevitable fate of people living between two cultures. While alienated from their original cultural heritage, the present seems lost to them because of their frustrating struggle. No matter how hard they try to blend in and

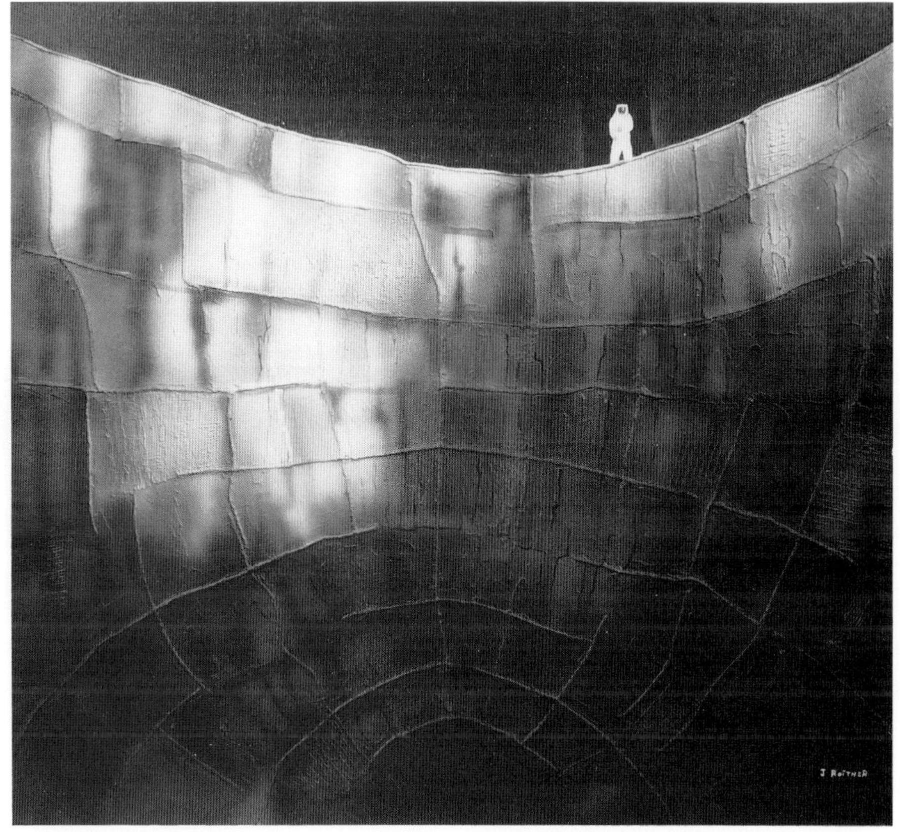

"AND SUDDENLY TIME BEGAN"   1970
acrylic on canvas
36" x 32"   91 cm x 81 cm
from the exhibiton "SPACE AND ELEMENT"

Crater on the moon which has not known time up to the moment when man appears at the edge of the rim.

JOSEPH ROITNER

totally immerse themselves into Canadian society, deep down the feeling of having been uprooted will not easily subside. They scrutinize their attitudes and values, brought along from the old world, until they face the great challenge of coming to terms.

Roitner looks into the soul of the newcomer and unmasks his innermost feelings. He tells us about the immigrant's guilt complex caused by not seeing aging family members left behind in the old country; of his hiding stark reality behind false pride when writing home so as to convey the news that one is succeeding when one is actually just keeping his head above the water. Roitner has a special talent for emphasizing conflict by means of interiorized dialogue between man and his alter-ego. His characters try to deaden the pain in their souls with tranquillizers, alcohol and hard drugs — yet Roitner's refreshing, genuinely compassionate concern for his suffering fellow-man —his neighbour — adds a special glow to any story, no matter how gloomy it may be. (A number of his poems and short stories have been published in the former Austrian publication, DER OESTERREICHER).

There is nothing cute about his stories — rather we are faced with in-depth reflection — just as "pretty pictures" are not the essence of his style of paintings.

To Roitner, art is an intellectualization of his life. Consequently, many of his works are of the abstract, antirepresentational type, and yet his innovative work is so fresh it seems crisp and tremendously powerful — even downright explosive!

He divides art into two levels:
1) imitation of nature that is faithful to the last iota of detail without the drive of creativity, and
2) the abstract of what is visible (as still existing in popular art that has not yet been polished)

differentiating between a) the technically masterful rendition of an object which requires, of course, great skill, and b) the creative skills that deal with inspiration but desist from slavish copying.

Roitner is fully aware of the fact that modern art is often considered an incomprehensible concept. But should that not be seen as a challenge rather than a deterrent?

His art, from 1948 to 1960, had rather Cubistic tendencies to the extent that colour was no longer tied to outward appearance and its imitation. Yet his compositions are carefully planned — their contents being subjected to laws of their own — and, often, the overall composition hits the viewer right in his viscerals.

Personally, he is often amazed at how little people in general are concerned with artistic ideas; the artist's philosophy of "taking in" life, trying to express its complexity. Maybe that phenomenon derives from the

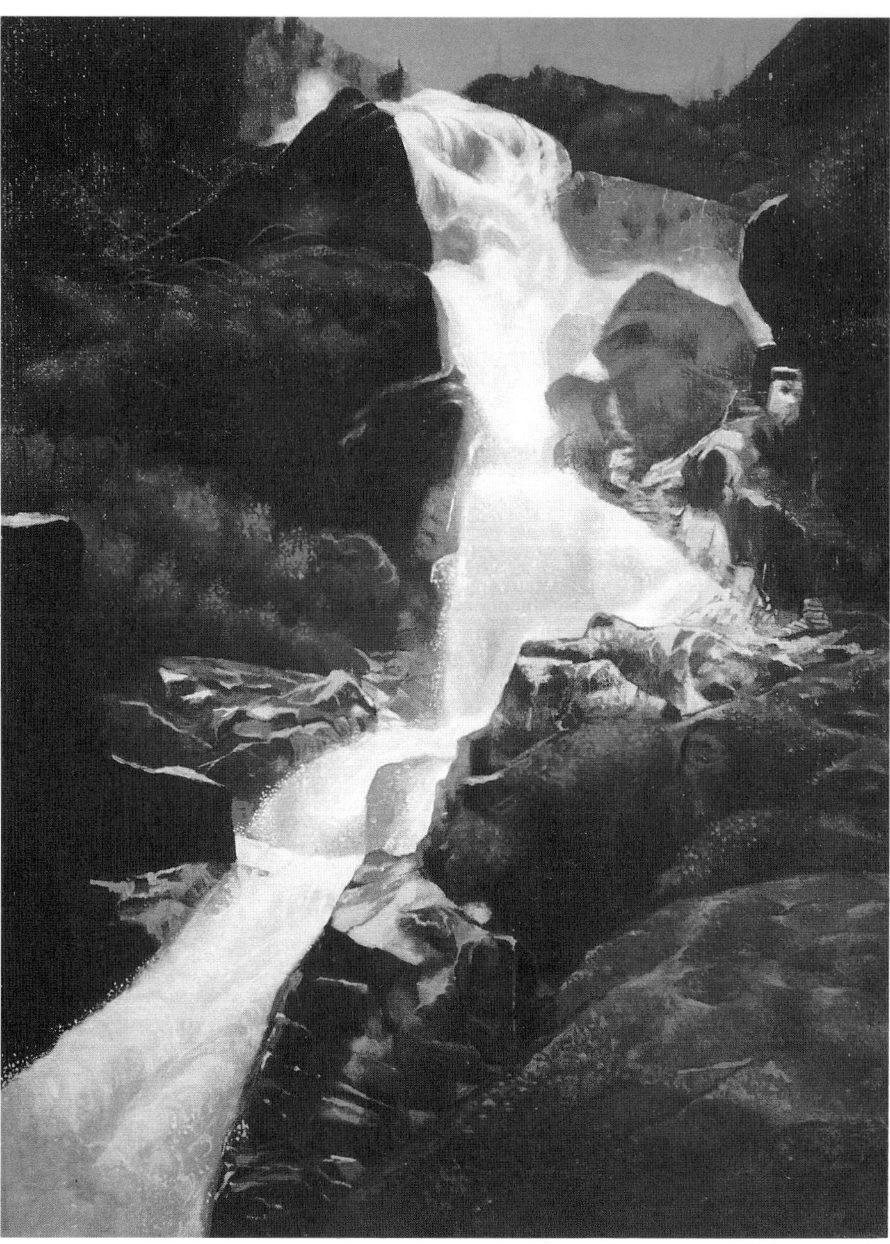

"WATERFALL" (Study)   1984
oil on canvas panel
18" x 24"   46 cm x 56 cm

searching for abstraction
within an apparent reality

fact that many people still equate art with luxury on which one should not waste too much of one's precious time, for time is money, and money allows one to buy art whether one understands it or not. And as to the so-called connoisseurs of art, they only honour the dead anyway…!

Why, then, does he delve so much into abstraction rather than universal concepts? Isn't "intake", via our senses, influenced by previous experiences — which through association and mental assimilation — lead us to perception?

As everyone knows, man see objects to the extent that they are familiar to him, and the science that surrounds an object or a property, is but one dimension. However, how can science reveal the myriad facets of the relationship each of us individually maintains with objects or the world in general which we perceive through our senses? Our relationship to things — which we consider fact and truth — depends upon our dimension. Thus "seeing" is not exclusively a matter of visual acuity but rather "intellectualized viewing".

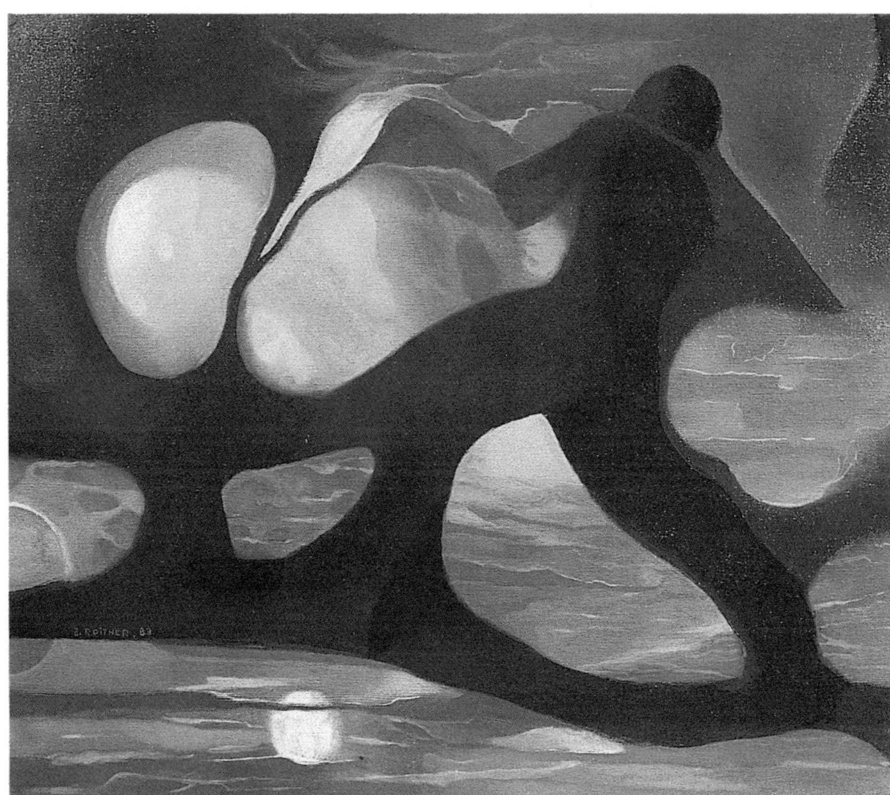

"TRANSITION" 1983 *oil on canvas*
26" x 22"   66 cm x 56 cm

The notion of travelling as it were from perhaps
a physical to a spiritual dimension.

In purely scientific terms, a rose is a flower just like any other. However, its appearance has led to our perceiving it in aesthetic and poetic terms having made it, throughout millenia, a symbol of many meanings. Didn't it gain importance in the course of our life at certain stages where it was, thus, no longer merely a flower with colour, form, and fragrance; not only a symbol with given properties, but an entity with innumerable destinations, our perceptions of it going far beyond its blooming and withering? Doesn't its existence — consciously or subconsciously — remind us of relationships as found in lovers, weddings, elegant festivities, and funerals? Even beyond that, roses became the ornaments of saints and — woven into Christ's crown of thorns — a symbol of heart-rending grief. Thus, one might safely state that objects leave, in individuals, an impression that depends on certain associations and situations. Every external appearance becomes a highly individualized perception.

Hence, according to Roitner, art has absolutely nothing to gain from so-called servile imitation unless objects can conjure up a relationship between what has been experienced and its meaning.

He also feels that there is no one formula — in terms of creative representation — through which one can assess a work of

JOSEPH ROITNER

art, nor is there any pat, direct sample or prototype against which artists have to compare creations in order to become masterly. Art makes statements — either in an abstract or concrete style — that are expressed in a more or less personal manner. A certain understanding without an explantion or a minimum of creative thinking on the viewer's part, is next to impossible. There is no such thing as art for everyone.

In Roitner's opinion, there is no work of art making a statement that is open to all in the same manner. According to Hermann Hesse, there is no other reality than the one which we carry within us. Both the external and internal world are truths of but a fleeting similarity.

Throughout his life, Joseph Roitner has made Art a priority, painting within a framework — be it reason, calculation, or emotion; never strictly following any trend or fashion. He kept on wondering about the bridge that should exist between painters and the viewers of their artwork. One way to cross that bridge would be to confront the artist for an explanation.

Finally, it should be stated that neither the text above -— in its brief attempt by way of excerpt from Roitner's prolific writings —nor the extremely limited selection of paintings, which span so many clearly marked periods of style, can do justice to the versatility of Roitner's creative output.

"THE SPIRIT IN THE DESERT"   *1984*
oil on canvas panel
28" x 22"   *71 cm x 56 cm*

The desert in its physical make-up is lacking in supporting life as a whole and yet most spiritual revelations have originated in vast desolation. Perhaps it is there that man is closest to his universe of abstract thoughts.

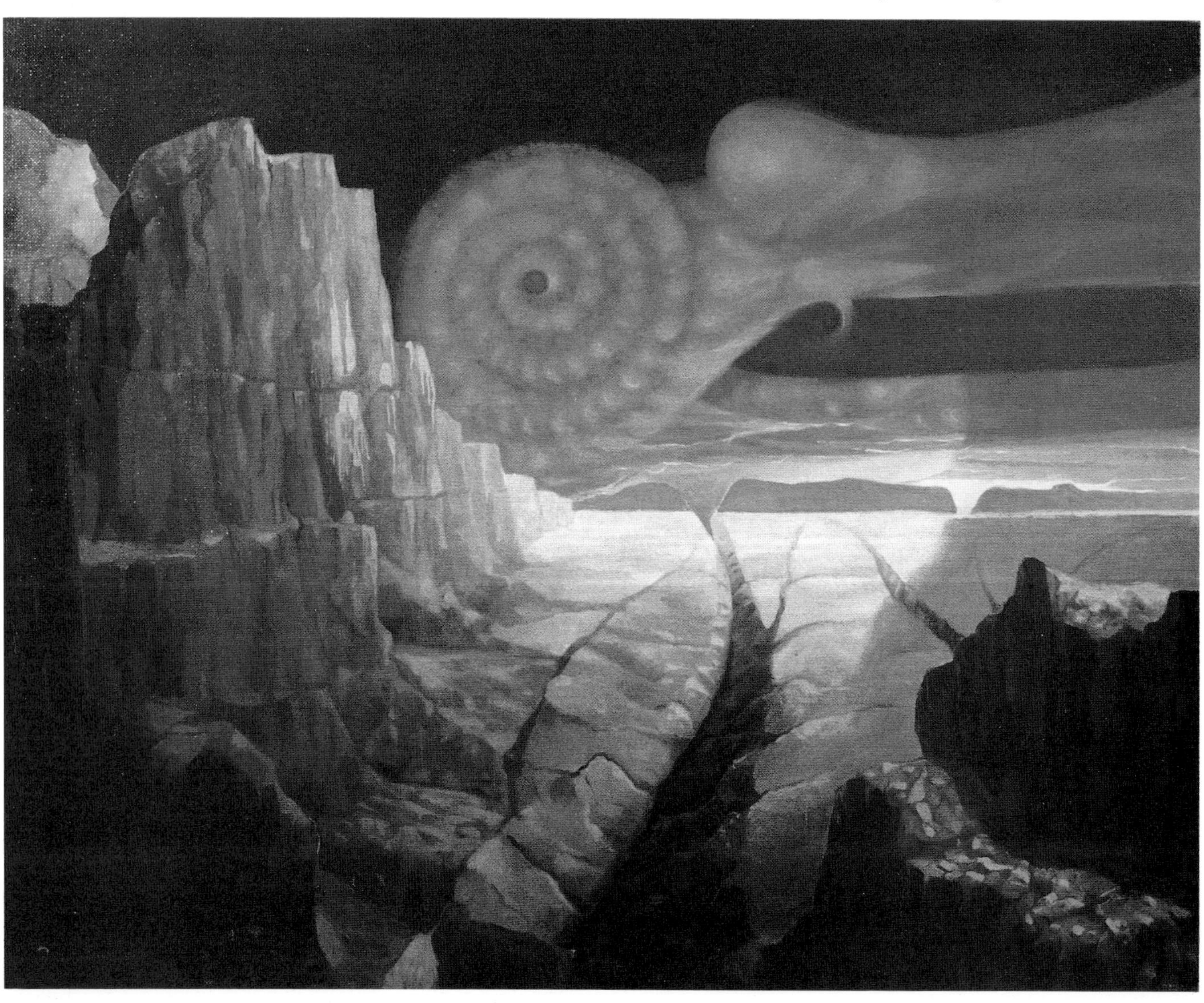

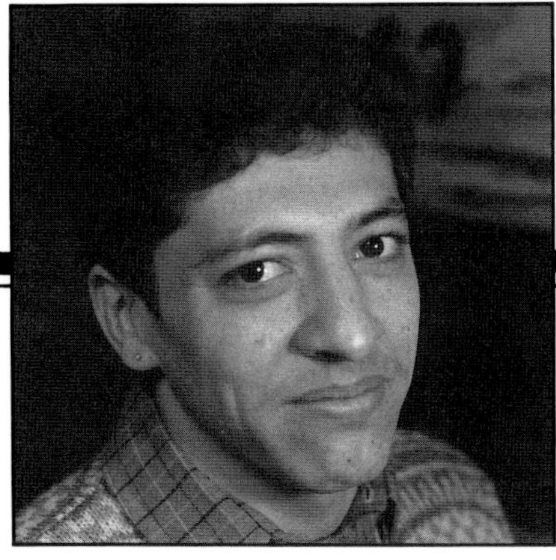

NELSON SEGURO

painter of great sensitivity, lover of the abstract
art historian dealing with present day problems of our society such as air pollution, exploitation, etc.
(excerpt in Spanish previously published in NUEVO DIARIO — Feb. 26, 1985)

Nelson was born on May 12th 1954, in Colombia, South America, where he lived in the mountains with his family for 3½ years.

They then moved to a small town where Nelson's mother had to struggle very hard to eke out an existence for a family of five; luckily, there was a grandmother to look after the children while the mother was at work.

When Nelson was ten, the family moved to Medellin where he attended high school and, upon completion of his studies, did community work amongst the mountain people for two years. He then emigrated from Colombia to Canada and is happily settled in his new homeland, proud to be a Canadian.

He is one of those who can only concentrate on inspirational art at night when his creative juices flow, unimpeded by outside disturbances or interruptions. However, he has no difficulty executing purely geometrical designs by day.

Nelson's greatest dream is to be a full-time painter some day, but meanwhile he is struggling along, working whenever he can in order to replenish his fast dwindling funds.

This artist is sincerely concerned with the world's present-day problems, a concern that becomes clearly evident in IN SEARCH OF PEACEFUL FIELDS which depicts mankind in time of trouble and conflict, trying to escape from the routine pace of daily life.

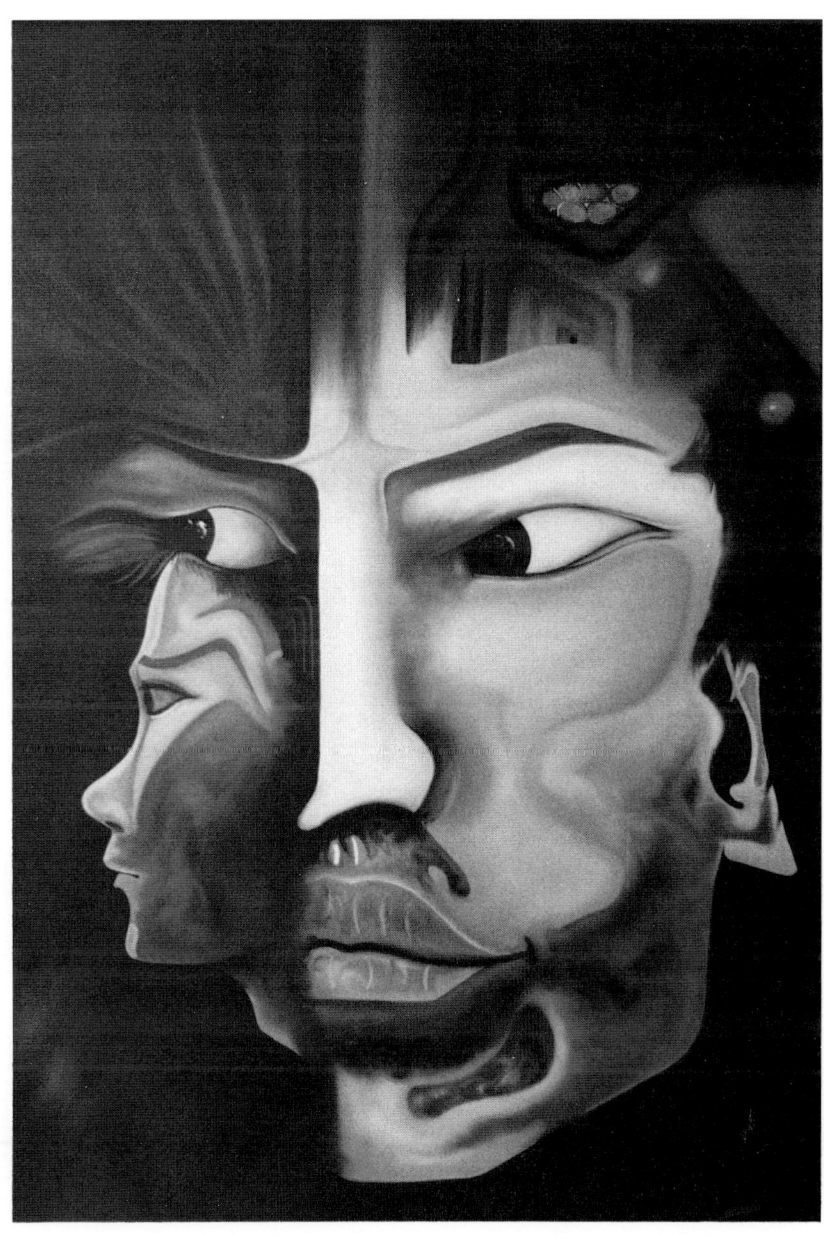

This painting represents Nelson's homage to the Oriental people he has known and with whom he established very strong bonds.
He shows a blending of South American and Oriental essence.

NELSON SEGURO

STRAY DREAMER, on the other hand, is an intriguingly structured composition telling us about an individual's problem; a mask symbolizing the painter himself and his confrontation with new space — his new homeland.

AUTUMN reflects his concern with environmental pollution and wanton destruction — colourful trees that are doomed to withering — their sapless white trunks standing out as warning signals.

This ecological involvement is also clearly evident in another painting of that series showing a young sapling with its roots exposed that has hardly any grip on the stones. The stones are actually kiliing the tree for lack of nourishment. In the background, we see the Hand of Providence with a book (the Bible?) in the heavily polluted sky above the soot and grime-suffocated city apartment block.

THE IMMIGRANT AND THE CITY

This could depict life in any North-American city where people come into contact with so many cultures. Yet do the twain ever really meet or do they merely touch and then safely withdraw to what is familiar?

Why can't one bridge the gap? Why is this worried face in the centre reflecting on the pros and cons of life in a megalopolis?

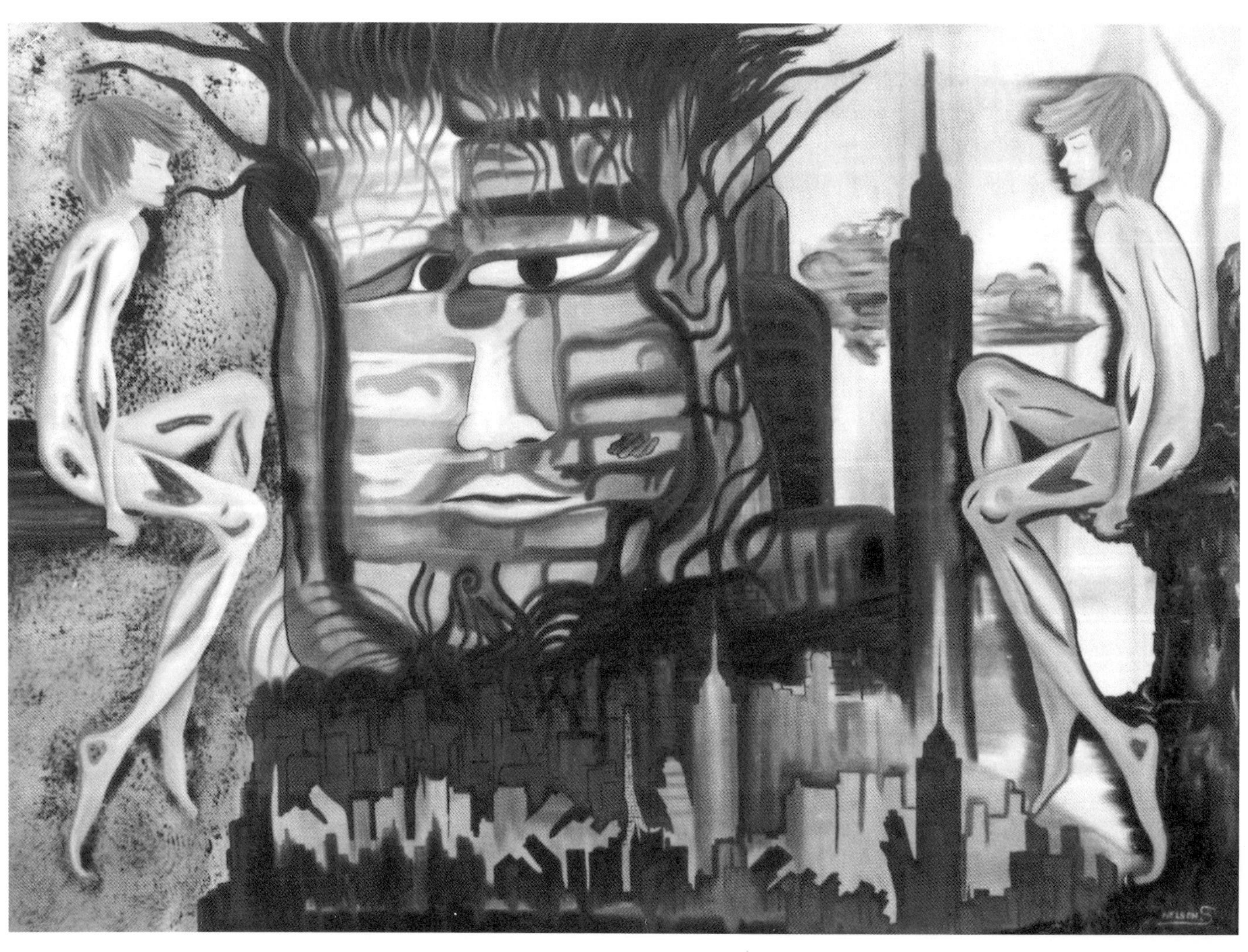

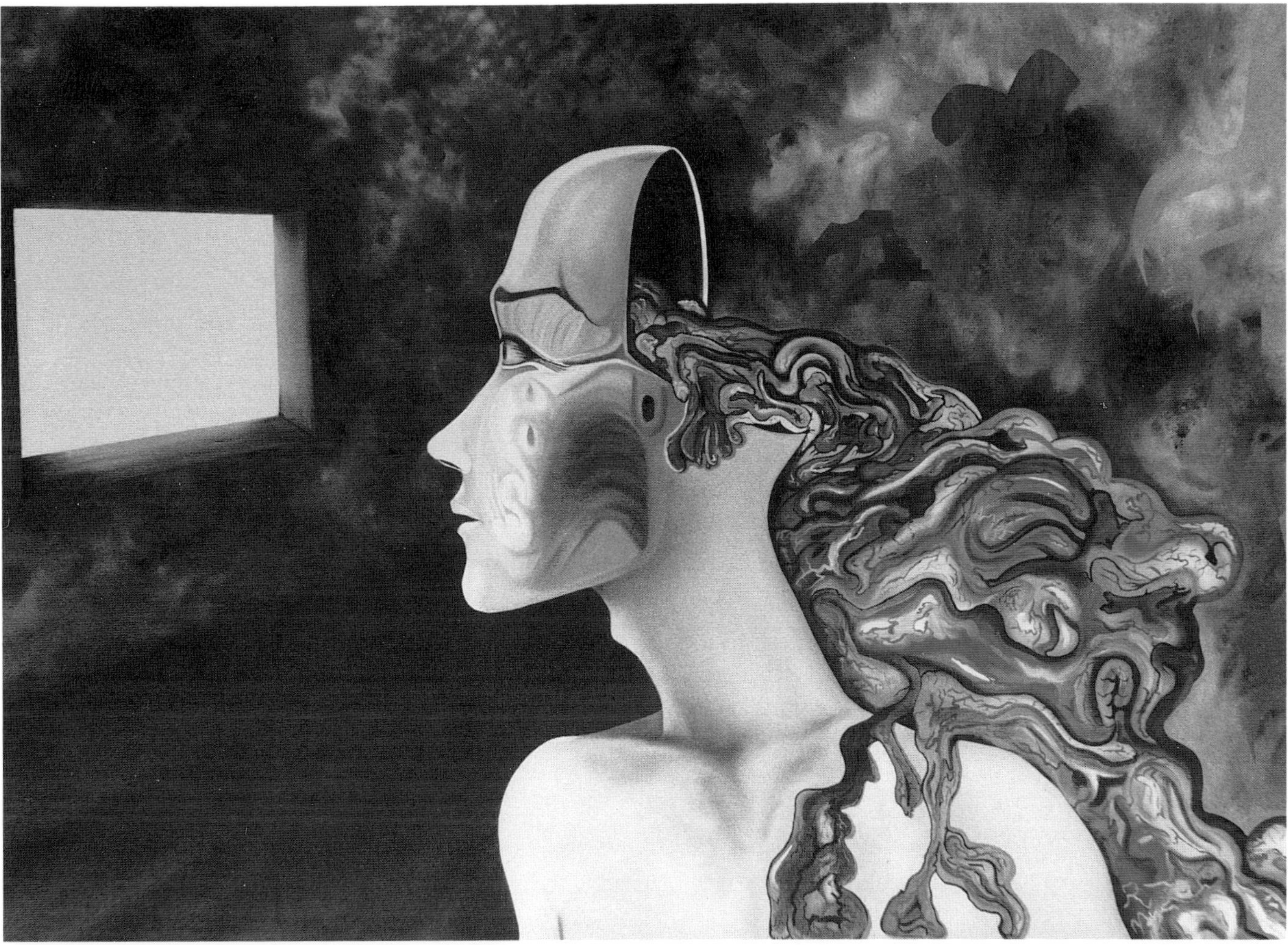

MY FIRMAMENT, FOR I WAS BORN
Another painting with a very positive note shows a window in a dark, empty room and an open

door symbolizing new vistas of the future opening up to the reflective occupant.
According to the artist's own explanations, the

brain laid open is a reaction against war and its atrocities, self-inflicted human suffering and environmental pollution being great concerns of his.

The topic of war and wanton destruction is picked up once again in SURVIVORS OF CRIME showing man left as the sole survivor on a planet where evil growth lurks everywhere.

The man appears mystified as to what has happened to his land, his earth. He wants to know who ruined it. He seems to be looking for the shadows of the past — after a nuclear holocaust.

But this picture, nevertheless, portrays a message of hope, for the beams signify resources still at man's disposal after war when the land is barren; resources that allow for a possible new beginning.

Some of the resources seem to be offering themselves to man, such as the one in his immediate vicinity looking in his direction but man, at this point, is only concerned with his own immediate disaster instead of looking farther ahead; instead of looking into the future where his resources lie. Of course, some of the resources are farther away and, therefore, more difficult to anticipate.

The older tree in the right hand corner is gnarled with worries and suffering, an agony of living that is further clearly expressed in the tortured twisting. Due to its age, its roots are deeper and it has managed to reach a more mature stage.

When viewing Nelson's collection of paintings, one immediately realizes that he draws very heavily upon the subconscious, such as recurring childhood dreams about his effortless flights during which he was totally devoid of fear and would always land safely. He would be filled with amazement and wonder at the serene surroundings portrayed in exotic, yet soothing colours.

A derivative from those dreams is ESCAPE — a firebird symphony effectively juxtaposed with a dark, ominous bird plummeting to the ground.

The dream motif is also present in NIGHT PASSAGE which features a weird type of dream; unfolding without end, kind of abstract — like an astral journey — something beyond reason, yet laden with symbolism. On the other hand, this particular painting also easily lends itself to the inter-

pretation of germination of evil'. We see a white homunculus from another planet which has implanted its seed in a monster of a woman who is ready to devour the universe. Yet the red bird (symbolizing love) emits golden beams (beams not featured in an earlier rendition of this very same painting), confining the growth of evil to a very small range.

Nelson does mood paintings of which DEPRESSIONS is one, created at times when Nelson feels that man is his own prisoner.

In those fragile moments, Nelson depicts people who totally lose track of reality and can no longer see the right solution to their many apparent problems.

Nelson feels that most painters are persons whose past hasn't been easy and whose ideas are of a rather philosophical nature.

Nowadays, one sees many painters but it takes more than merely wanting to be an artist in order to deserve that title. A painter should be able to develop his ideas on his own, based on his knowledge, intuition and life experience.

NELSON SEGURO

As long as an artist can survive, money should be of secondary importance — a means to keep him going, but not a goal.

As to ordinary art critics, a painter should not worry too much about them. Once the artist completes one of his paintings, that particular piece of work may cause some people to laugh at it while it may be a masterpiece in the opinion of others. Unless you are an artist at heart, you cannot grasp the depth of the true creator's mind.

The colours, lines, shapes, shades and shadows are the reflections of the true artist's mental journeys. At times, he travels far away through the space of his existence. The sky seems to be touching his head without hurting him. The space through which he travels seems to show him the beginning of creation and the unknown limits of the universe. Then, when he turns back to contemplate what he has done, he can — full of satisfaction — clearly see his past; his world, its magnificence and even his near future. He may not be the greatest, but he had done his best. He may not be the smartest, but he has a genius of his own.

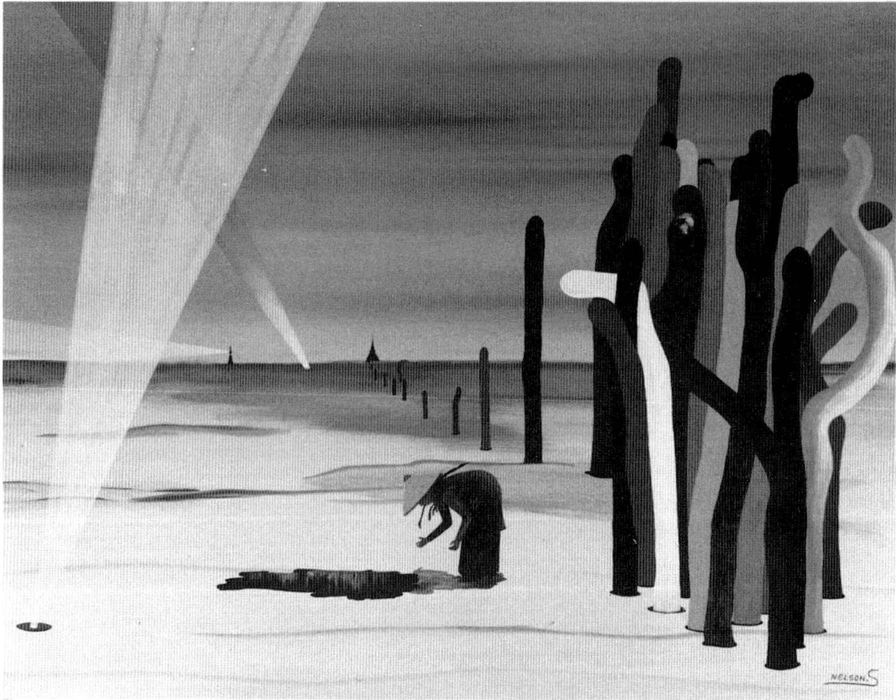

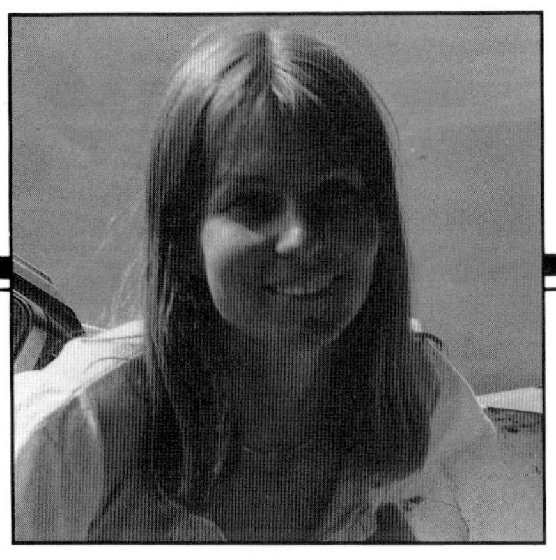

LIANE SKELTON

(excerpt published in the Summer '85 issue of THE SPIRES Cultural Community Focus.)

nature painter par excellence

Liane, a warm Sagittarian, was born in Etobicoke in December, 1956, of French-Irish stock.

Her love of wildlife and nature goes back to her childhood when she would explore the family island near Parry Sound.

All through high school and university, she continually carried on artwork but more or less as a sideline. At the time she did not feel that art would become her career — it seemed to be an impossible dream — an ideal she so desperately wanted to have come true.

Meanwhile, she progressed through university, studying sciences with emphasis on biology and ecology. She graduated with a B.Sc. from the University of Waterloo, also taking courses in sculpture and illustration.

She always kept up her artwork and would paint at home during her leisure

Water colour TURNING COLOUR

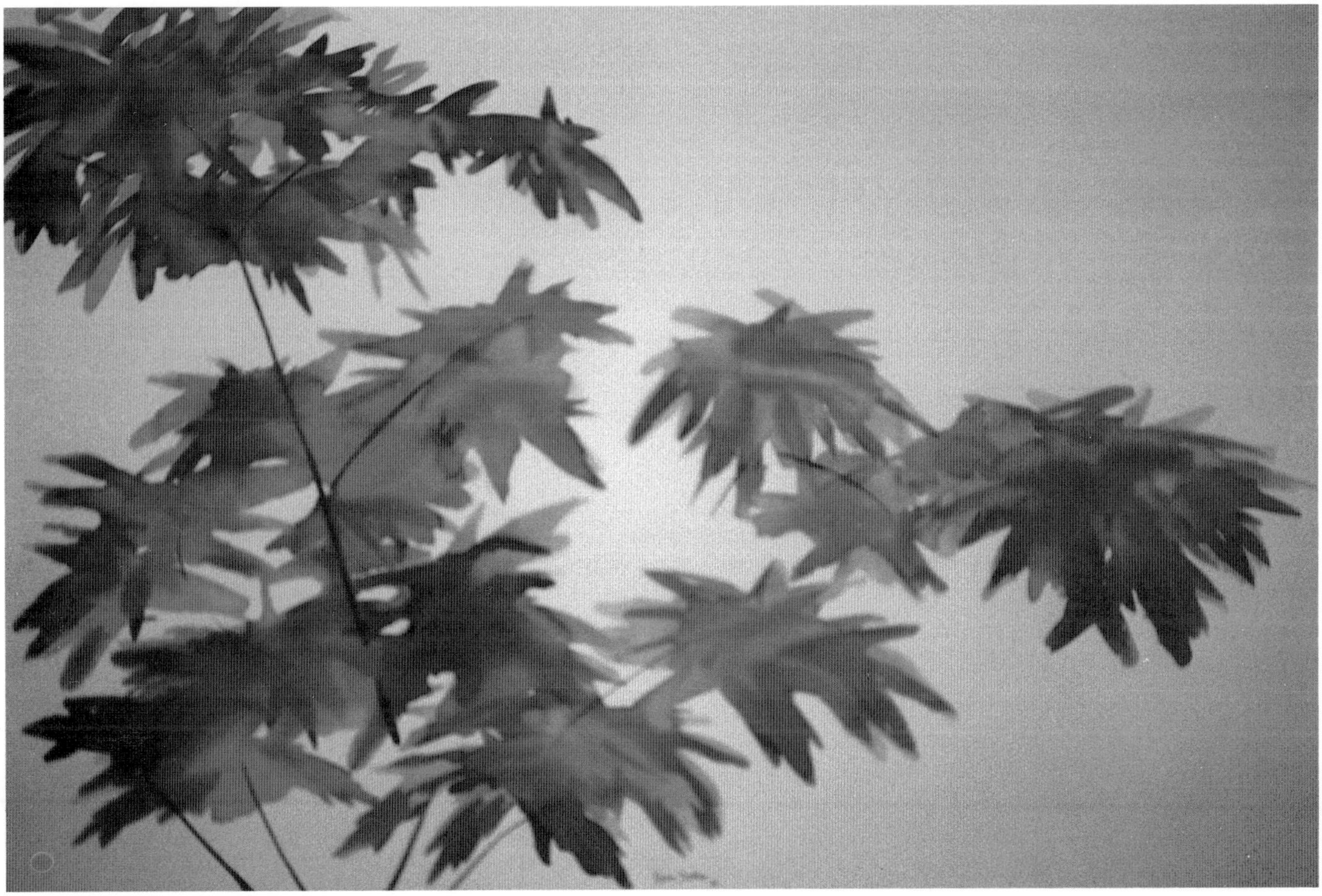

LIANE SKELTON

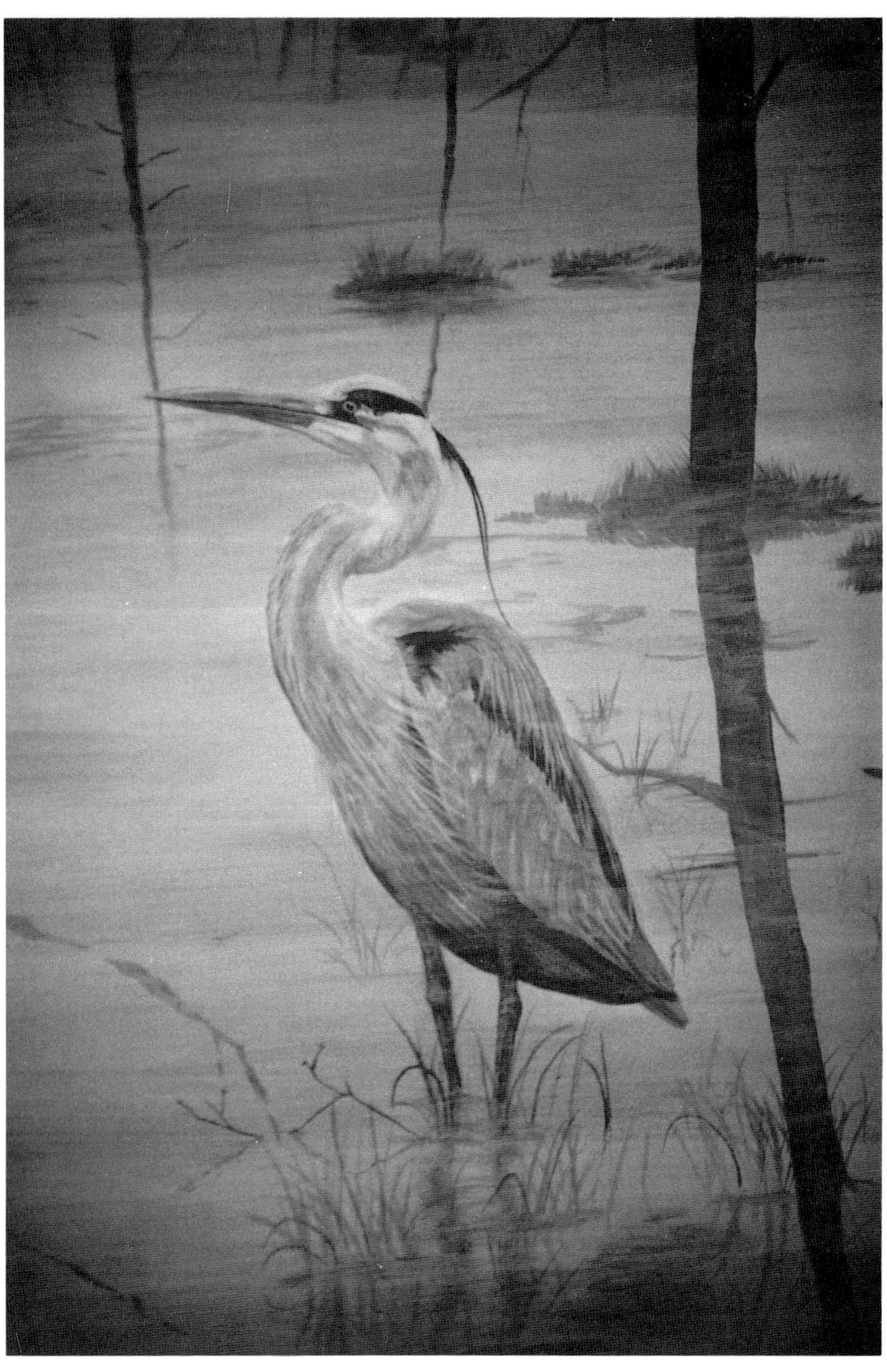

detail of oil painting,
HERONS AND TAMARACK

hours when she did not have to study or write exams. It was a release. And it was while at the university when Liane was studying so many analytical things, that she realized a non-fulfilment of the aesthetic side of life — a yearning that became stronger and stronger as time went on. Consequently, she later continued her studies in art at the OCA, Sheridan, and the Haliburton School of Fine Arts.

Following graduation she had no problem finding a job as laboratory technician with the Ministry of the Environment, working with the Acid Rain Programme. And although it was challenging indeed, it was at the same time stifling her artistic soul that was simply crying out to express its love of nature and share those feelings with the rest of the world. She dreamt of a position that would allow her to protect and preserve nature. Yet instinctively, she already knew that she could probably better achieve that goal through the interaction between people and her artwork.

Having worked as a lab technician for two years, she then found a job downtown with the Ministry of the Environment as environmental field technician with the Acid Rain Programme, outdoors being in charge of sampling sites. The work developed in a direction which she did not want to pursue.

At the same time, she joined a group of Co-op artists, called ARTISTUDIO, in downtown Toronto where the artists worked in the back of the store and displayed out front.

By 1982 her work had become more popular allowing her to gain some financial independence. This helped make up her mind in favour of the career of her dreams.

In November, 1983, she participated in the Juried Art Show at the Etobicoke Civic Centre, being a member of Arts Etobicoke. It won her recognition from private collectors in Texas and remote corners of the world, her work being marketed, as well, here at home by The Ontario Craftsman on Yonge Street.

In June, 1984, her work was featured in the Caledon Art Show, ART IN THE CALEDON HILLS.

Now Liane was encouraged to become more experimental and did screen printing on cloth. For her original designs she found an outlet, called SPLASH, on Queen Street in the Soho district.

During that summer, Liane joined the Haliburton Highlands Guild of Fine Arts and bought herself a houseboat near Bobcageon. Here, immersed in a true natural setting, she experienced a tremendous creative outburst, producing a substantial body of work for the exhibition in Haliburton.

In November, 1984, she held a one-woman show at the Campbellville Art Gallery. This resulted in an almost total sellout which proved such an exhilarating experience for her that she decided against a steady job with regular pay cheques, in favour of a full-time career in art. Finally her dream had come true!

SERIGRAPH, LOON

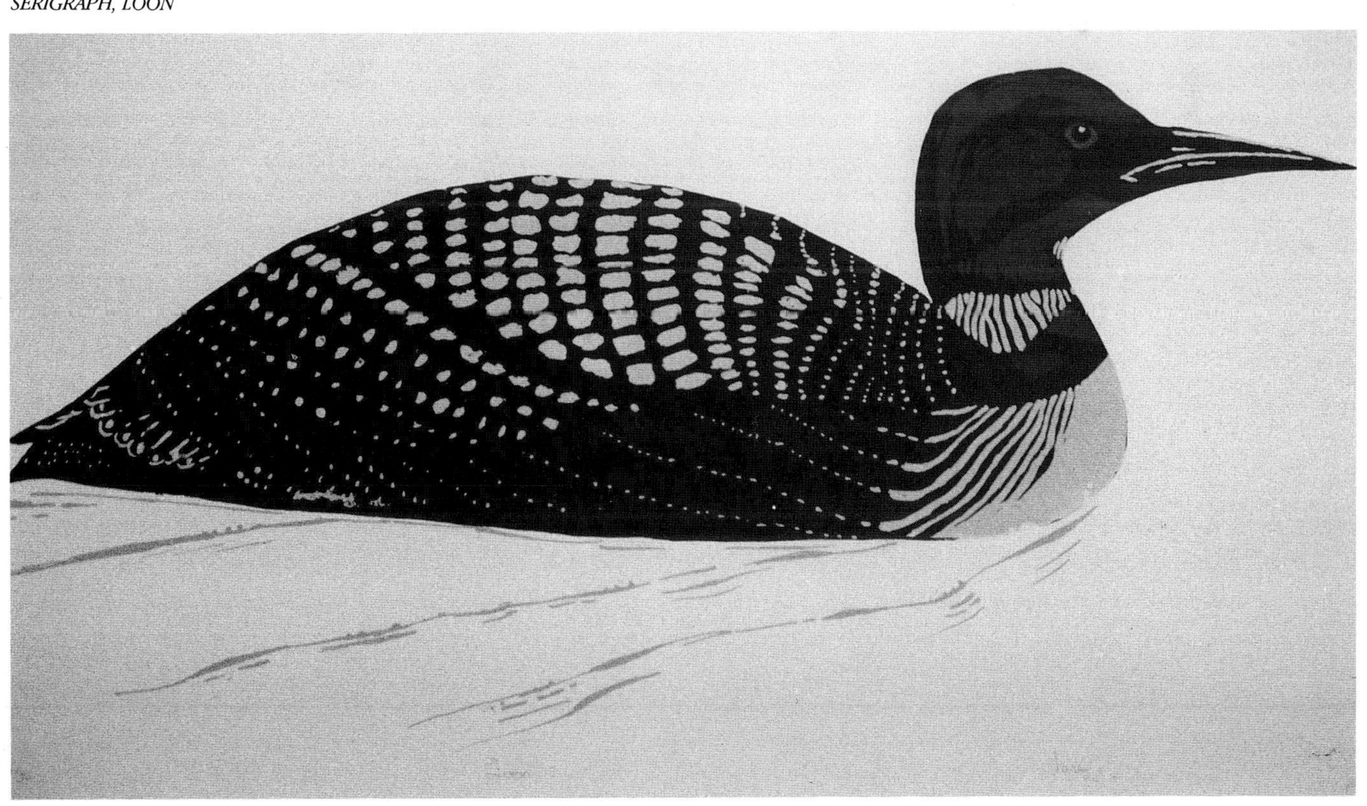

LIANE SKELTON

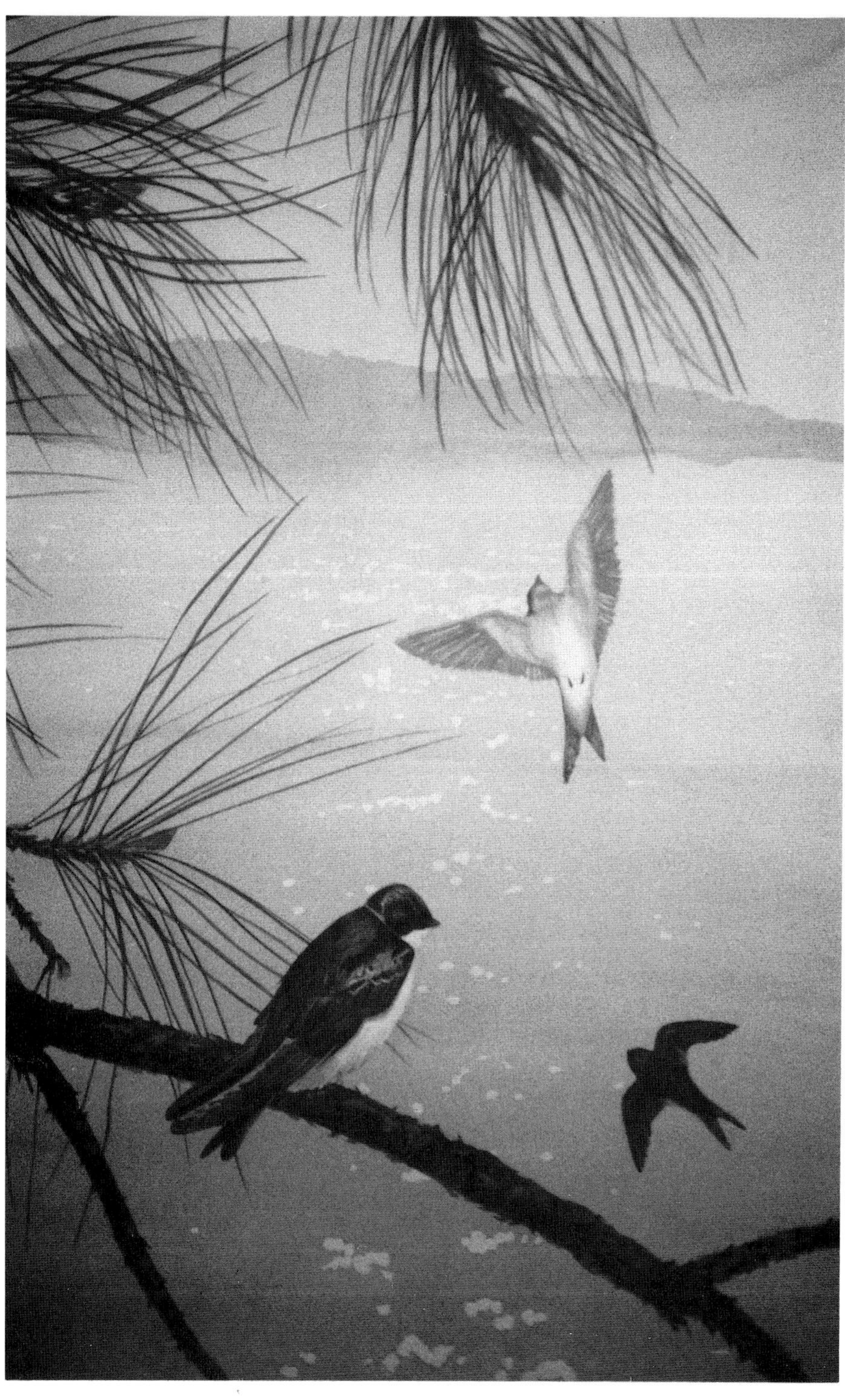

water colour and gouache LAZY DAYS

In February, 1985, she participated in the 16th Anniversary Show of Gallery Artists in Collingwood, at the Crow's Nest. This led to increased sales from her home and at craft shows resulting in quite a few commissions.

In March, 1985, she held a one-woman show at the Lakeshore Lions Centre where her work was extremely well received.

Now Liane knows she will never turn back on her decision.

Apart from the water colours and oils, she has been experimenting with serigraphs ever since she joined the Co-op in 1982. The technique involves making a stencil on a silk-like fabric for every colour in the print. Ink is pressed through the fabric with a squeegee onto the paper and each colour has to dry separately before the next colour can be applied. Liane uses three methods: the photographic, stencil-cut, and hand-drawn techniques. It is rather time-consuming but, on the other hand, an extremely popular medium — commercially and for print lovers. There exists a considerable market for limited edition style prints.

Besides, she had an exhibition of recent water colours at the Richview Library Gallery from June 3rd to June 29.

Liane's artwork clearly reflects her personal bond with nature and her appreciation of nature's purity while simultaneously evoking strong feelings for nature in its viewers.

To quote Liane verbatim:
"My love of nature and its preservation, travel and art have finally come together in a career I intend to pursue for a lifetime."

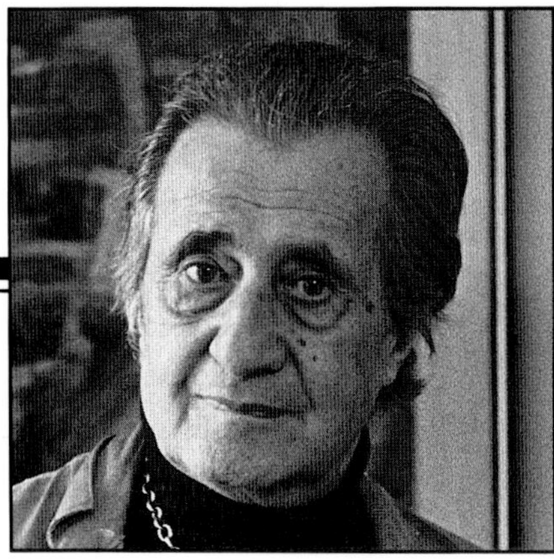

FREDERIC STEIGER

versatile painter of the abstract and excellent portraitist who captures the soul of his model

(previously published in the 1981 winter issue of THE SPIRES CULTURAL COMMUNITY FOCUS*)*

Frederic Steiger, well known in the art world since 1936, has developed his own strong, unique style with a pallet knife as his only tool.

This renowned artist was born in Roumania. Due to hectic wartime events, he moved to Czechoslovakia and then to Austria. Thereafter, he has made Canada and now Etobicoke, his home where he has been painting ever since.

Steiger initially settled in Saskatoon where his painting, the DROUGHT, earned him instant success and fame. That painting captures, with heart-rending appeal, the depression and disillusionment in the face of a farmer who sees his land and crops devastated by merciless elements.

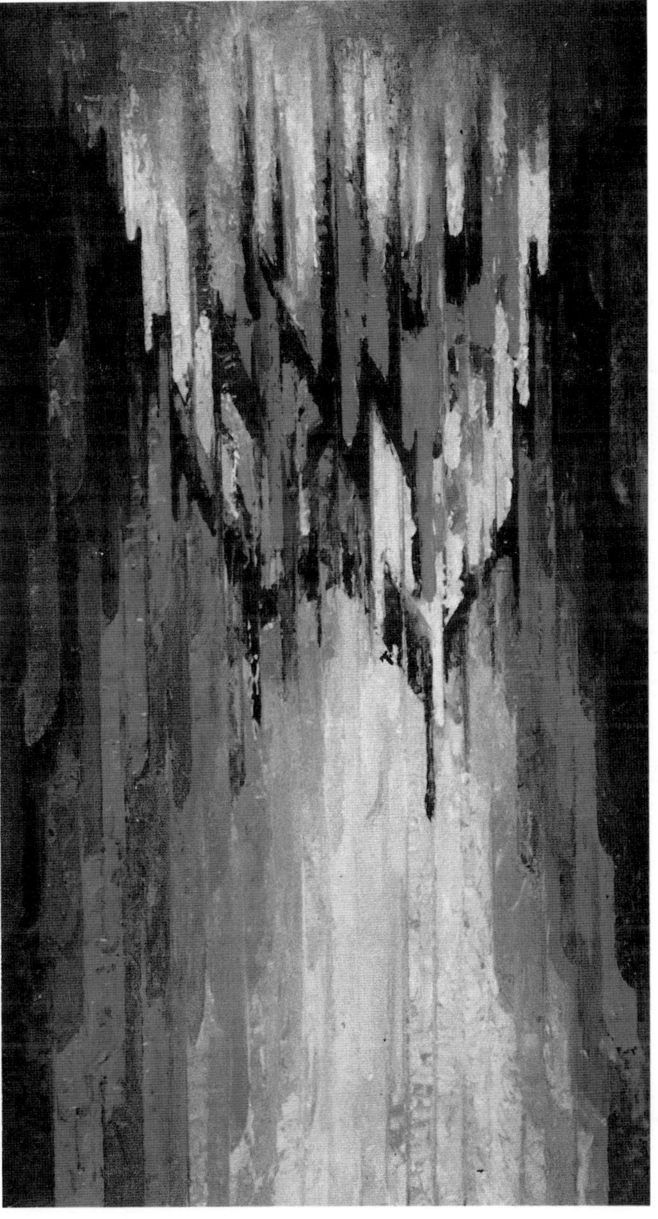

CANADIAN GOTHIC
medium: oil (painting knife)
36" x 20"   1978
in a private collection in London, England
(Mr. and Mrs. Allan Swingler)

FREDERIC STEIGER

This painter is particularly touched by
the beauty of simple people observed in
everyday life. He takes pleasure in depicting them in natural poses and — as a true
artist — always goes after the essential. He
goes for the real person — for the man
behind the outer trappings — for the soul.

On the other hand, he also does, of
course, many portraits of leading personali-
ties. The one of Premier Bill Davis deserves
special mention, as it truly reflects the
Premier's charisma, optimism, self-
confidence, and strength.

To get all the proportions, he starts by
doing the first basic outline in charcoal. In
the case of portraits, he then focuses on the
eyes, an important aspect in his paintings,
since they are what is most expressive in
people. He then works around them, and it
takes him an average of two days to complete a portrait.

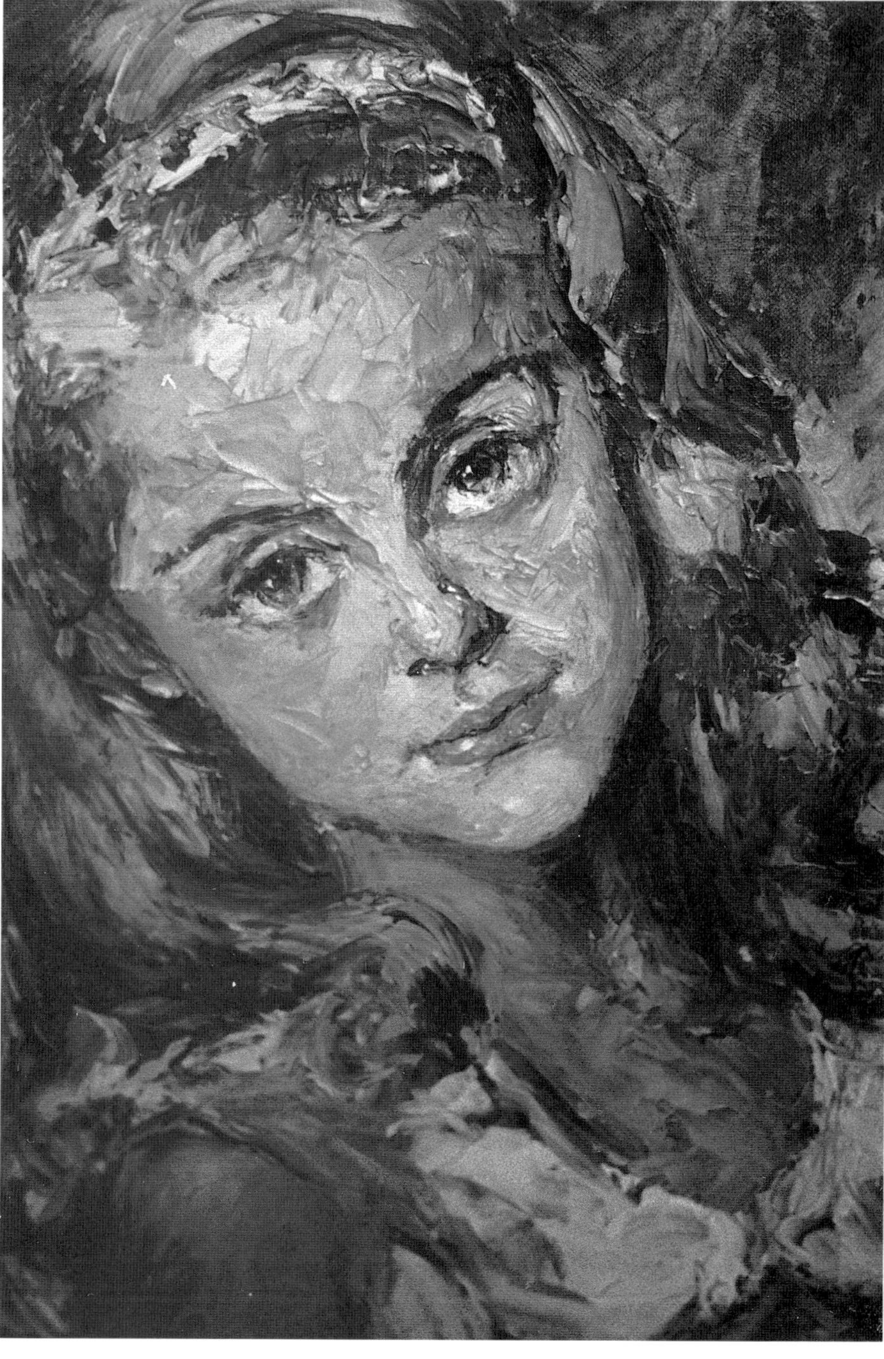

STUDY OF A FIVE-YEAR OLD (detail)
medium: oil (painting knife)
20″ x 16″   1950
in a private collection
(Dr. & Mrs N. Mittler, Toronto)

At times, Steiger lets his imagination take flight which results in paintings such as the Bacchanal, an orgy of colours in pointillism style — warm orange hues blended with touches of yellow and light blue — inspired by the glowing colours of the Canadian Indian summer.

With but a few strokes — strokes that almost escape the eye — he depicts people and arrests their movement. He does so with the absolute control of a master. Rarely can one detect such powerful economy of lines: three vertical strokes of different length, side by side, catching the movement of a parent accompanied by children. This creates a truly amazing optical effect!

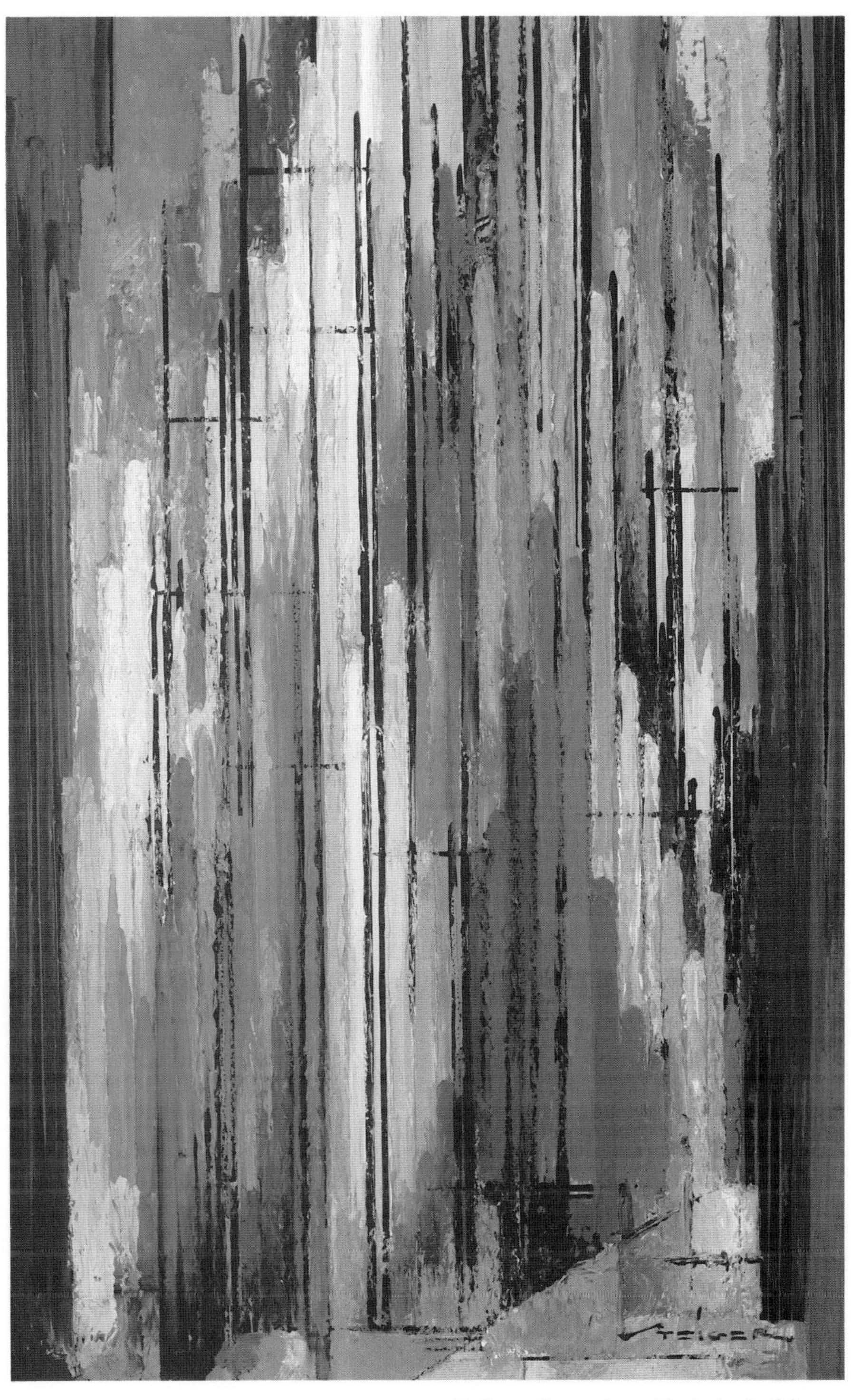

Medium: oil on teakwood (painting knife)
34″ x 20½″   1964
in a private collection —
Mr. & Mrs Pentti Lauren, Rodwell Manor, Somerset, UK
FROM THE PAINTERS OF CANADA SERIES, HALLMARK CARDS CANADA

FREDERIC STEIGER

Steiger is very fond of the countryside; in particular, of old barns. From time to time he takes a few photographs of these to reinforce his memory, and then adjusts the colours to the seasons.

Although his architectural paintings are abstract, they are nevertheless very realistic. Here, his style is almost overpowering. Everyone of these paintings seems a spatial symphony. Particularly impressive are those structures with a momentum of upward movement — created with some deftly applied, textured strokes creating an impression of an upward surge that seems to symbolize the artist's innermost yearning.

"Painting uplifts me", states Frederic Steiger. "I like strong lines."

Modestly he adds:

"It may be a means of personality compensation", for although highly talented, this artist is neither pushy nor aggressive.

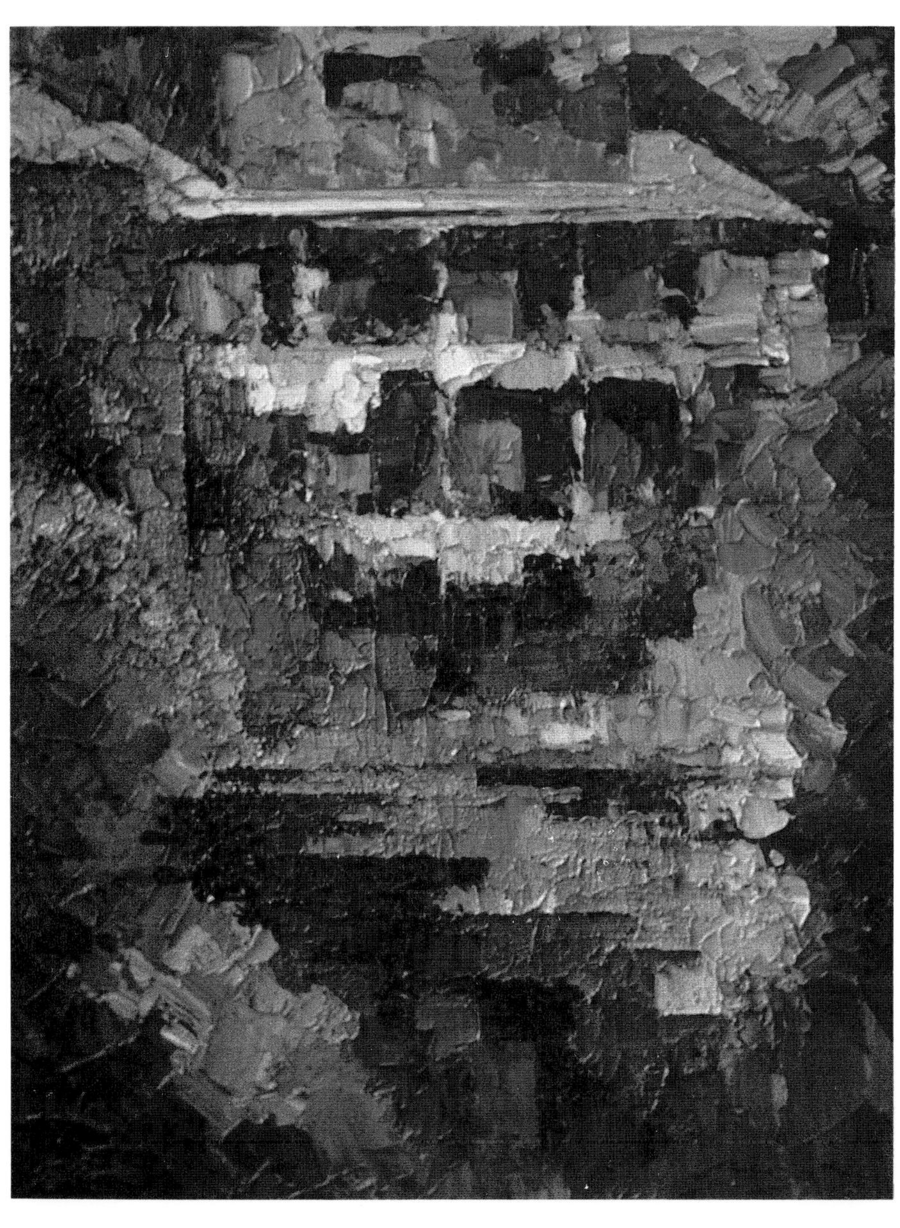

ELORA, ONTARIO (detail)
medium: oil (painting knife) 1982
30" x 24"

(see Richard Gordon Taylor's ELORA *— two artists depicting the very same spot)*

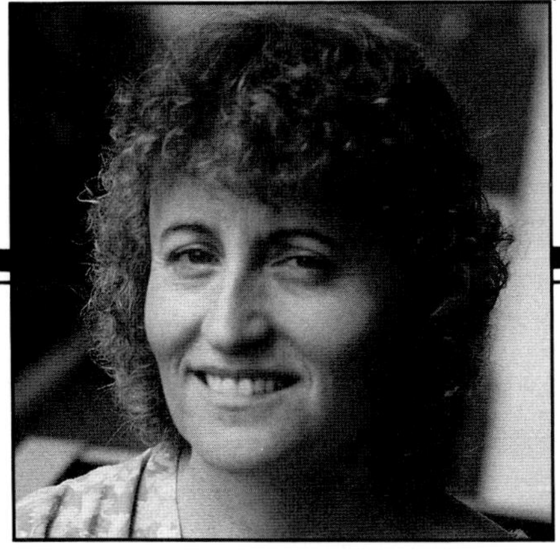

SHULAMIT

dedicated painter, unique colourist, with a very strong sense of structural balance

(excerpt previously published in the ANTHOLOGY '83 by the EWG, Etobicoke Writers' Group)

Shulamit (Shula Steinberg) who came to Canada in 1953, was born on November 28th, 1941, in Rovno, Poland. She grew up in Russia where she spent the first five years of her life in complete isolation without any playmates. She only had animals to play with and therefore identified with them.

When questioned about the dynamic nature of her art, Shulamit comments as follows:

"It took me several years to realize that I have to paint. If I didn't, I would be spiritually ill — an incomplete human being.

"Some people take it or leave it, but I can't leave it. I've tried to do everything else from teaching to dream interpretation, but I have always known that painting is the one thing I have to do. With me, painting is not an ambition but a fulfilment of my soul. Painting is something that comes from my heart.

"In my paintings, people are my prime concern. I guess I see people in a broader sense than their particular religion or culture, since I believe that the human psyche is best enjoyed when expressed in a visual way.

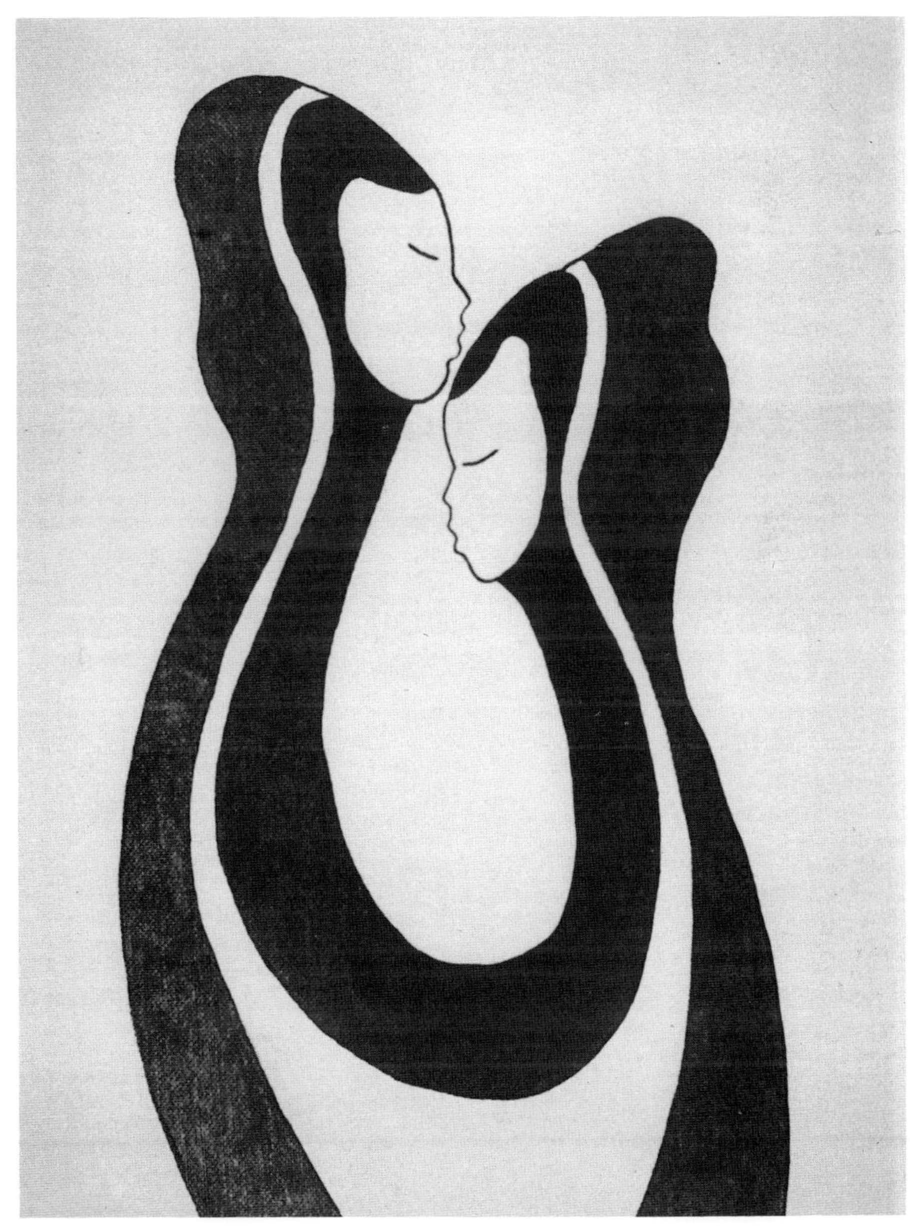

MOTHER AND CHILD
concept in Eskimo tradition
This drawing is a masterpiece achieved with an incredible economy of lines. the child is so close to the mother that they form one unit — contrary to some modern disruptive trends.
To Shulamit, this particular series of paintings is a comparative study, highlighting a bond that used to be very storng but is loosening more and more in our present-day society.

SHULAMIT

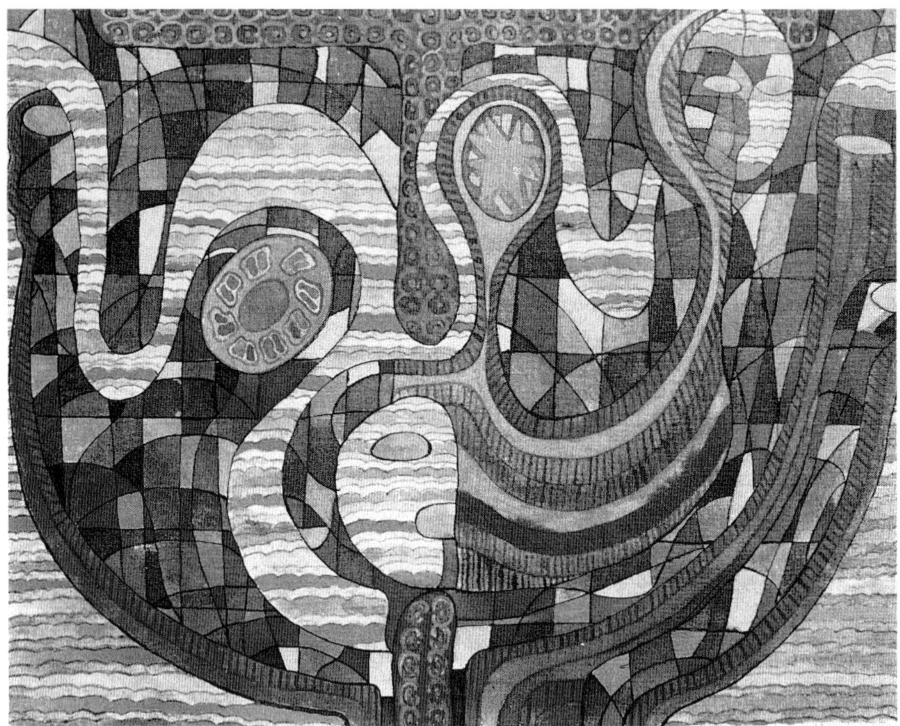

FAREWELL (completed in 1979)
medium: pen and ink
This is a truly psychic painting based on a life reading of a very close friend who passed away. He was a naval officer who had loved the sea, and the sea somehow seemed to be with him at all times.
He also identified very strongly with his Viking heritage of the past, and thus the main motif of this painting is the Viking ship and Viking spirits.
However, in this painting we also find the cross and sword symbolizing that the man was a warrior who bore his cross very well, and the nymph spirits and sea goddess always guided and protected him on his journeys.

"I usually depict the worst (i.e. suffering) in a calm harmonious way and in very simple forms. So much drama and misery — yet in a very simple but stark, to-the-point manner (ref. Eskimo woman devouring her own child — having passed the ultimate barrier of human endurance). It's all there, and very graphic.

"I believe in basic simplicity of style and profound meaning through economy of painting in two to three lines. Many of my paintings are childlike, in a sense, because the are based on memories of earlier experiences. I am very close to the child within me, because I never really had a childhood. I still view the world through the eyes of a child, always full of hope that we will have a world free of war and violence.

"Many of the paintings I do now, share people's perceptions of a person's many lifespans, in the hope that they would perceive themselves much greater than in terms of just their ordinary existence, tapping into that part of themselves (ref. Liz — expansion of psyche on a multi-dimensional plane). I also perceive people, in life, that way.

"I had one bad experience, though, in high school. I had always painted until then. I used to spend hours outside of school drawing, until I had a teacher in high school who nearly failed me because I could not draw in a three-dimensional form. It had such a devastating effect on me that I did not draw for ten years. I was shattered — I really was!

"I realized, however, that the drawings always haunted me in my dreams and I dream a great deal in paintings. Finally, when I understood my dreams, (I studied dream interpretation at that time), I recognized that I had to go back and paint again. At that point, I switched my major from English to Fine Arts and formally enrolled in the Fine Arts course at the University of Manitoba where I studied for two years. The interesting thing is that my art teacher liked my particular style, so he encouraged me to go on, on my own, saying that schooling might take away from it. And that's what I did.

"I completed my B.A. in Art History and specialized in Eskimo Art, because I love primitive art. I paint in a two-dimensional style which, I feel, is in a sophisticated way in the tradition of the primitive artist.

"George Swinton's encouragement gave me a real push in my art. He was my art teacher at the University of Manitoba, and later my thesis adviser in Eskimo Art at Carleton University in Ottawa. He was probably the major teacher in my life, who recognized my potential.

"My first major set of drawings was done in lieu of a term paper and was based on the Eskimo life — its joys, and sufferings.

"It was a slow beginning due to having a full-time job, raising a family, and being a single parent. So I am not a prolific painter because my work is done at night. Yet, despite the fact that I am not prolific, I am a very consistent painter and have reached the point now where commissions are steadily coming in. I have begun to sell privately, the commissions I get mainly being requests for life readings in a visual form.

"I have a style of my own which has changed, though, from the black and white graphic works in the early Seventies, to colourful pen and ink work in the late Sev-

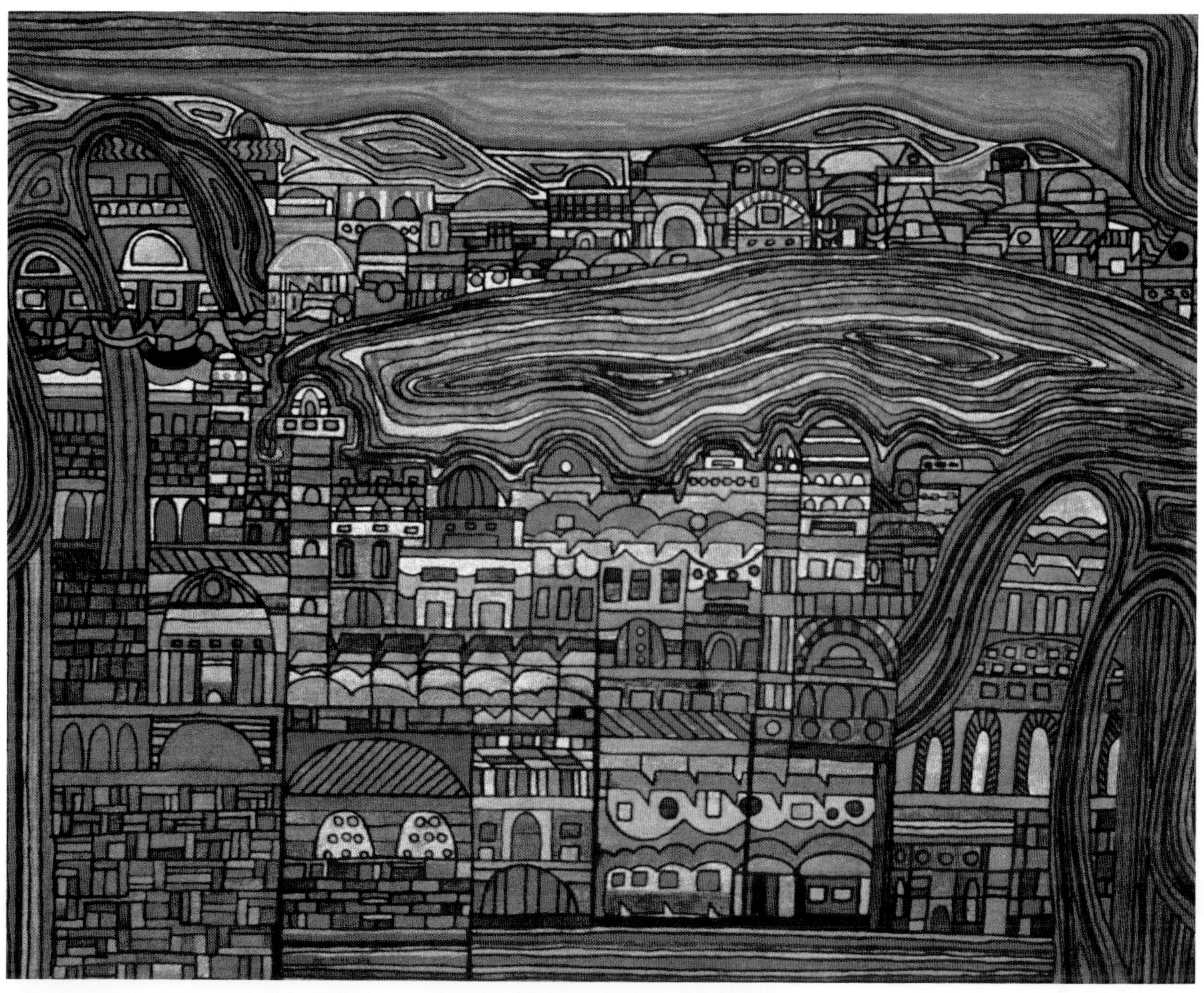

*TIBERIUS done in colour medium: pen and ink
1979*
*This painting depicts her favourite city in Israel
or — for that matter — anywhere in the world,
for it is a city where Shulamit had her first religious experience when she went with her class
on an excursion to visit holy places and old
synagogues.*

*It had a terribly moving effect on her, to
stand in a place where history was taking her*

*back for centuries and centuries, and she felt
part of it.*

*It is a painting of fine details. Shulamit
used several overlays of different blends of
colour before she arrived at its present rich deep
hue. It is a painting of old buildings and walls
— permeated with serenity. TIBERIUS is a city
where Shulamit wanted to live forever — a city
that left an indelible impression on her — (ah)
the unforgettable sunset on the Sea of Galilee!*

enties. I have now incorporated oils, in
addition to my pen-and-ink drawings.

"I also have a keen interest in landscape and architecture because I view cities
and landscapes as extensions of the human
psyche. I like to harmonize and bring
together a combination of forms that are
natural and man-made, such as buildings
(ref. TIBERIUS).

"I have a passion for balance and
order, in nature as well as in one's inner
self. The inner spirit of man restores harmony in a world that often suffers from
blatant disharmony. Maybe it is my particular way of restoring peace, which is the

meaning of my name (Shulamit = Shalom).
I also hope that my paintings will give
people peace and stir a deeper awareness
of life.

"I guess my own goal, too, when I
think of projecting the future is to show
how that totality of cultural diversion has
affected my present thinking. I am now in
the process of doing a series of historical
paintings based on my past; my heritage,
and my historical journeys from Poland,
Russia, etc. like the European, Israeli, and
Canadian journeys.

"The one objective I still hope to
achieve, is doing work of a mural nature. I

really want to leave a legacy to my children
to show them where they come from. This
would be an autobiography in a painterly
style, a goal in addition to what I am presently doing.

"European wartime events made me
exceptionally sensitive to any kind of prejudice or violence. If there is anything I
have to say in any of my work, it is that I
abhor disharmony of any kind. I want to
make a historical statement in the hope
that we won't repeat history in that form
again. I am very concerned about another
holocaust that is global — a nuclear
holocaust.

SHULAMIT

"We have so much that our energies should go into sharing and caring rather than hurting ourselves. What more can anybody say? I only think to live for this harmony — this outcry for peace.

"As to advice to other artists:

— believe in yourself — in your unique style — and do not judge success in monetary acclaim. The greatest artists are often very poor in monetary terms — talent not being equated with financial gain;

— strive, truly, to bring out the most honest in yourself;

— never compromise by destroying your style — not even for great commercial gain! It would be the beginning of the end for an artist. It is like Faust selling his soul."

Since Shulamit grew up in Russia, quite a few of her paintings deal with that period of time — representing wartime memories.

She painted several church windows, for she was born in a church (converted into a hospital during the war) and the first images she remembers, are church windows — windows that symbolize to her the incredible fragility of life. Although Jewish, her first identity was Catholic since she was brought up in a convent where she herself led a fragile, wartime existence.

Shulamit, who also teaches dream analysis, does a lot of psychic paintings such as LIZ OF MANY LIVES (medium: pen and ink) — the portrait of a woman who lives in the heart of a large city which is sprawling around her. Yet she is a nature lover from the bottom of her heart. Therefore, Shulamit depicted her mind as a sanctuary of fish and birds — in the midst of the city. The birds symbolize the fauna of the Northern tundra of which Liz is so fond.

As Liz identifies very strongly with the Canadian native peoples, Shulamit depicted her with an Indian braid. However, Liz is Danish by birth and she has an Icelandic nose.

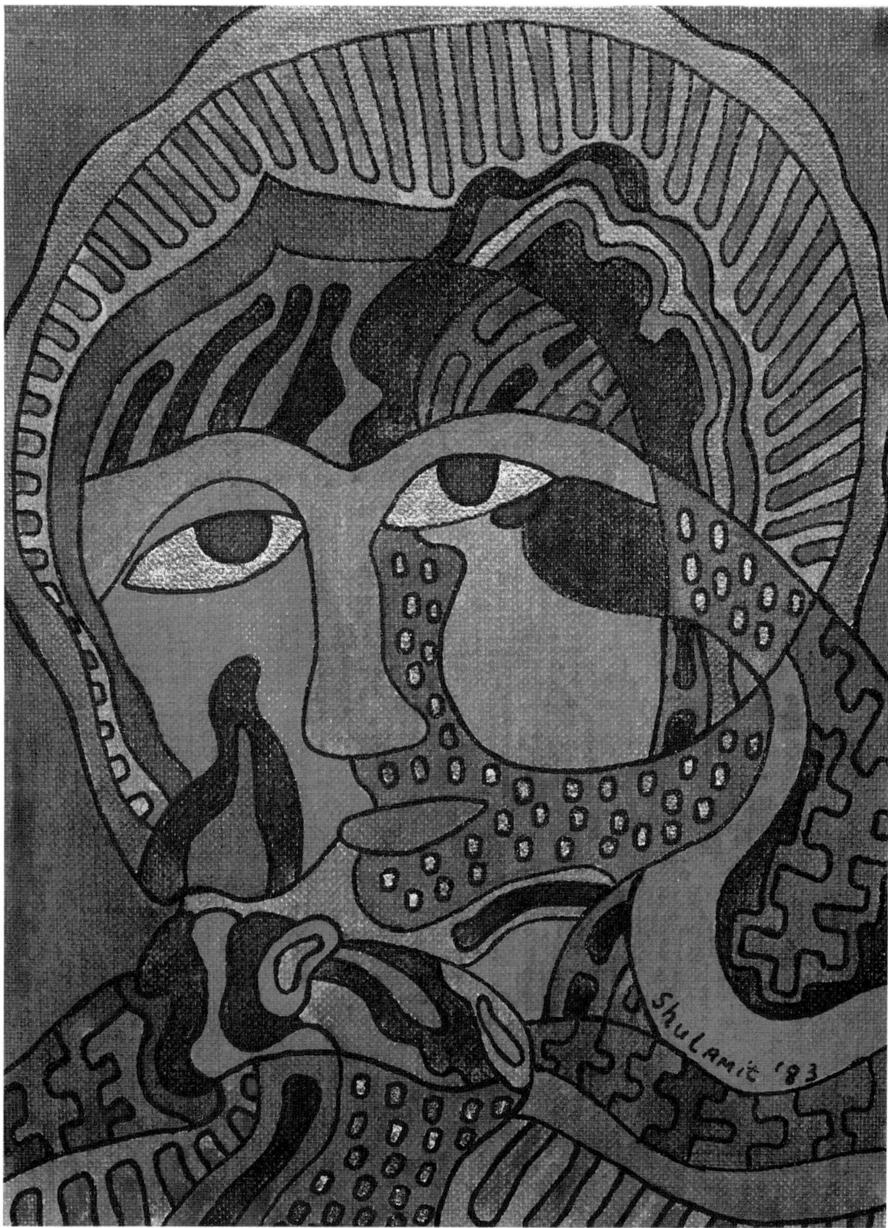

1983   ICON   done in India ink 9″ x 12″

A mosaic of such a powerful compositional and colour effect that it evokes an optical after-image in the mind of the beholder, the face triggering a gamut of emotions.

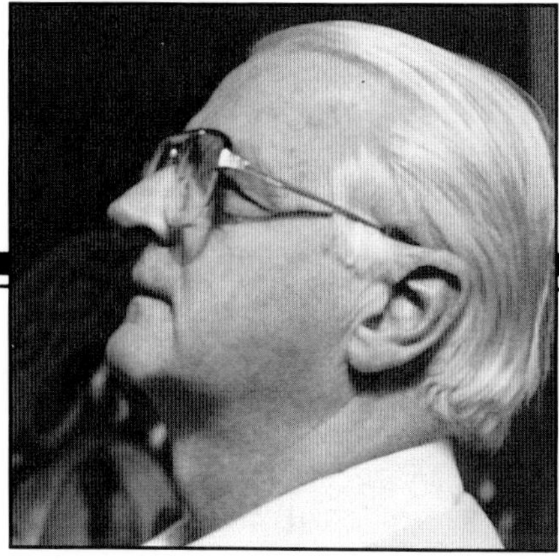

IGOR P. SUHACEV

a rare blend of unique talents — specialized in iconography, stained glass work, mosaic, architectural design, portraiture, and fairytale illustration as well as surrealistic abstract art — a humble man — his art comes from his heart and is uplifting, interesting, and entertaining all at once.

Igor P. Suhacev was born in Zagreb. Yugoslavia, on November 21st, 1925, into a family with a tradition deeply rooted in ecclesiastic mural painting, mosaics, icons, and stained glass windows.

In Yugoslavia he studied initially under his father who was, for a while, doing murals in the Yugoslav Parliament.

After the war, he studied in Germany at the Hamburger Akademie where he was enrolled in secular art and — parallel to those studies — attended a small, icon-painting school for refugees — an institute where his father also taught fresco techniques. After all, sacral art is not that far removed from the secular, since all art originated from the sacral.

When starting out, Igor was, for some time, under the influence of Duerer, Rembrandt, Cézanneand French impressionism.

Inspired by Puschkin's fairytales that exerted a very strong influence on him during his childhood, he did those superb illustrations of enrapturing luminosity of TSAR SALTAN and THE GOLDEN COCKEREL at the mere age of 19, "a type of fairytale illustration that is close to popular art and which the Slavs carry within themselves all their lives." And this comes easily to Igor, as it flows effortlessly from his subconscious.

As of the end of 1949 he worked for seven years in Ethiopia for the emperor Haile Selassie through the Ethiopian Ministry of Public Works, decorating two churches in stained glass (murals and iconostases)*, designing a military hall and several lions — those imposing protectors and guards — coats of arms, and two thrones, etc.

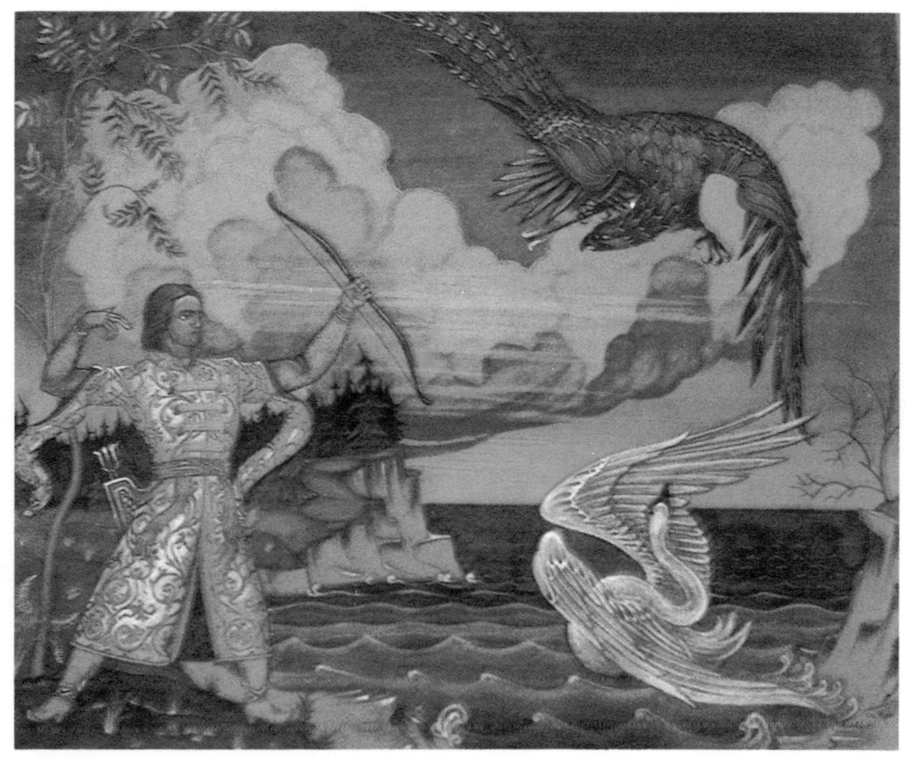

ICONOSTASIS:

a screen or wall (separating the sanctum from the main part of the church) on which icons are displayed.
done in collaboration with his father
stained glass window
HOLY TRINITY church in Addis Ababa

IGOR P. SUHACEV

He emmigrated to Canada in 1957 where he decorated Ukrainian, Slovak, Serbian, and Russian churches.

He did two churches in Toronto — by himself — and one church, the St. Nicholas church, — in collaboration — four churches in Hamilton (murals and iconostases); two churches in St. Catharines (murals and iconostases); one church in Montreal (murals); one church in Roblin, Manitoba (mural and iconostasis); one church in Yorkton, Saskatchewan (mural and iconostasis); one church in Ituna (murals); some icons for Chicago, USA, and some icons for London, England.

He also did portraits purported to be truly amazing likenesses.

When asked:

"Did you ever paint your wife?" he replied:

"Not yet. As you know, inconographers only paint saints. And sainthood quite often comes from martyrdom."

Suddenly an amused smile flickers in his eyes."

"Hmmm…but since the eastern orthodox philosophy considers marriage as having an element of martyrdom, she might qualify after all."

Besides, he enjoys landscape painting and also engages in abstract surrealistic painting. As to abstract art, it mainly involves a concept that is clearly visible in his mind before he actually executes the painting.

Igor Suhacev is a restless artist whose mind always needs diversity and whose interests span the vast range from the classical tradition to the supermodern — in painting and architecture as well as in his taste in music.

As to his religious art, there exists a very sincere attachment to his work rather than commercial consideration. He paints out of strong feelings but not to satisfy demand, and he derives such personal enjoyment from his work that the monetary aspect is secondary.

"One has to profit from daylight plus artificial light to avail oneself of optimal conditions. Otherwise, with artificial lighting alone, you might be horrified the next morning, to be faced with murals or vault decorations that look as if affected by jaundice."

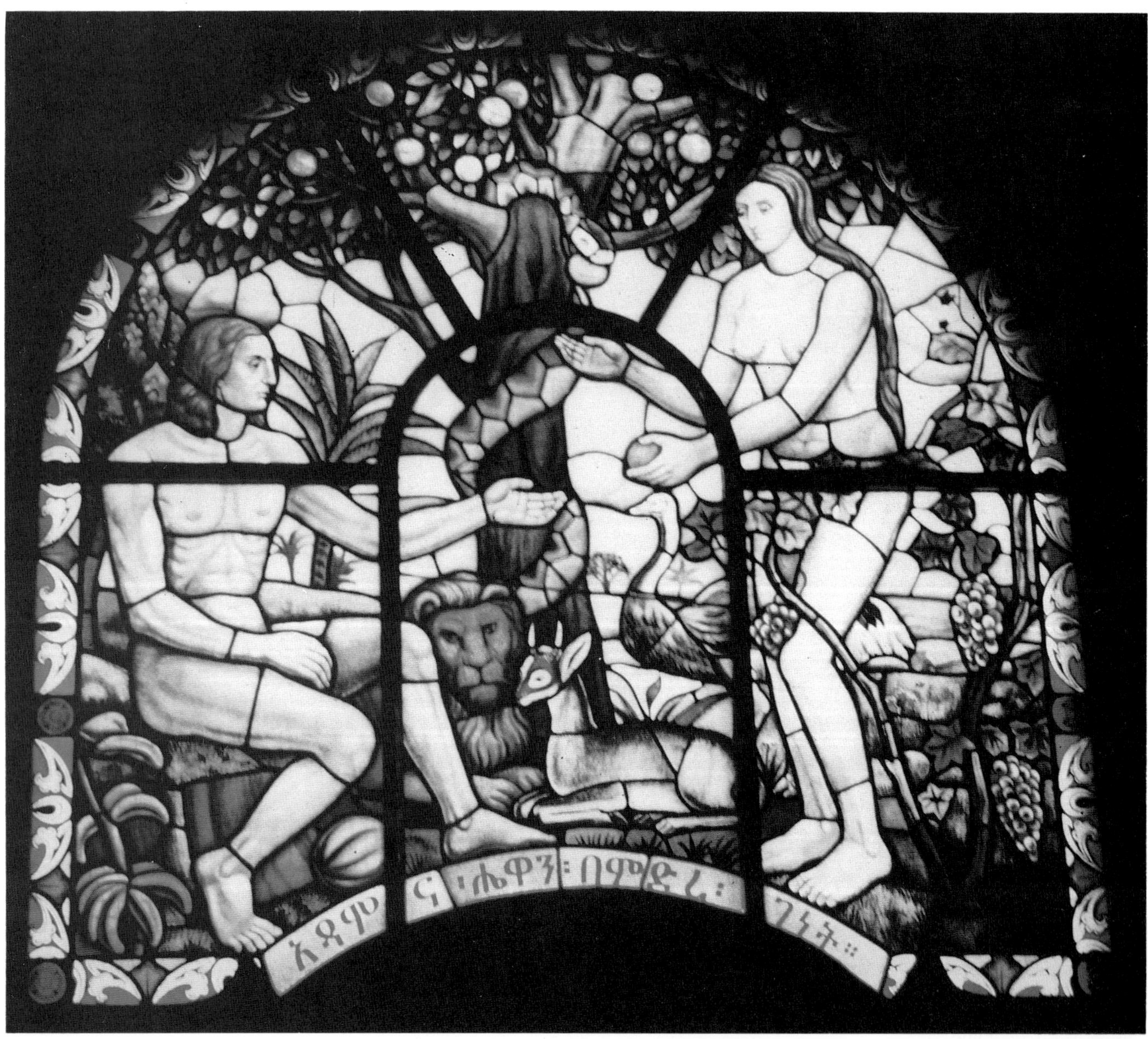

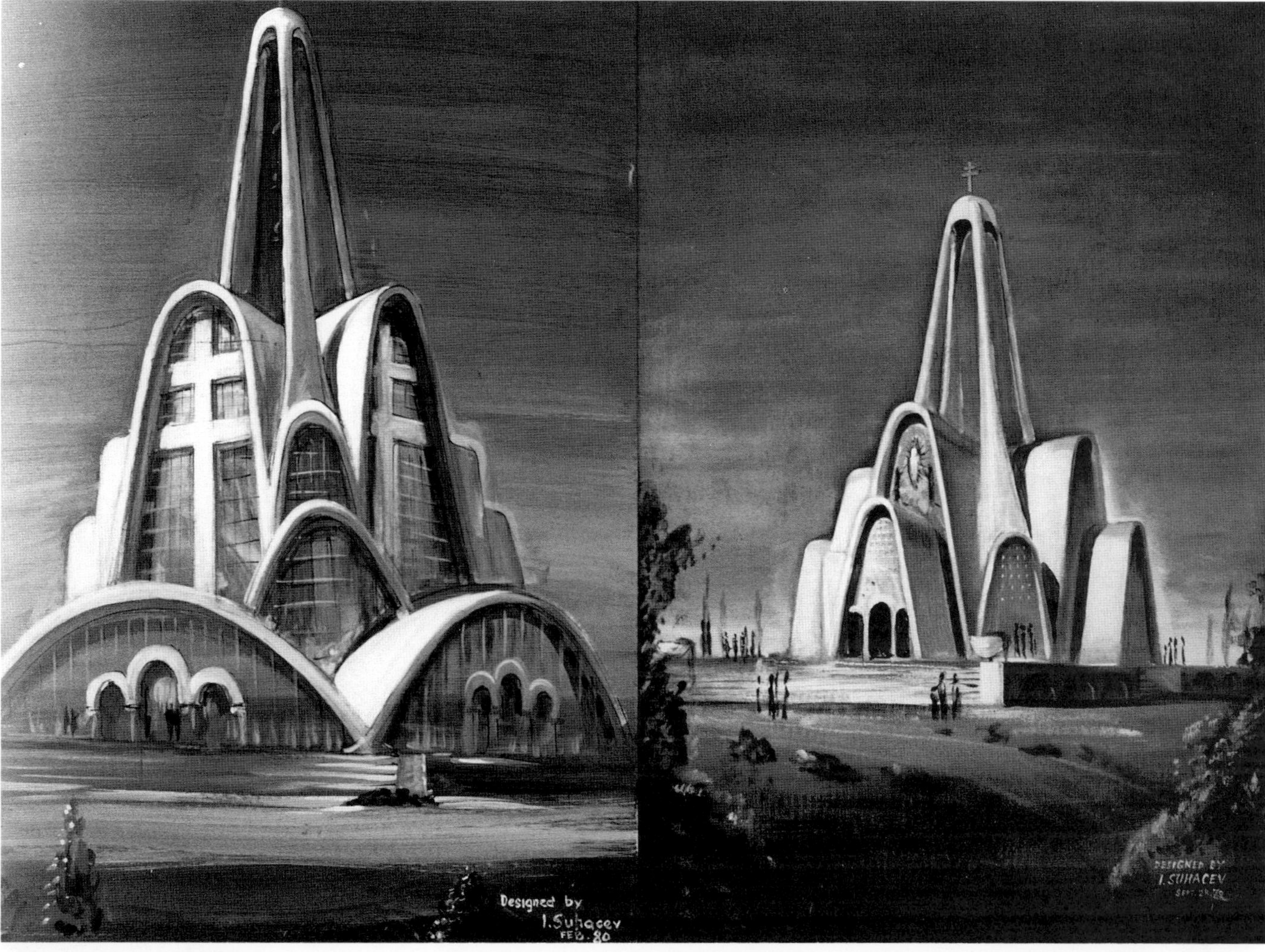

design for a Slovak cathedral

Igor was invited to Rome by Cardinal Slipiy to complete the decoration of his cathedral.

Being part of the reception line, he also met His Holiness Pope John Paul II, at the consecration of the altar of the Slovak-Greek-Catholic HOLY TRANSFIGURATION church

Of course, everyone knows that it is not easy working high up on scaffolding — suspended in the air — fastened to a safety belt and painting for hours on end in a position that is not always the most comfortable. Apart from genuine feeling towards religion, an appreciation of tradition, a love for what you are doing and — obviously, artistic skills — stamina and good health are also of critical importance for this particular type of artwork.

In addition to decorative work, Igor also designs churches bearing in mind the religious relevance, environmental affinity, contextual adaptability, and cultural specificity. He focuses first on considerations such as air, light, colour, form, being aware of structural advantages to be derived, as in this case, from the Slovak type of cross, for instance. His spires surge into the sky in an admirable purity of line.

(Steve Roman Foundation) in Markham, Ontario.

In architecture, he appreciates the Romanesque, Gothic, Baroque and contemporary styles. He does not delve too much into the abstract and shies away from being too subjective., believing instead in universal accessibility.

In general, he quite loves realism and does not feel that it is out of place at the end of the twentieth century. He strongly suggests that abstract art is actually just a revolution and reaction to the 19th century extra-realism — a religious or cultural revolt against the traditional. However, strictly copying gives Igor neither pleasure nor satisfaction, nor does it provide any challenge.

He finds surrealism too objective although he sympathizes with it. He feels that people experienced a kind of boredom arising out of over-saturation and hence abstract art may be interpreted as a type of counter-balance because the 19th century was almost photographic in its rendition. Hence, abstract art was felt to be a breath of fresh air but he considers it, nevertheless, a culture that cannot exclu-

sively exist all by itself. However, he can see the validity of abstract art such as unusual spatial sculptures that break the monotony of routine life. This validity seems logical when we see, for instance, the abstract sculptures in front of the Sun-Life Building, the City Hall or the Art Gallery of Ontario where they fulfil their function. We need the mysterious, unexplainable, and irrational.

Almost daily Igor browses through architectural and art history books with the same enjoyment someone else might derive from comic books or watching sports events.

He considers painting and architecture as having reached their pinnacle during the Age of Monarchy, the Age of Faith and the Age of Princes, most of whom had the means and taste to encourage them.

His knowledge of the history of art is exceptionally profound and it is his opinion that the Ancient Greeks were never surpassed — Renaissance or no Renaissance. To him, their art is perfect in its extreme restraint of line — aesthetics being their religion.

IGOR P. SUHACEV

As to the past, he also highly appreciates German art of the period of Romanticism, and the French art prior to the revolution (Louis XIV and XV).

Besides, he feels that religion is definitely not out of place in the 20th century, as propaganda would have us believe — or not even Humanism could quite supplant religion. Hence, iconography is particularly dear to his heart. He was born and raised in Eastern orthodoxy which includes the whole eastern orthodox view. "But —being also a western person — he is a great admirer of realism and never wanted to be, exclusively, an icon-painter."

Icons hold a special place in Eastern orthodox faith and form an integral part of even the humblest home. Particularly, women who had no one else to turn to, would — for centuries — take their sorrows and griefs to the images of the Mother of God, the epitome of love, who — they believed — could understand them and would disregard their failings.

Iconography is a pure and very rigorous discipline where copying is virtue.

Those highly symbolic icons are subject to strict tradition as ruled by Council in the time of Ivan V who stated that icons must be faithful to the consecrated type so that icon-painting was not a question of originality, but a question of faith.

Yet artists have managed to break away from that order of Ivan V through skilfully changed nuances of expression, special colour effects and stylized halos done in filigree, gold leaf or being encrusted with precious stones or semi-precious gems.

Igor P. Suhacev has a sound knowledge of theology allowing him to paint in accordance with the established dogmas and ecclesiastic tradition, it being the very idea of iconography to serve religion and tradition. This holds true even more so now, since most of the churches behind the Iron Curtain are closed which gives rise to the artists' strong urge or pressing need to create — an urge that should not be repressed.

Suhacev feels that, unfortunately, great damage has been done by some modern artists because they dishonestly pull the wool over the public's eyes —something that is proving generally detrimental.

Igor Suhacev is a truly multicultural and multilingual artist who speaks seven languages, namely: Serbian, German, Russian, Ukrainian, French, Italian, and English …but for the past twenty-five years he has done all his reading exclusively in the English language.

He is grateful to Canada and happy to reside in a country where even non-commercial artists can do well; where refugees want to donate decorations to churches and bring their traditions to Canada in order to share them with others and, hopefully, enrich Canada with the uniqueness of their styles.

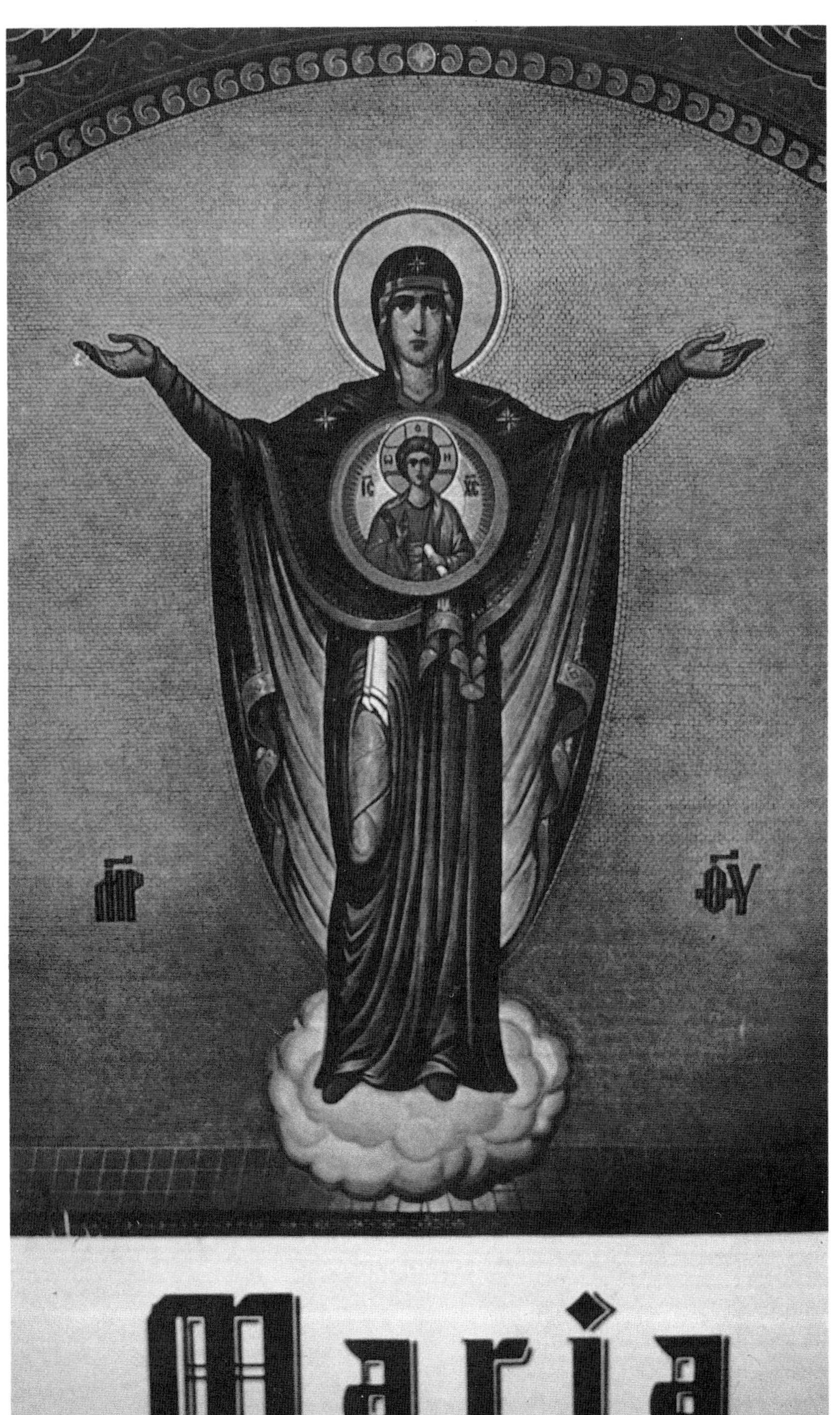

15-foot icon
behind the altar
in the Slovak cathedral in Toronto

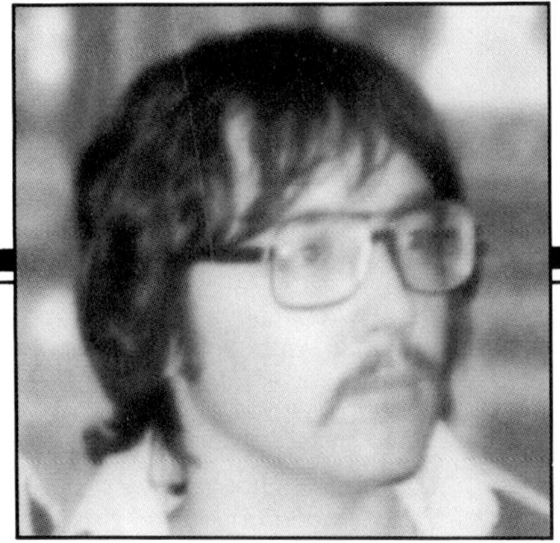

RICHARD GORDON TAYLOR

outstanding painter and illustrator

(excerpts previously published in ERIN MILLS REVIEW *— Sept. 3, 1980* THE SPIRES *Cultural Community Focus — 1980/81 Winter issue.)*

Richard Gordon Taylor was born on July 12, 1950, in Fergus, Ontario, and raised close to the Grand River.

As a second- and third-year college student, he had a couple of one-man shows in the Mississauga Library, and was also chosen as a participant in the Young Canadian Painters exhibition at the Scollard Gallery.

Besides, many of his paintings were featured in a Father and Son Show at the Malton Community Centre in November, 1977, and he also had a Pen-and-Ink Show in 1979. In 1980, the Mississauga Central Library was the site of his 5-year retrospective show.

"Fancy that! He comes home and with a nod for a greeting, he withdraws to his study and lies down on the chesterfield — eyes closed — without giving any thought to food. At times, he lies there motionless for hours on end." That's how Krista describes Rick during the second stage of his creative process.

For, as I learned from Rick, first comes this onrush of ideas — acompanied by shapes and colours galore — which he then subjects to a careful mental screening — sometimes for quite a few hours. Only then does he rush to his easel where, seized by sheer frenzy — his hands keep on working the canvas until the early morning hours.

However, Rick does not rely exclusively on those truly creative bouts but is extremely disciplined. He never lets a single day or night go by without painting or doing some sketches — 'for what would a piano player be without practice?' comments the painter in a rather nonchalant manner.

Rick, who teaches art on a professional level, has been painting for the past ten years, taught for two years before graduation from Humber College, then attended Guelph University from whence he pro-

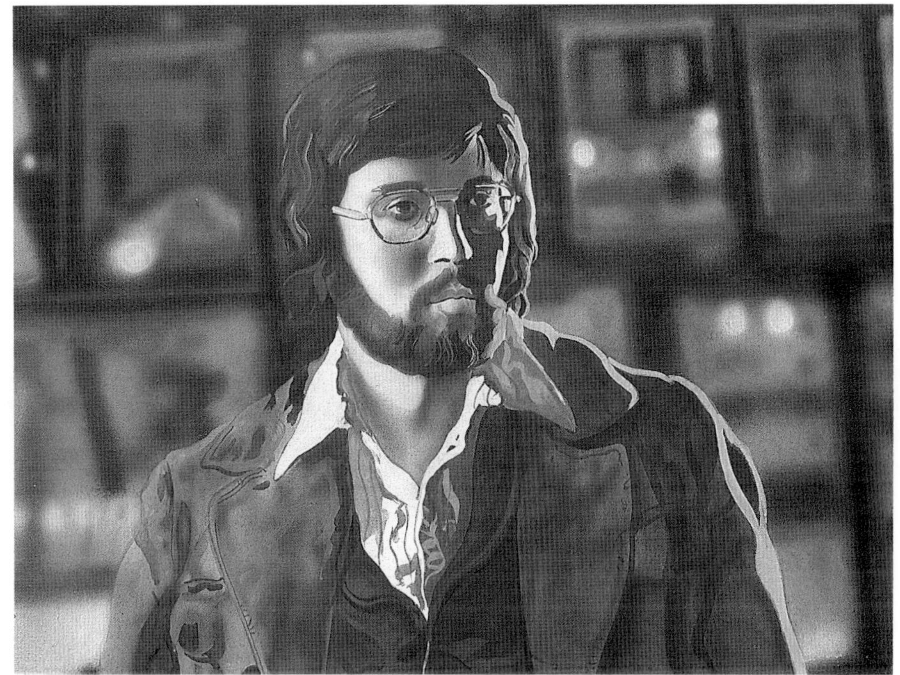

SELF-PORTRAIT (airbrush)

RICHARD GORDON TAYLOR

ceeded to York to get his degree. He is now a full-time elementary school teacher.

Rick also accepted many private commissions — being much sought after due to his special sensitivity and in-depth penetration of the often deeply hidden traits. THE GREAT GATSBY painting with focus on a single elegant rose arrangement in the foreground places the main emphasis, however, on the background figure —the forceful but simultaneously constrained lines so aptly characterizing the man..

Rick enjoys, particularly, those commissions that allow a certain margin for his mind to roam freely.

Besides, Rick also illustrated books presenting Canadian Indian settings and Canadian festivals such as Halloween, Christmas and Easter — scenes for which several of his students served as models.

Interviewer: Rick, you really know your medium — I would guess your painting goes back a long way.

Rick: Yes, I have been exposed to materials such as brushes and paints from an early age when I used to accompany my father, a lettering man by trade, on his commissions. He always encouraged me in my endeavours and spent a lot of time conveying to me an insight into design. Dad also taught me the beauty of clean stationary lines — clean lines having, however, a life of their own — expressed in relative fluidity.

Interviewer: Oh, I see what you mean when I look at these sketches where even the wood is alive, where the grain patterns speak of great discipline on your part. But don't you feel conflict, at times, between the freedom of freely flowing lines and those rigorously clean lines?

Rick: Life is conflict — art is conflict, but forces stronger than man blend it all into an intriguing oneness, as it were.

I actually started out doing oils, dabbling for some time in the abstract which I enjoy a lot. Next came a pen-and ink phase from which I also derived great pleasure.

Interviewer: As to frequently recurring motifs, do the wire and fences, in some of your latest paintings, mean anything in particular?

Rick: They are a sign of restraint to me, restrictions I willingly impose upon myself. But don't overlook the kite recurring throughout the entire series of my Toronto street scenes. That kite actually symbolizes me. It seems very free although it has actually no control as to where it goes.

Interviewer: Besides, like CAMUS' OUTSIDER, it looks on but does not participate in the life of the crowds below.

Rick: Significant correction: it participated and was then airborne to the position of looking on.

Interviewer: Do you ever work from photographs?

Rick: Yes, but only to a certain degree. I take plenty of photos, as you can see, but use them merely as reference to refresh my memory. Photographs do give me the form, but not the substance. Besides, I change the moods a lot.

Interviewer: Almost all your landscapes contain water bodies of some form or shape.

Rick: I was born and raised on the banks of the Grand River. I played by the river, and although I was at times even a bit afraid of the river, I have always felt attracted to water.

Interviewer: Could the water motif, somehow, be equated to mirror symbolism?

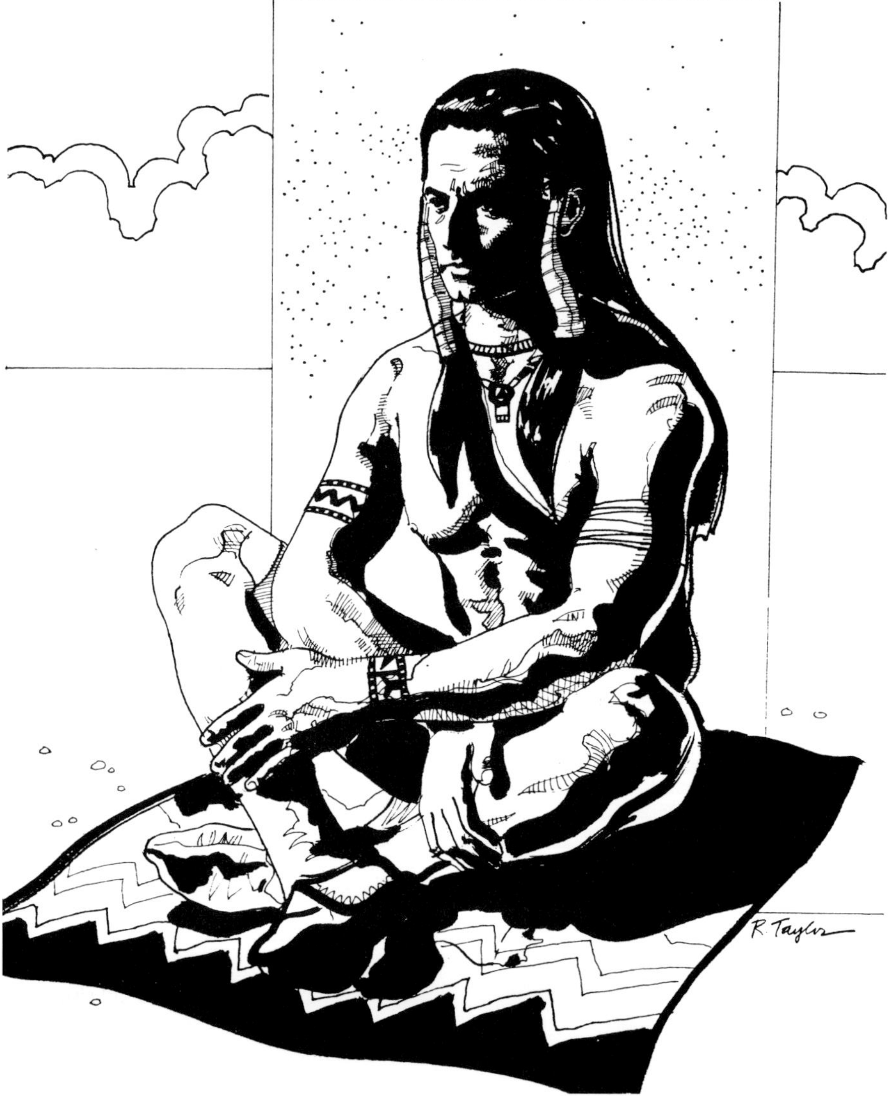

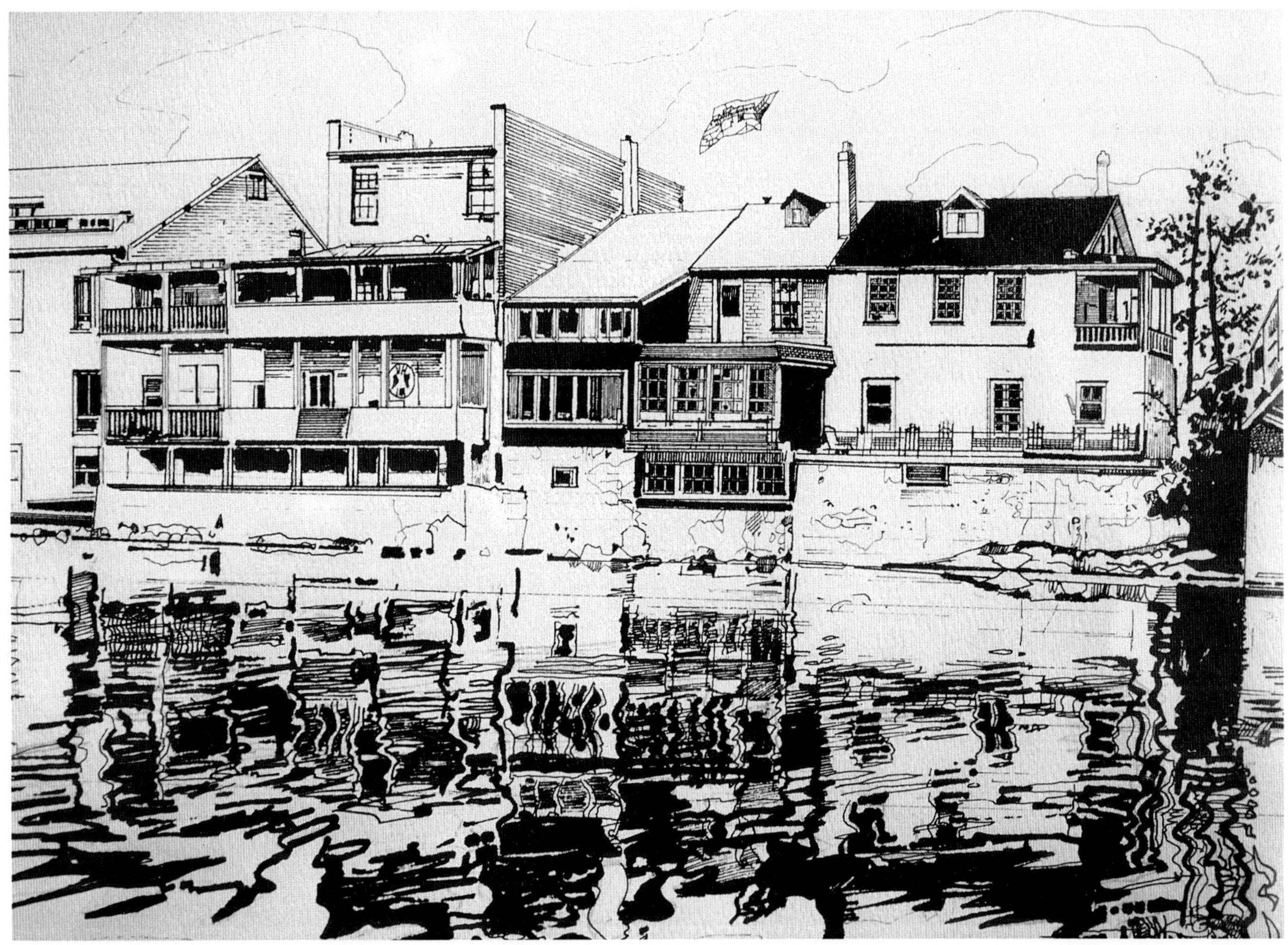

*ELORA, ONTARIO (see Frederic Steiger's Elora —
two artists depicting the very same spot)*

Rick: In a way, yes, because both conjure up interesting images of reality in unreality. Water is life. Life is reflection, for by the time the artist converts an event or happening into an artistic experience, something has already slipped — and the work of art is thus a reflection, or to quote BERNARD MALAMUD: DUBIN'S LIVES … There is no life that can be recaptured wholly, as it was.

Interviewer: Does the change to more soothing orangey tones imply anything?

Rick: You mean in terms of personal change?

Interviewer: Yes.

Rick: Not really, since all of us are always caught in a constant state of flux.

Interviewer: Not only your landscapes but also some of your "timetrippers" (a series of paintings showing the artist in his process of maturing) are set in warm, orangey colours and hues. Does that particular colour combination imply a certain mood of Fall, or the peacefulness of fulfilled youth?

Rick: No, not quite. Try a whiff of nostalgia instead.

Interviewer: Besides, the brown reminds me of old photographs.

Rick: Yes, it is similar to a dream where you can't quite remember the exact colours, like looking back on childhood with bits and pieces of childhood memories surging up from the subconscious. Besides, people can easily relate to and share the underlying feeling. Yet, painting in those shades also may make one a little bit sad since they reflect something that is irretrievably lost in the past.

RICHARD GORDON TAYLOR

Interviewer: Are you, in any way, preoccupied with time?

Rick: Ah, time is a major concern of mine. Take the timetripper series, for instance. Outwardly it is, of course, a sort of device that links paintings. The timetripper can be in any setting, be it realistic, time-alientated or romantically stylized. As he gets older, I get older.

Rick looks back and reflects on events — wishing there were things that could be done over again. Man's yearning to go back in time!

Yes, the idea of continuity is very much like a character in a book.

Interviewer: Do you follow any particular school of painting?

Rick: No, at least not knowingly but I am definitely influenced by Vermeer, Degas, David Milnes and some of the old magazine illustrators towards whom I feel drawn on account of their sense of drama.

Interviewer: Do you still do figure drawing?

Rick: Yes, that is a field I particularly enjoy although I have slightly shifted to a combination of focusing the figure within a certain spatial composition.

Interviewer: Your lines are powerful.

Rick: They have to be, for my figures are solid, positive figures — figures you can count on.

Besides, I like my figures against warm, light-flooded backgrounds — settings permeated with coziness exuding an atmosphere of peacefulness, people totally in unison with their environment, in their favourite corner so-to-speak.

Interviewer: Your loving attitude towards all mankind is so refreshing.

Rick: Well, I cannot stop this warmth despite my having been afraid of oversentimentality at times.

Interviewer: One last question, Rick. Do you ever get mental blocks, the so-called dry spells?

Rick: No such problem because I have so many creative ideas without sufficient time even to execute them all — always more ideas that I can handle. No. thank God, a dry spell is something I don't know, for even if don't paint, I always work on my sketchbook. (Rick's place is littered with sketchbooks).

TOUCHDOWN TORONTO

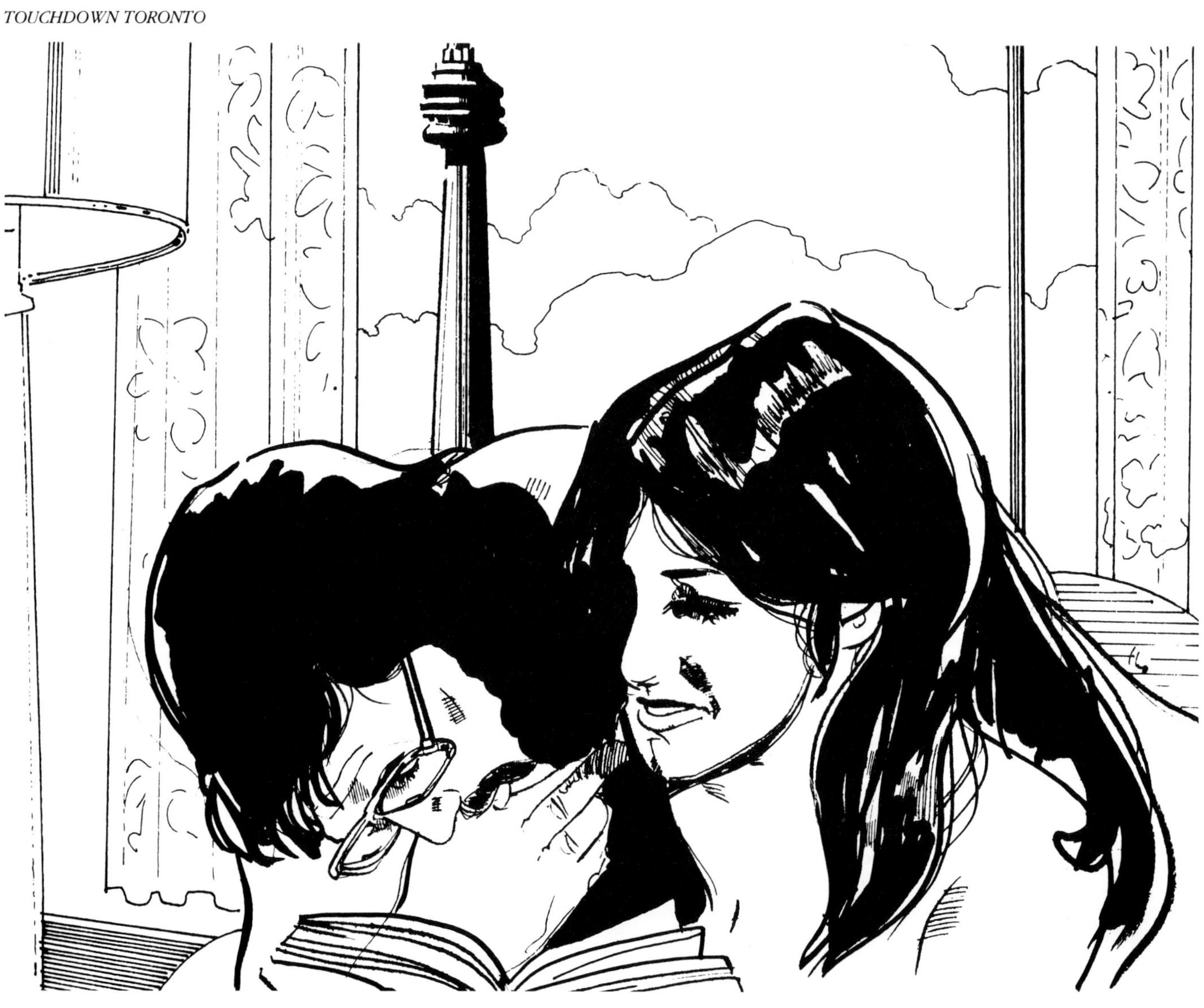

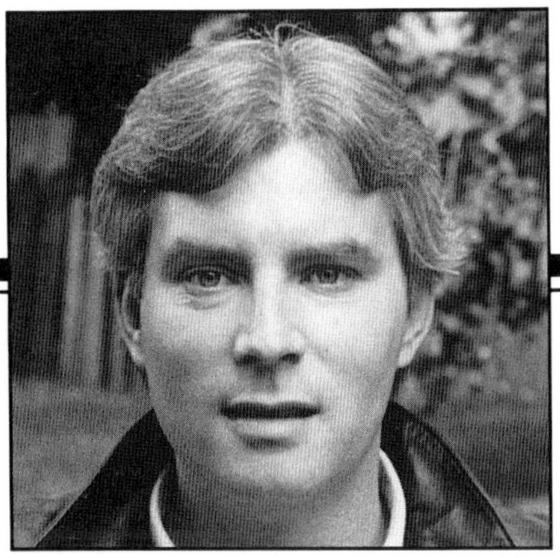

IAN WALLACE

amazing combination of children's book writer and illustrator who enjoyed his first instant success at the mere age of 25

(excerpt previously published in the Winter 1983/84 issue of THE SPIRES Cultural Community Focus?

Ian Wallace, a truly impressive, dynamic, handsome, 6-foot tall, independent-minded Aries born in 1950 in Niagara Falls, Ontario; a young man with sparkling blue eyes which radiate an infectious warmth that invites spontaneous communication; a young man with a frank look of infinite kindness.

Ian, who graduated from the OCA (Ontario College of Art) in 1974, is a perfect blend of writer and illustrator, and although he enjoyed the intoxicating sensation of instant success at the mere age of twenty-five, after only a fortnight of writing when he had his first best-seller (with Angela Wood), he is totally unaffected and very modest.

He also won several coveted awards for his work, and his book THE SANDWICH was named a Canadian Classic in April, 1981, by the Canadian Children's Book Centre in Toronto.

He hopes to write for and read to his own children some day, since he really enjoyed having his grandfather read to him when he was a little boy.

Until now, I had always thought that LE PETIT PRINCE by St.-Exupéry was the ultimate in the philosophy and children's book genre, but after having listened to the deeply stirring recital of Ian Wallace's THE SANDWICH, I could not help thinking:

>"Warum in die Ferne schweifen, wenn das Gute liegt so nah?"

(Why search so far afield
When good things are so near?)

This writer and illustrator reaches beyond our national boundaries, being a great humanist who is not teaching yet provides a powerful philosophy, a touching multicultural message, coming from the

JULIE NEWS
(out of print)
published by KIDS CAN PRESS

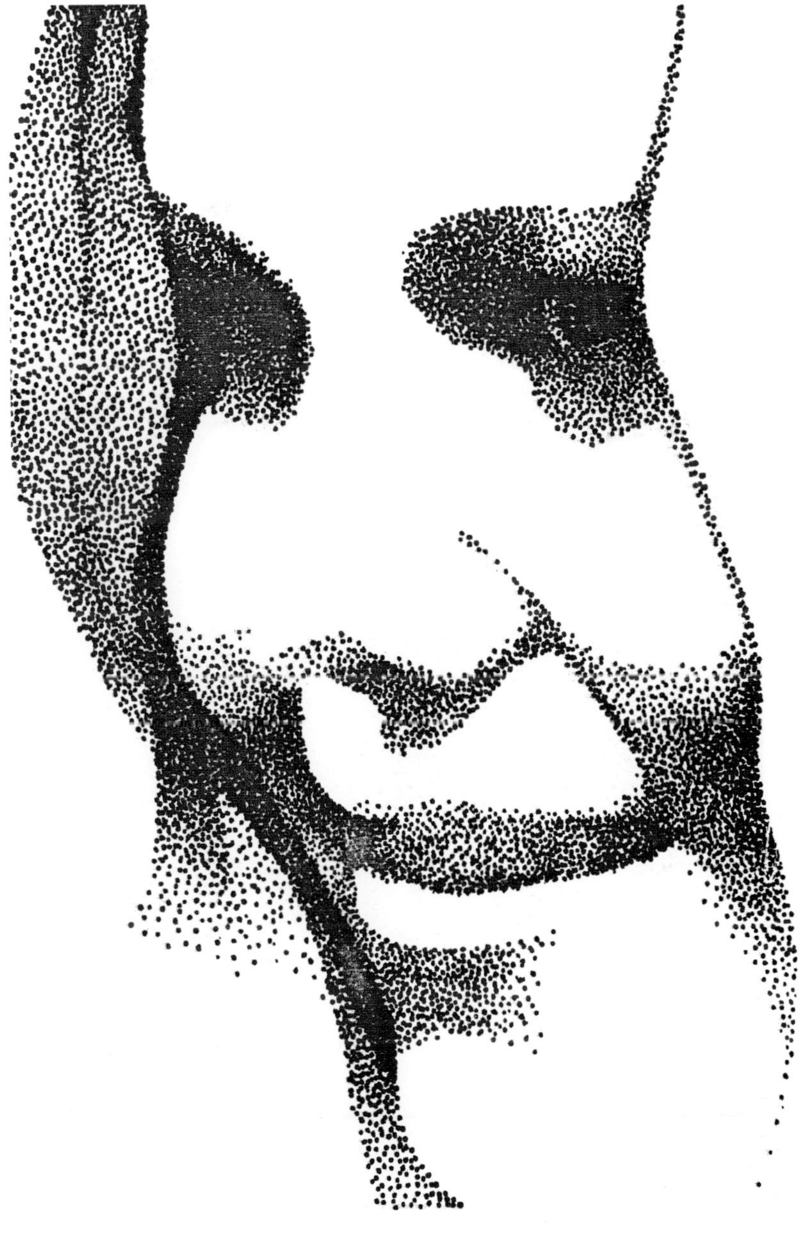

mouths of children in a simple language that is truly theirs.

His books have universal appeal because children from all around the world can easily identify with his characters and themes.

THE SANDWICH is the deeply moving human experience of a little boy by the name of Vincenzo, who is laughed at by his peers just because his sandwich is and smells different from theirs. However, the story ends on the promising note of all of the unknown. Instead of a negative deduction à la…who laughs last, laughs best… the book concludes on the positive note of beauty in diversity.

Ian Wallace is a master in characterization within the framework of dialogue. His children are children of our era; intelligent individuals, who even question adults:

father:-   Fresh bread out of Fiore's oven — it's the best bread in Toronto…

son:-   Yeah, but I haven't tasted any other.

Wallace also brings out the cruelty that is already latent in all children, particularly at the expense of one, singled-out child.

….Vincenzo eats stinky meat… but then tempers it with compassion, showing how those words make the boy's heart bleed who is slighted, just because his food smells strange, looks different and is new to them…aspects that sum up an entire philosophy of life.

But although momentarily cruel at times, his children are never totally insensitive — a fact that Ian showed by means of one single question when Rita asks: 'How is your Nonna?' — a question that speaks of care.

Then, relief! The child finds the answer. Remembering his father's words, that he has nothing to be ashamed of, he finds strength within himself and joins them in their laughter.

Whenever Ian has asked children whether they had ever been hurt themselves, they have told him quite frankly that they had all been laughed at, at some time or other, or had ethnic labels attached to them. Even at their young age the children know the feeling of hurt and that very experience provides plenty of scope for improvement; for the successful eradication of prejudices.

Wallace's particular beauty lies in the simplicity of his style; in the celebration of creative imagination carried over into adulthood (THE CHRISTMAS TREE HOUSE) and his truly loving approach to people, refreshingly encompassing our elderly as well. Ian Wallace is not affected by the so-called youth cult. His people are young and old; real people who have their feet firmly planted on the ground. It is heart-warming to read that the elderly couple in JULIE NEWS, the Simpsons, are active pensioners forever engaged in the highly symbolic art of gardening.

These characters are probably inspired by people Ian knows personally such as his grandfather — a small but strong man who happily plunged into his second marriage at the age of 81. No wonder this young

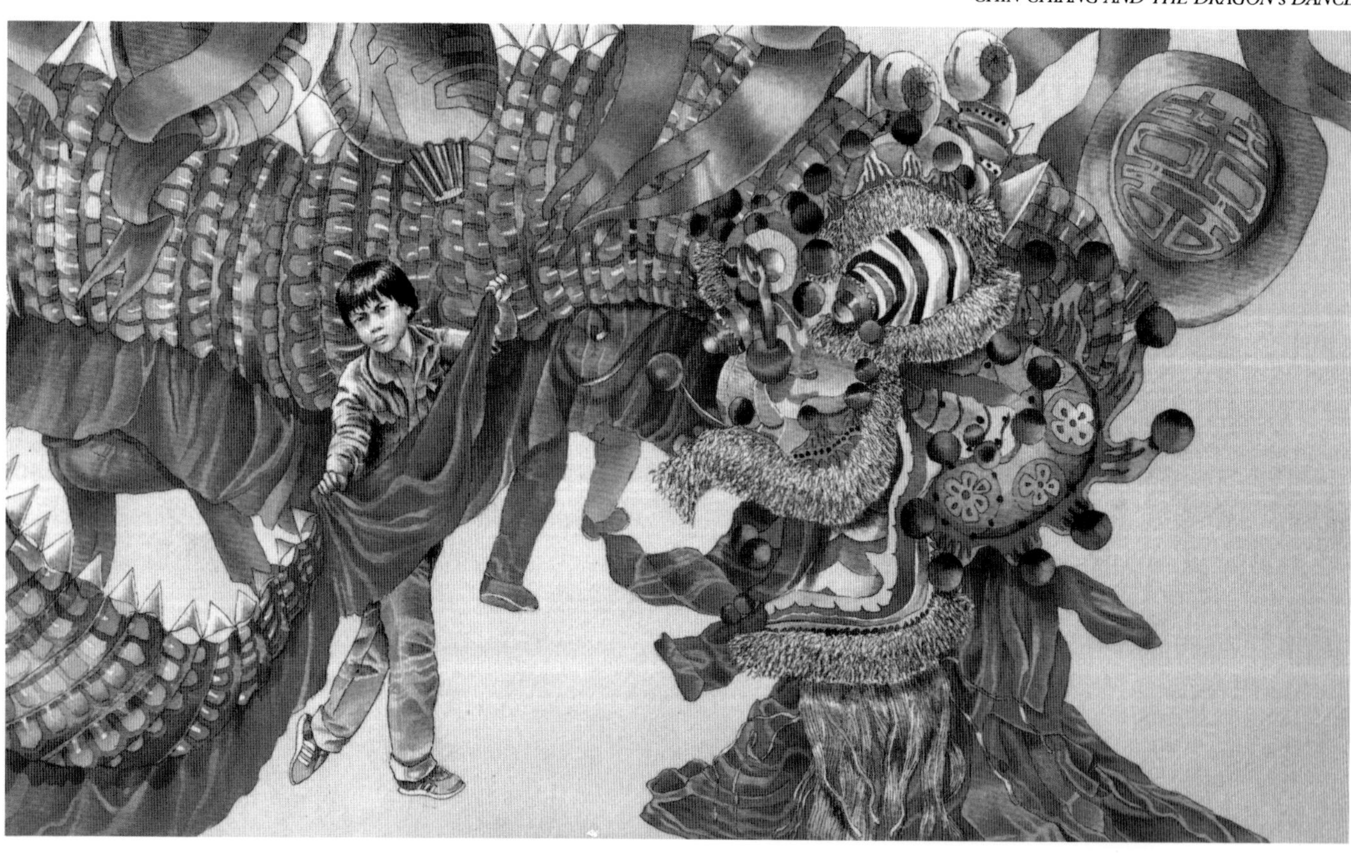

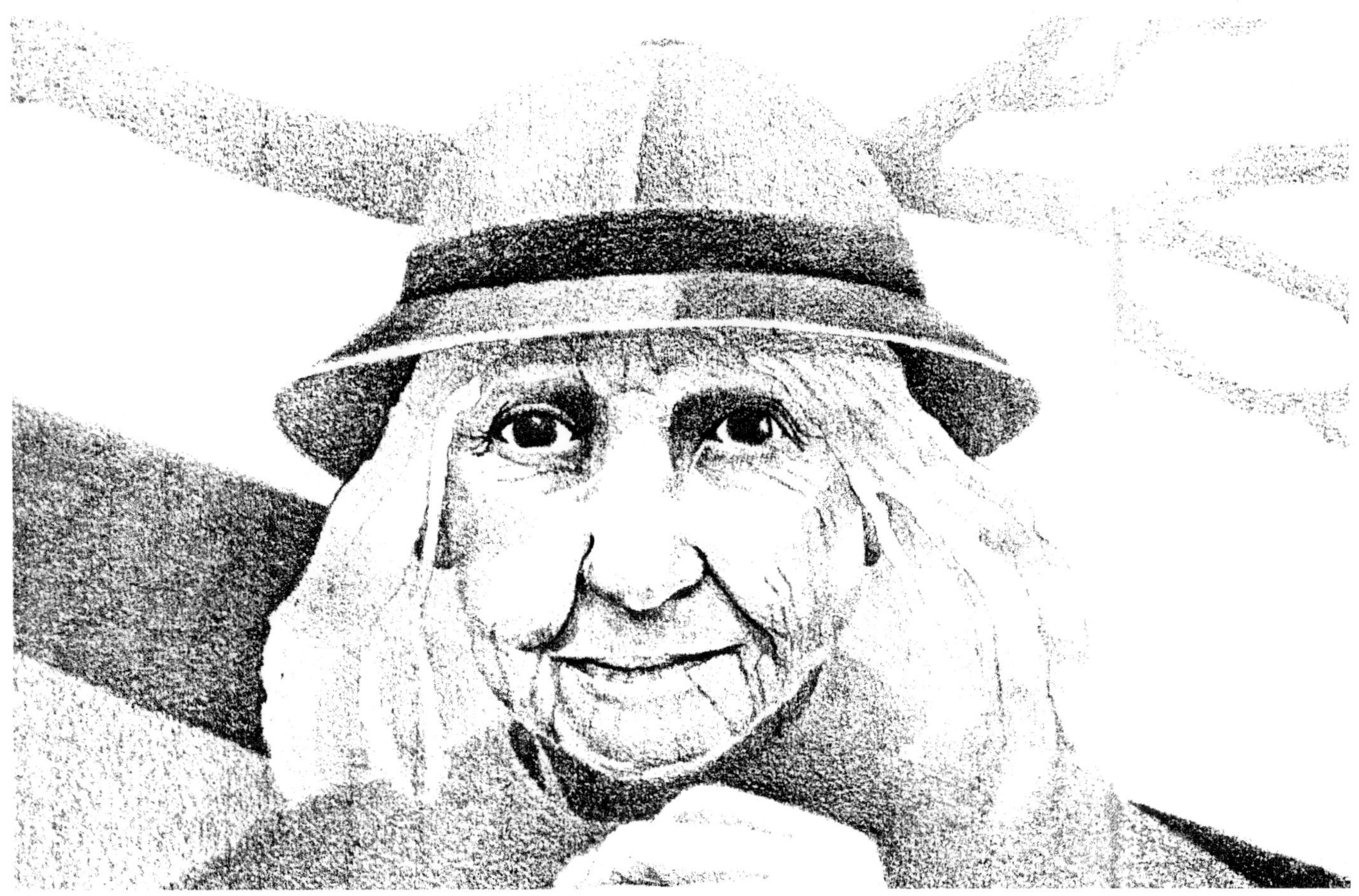

DON VALLEY ROSE phantom illustration out of
THE CHIRSTMAS TREE HOUSE
(*available from* KIDS CAN PRESS)

author enjoys such tremendous popularity with people of all ages!

The cover of JULIE NEWS is done in cut-out letters in order to create the desired scrap-book effect, while a hint of nostalgia is produced by a sketch of the elderly pensioners done in pointillism evoking an association with petit point needlework and the mores and customs of a bygone era.

JULIE NEWS is a book about an extremely positive, vivacious, concerned and caring papergirl (instead of the stereotype paperboy) who is full of confidence knowing…she can be whatever she wants to be if she wants it badly enough…and on her daily TORONTO STAR paper route in Cabbagetown she comes, of course, into contact with many types of people who touch her life and whose lives she touches in return.

Wallace still further enhances the beauty of his stories by his superb artwork, conjuring the fairytale-like effect of an inviting winter wonderland by touches of grey, in THE CHRISTMAS TREE HOUSE.

Yet, for all his success, Ian does not rest on his laurels, but is constantly bubbling over with new ideas.

His above mentioned work, a truly fascinating and touchingly illustrated book, is about the hero, CHIN CHIANG, whose most cherished dream was about to come true when the New Year approached. But instead of seizing the coveted opportunity,

He also subtly injects profound symbolism. How touching is the gesture of Don Valley Rose who hands the children the key to the Tree House, their palace and safe refuge. She shares, so generously, this house that has…a window to the East and one to the West, one to the North and one to the South. Yes, Ian is open to any culture …a fact that is also clearly reflected in his artwork, for he spares no effort when it comes to in-depth intercultural observation. Ian sometimes spends weeks doing research with painstaking dedication to discover a particular motif, one special characteristic that could be vital to an illustration's authenticity, as in CHIN CHIANG AND THE DRAGON'S DANCE.

CHIN CHIANG becomes scared and runs away. On his flight he meets PUI YE an old cleaning woman who had shared the same dream. Gently the child prepares the adult to take his place. However, they get lost in the crowd on their way and…CHIN CHIANG's dream comes true despite his will, the child managing to draw his adult friends into sharing the joy, thus closing the magic circle of the old involving the young, and the young in turn passing on knowledge acquired from his elders to other old people and bringing the elderly together.

This truly wonderful book is to be enjoyed, not only by children, but by the entire family.

Q: Ian, how did your writing for children come about?

A: It was by sheer accident, actually. I graduated from the Ontario College of Art and did not have a job. It so happened that I was having a drink when some people from Kids Can Press, sitting next to me, mentioned that they were looking for an illustrator.

I told them that I would be interested and was hired on the spot.

IAN WALLACE

Q: Did you do any writing before?
A: I have always enjoyed writing. It was just that the idea of putting writing and illustrating together had never even entered my mind.

I particularly enjoy writing for the young. It's challenging. In a picture book you have to create a magical world in, say, twenty-four pages that could easily be 200 pages where adult fiction is concerned.

Q: Do you ever 'try out' your writings on children prior to submitting a manuscript for publication?
A: That goes without saying. I enjoy reading my work aloud to friends and children alike. I am always interested in their reaction.

I love children and, in particular, their amazing spirit. They are quite spiritual beings and they are bright enough to notice when someone tries to put something over on them.

I would suggest that anyone interested in writing for children, write **to** them but never **at** them — to give children credit for who they are.

Q: Do you have any special aspirations?
A: To become the best children's writer/illustrator I can be hopefully standing alongside Sendak/Mayer and The Dillons.

Besides, I hope to help eradicate the problem of prejudice by making children question their treatment of others and their reaction to them.

Q: You set yourself a lofty goal.
A: I am convinced it can be done.

I expressed in the ONE AUTHOR'S TOUR article in the IN REVIEW magazine, *"....it is the right of every child in this country to see his/her face reflected in a book."*

Q: Is there any special advice you would want to pass on to junior writers?
A: To have perseverance in writing.

Q: Should they listen to criticism?
A: Of course, as long as it is constructive and justified. If you agree with the criticism — then make the necessary changes. But if you do not — then stand by your viewpoint. But never give up.

PUBLISHING CREDITS

1985: illustr. VERY LAST FIRST TIME by Jan Andrews children's book published by Douglas & McIntyre, Vancouver & Toronto.

1986: February — March 23rd, 1986 AGO — Walter Trier Gallery "CHIN CHIANG AND THE DRAGON'S DANCE exhibition covering 17 original water colours and special displays demonstrating the different stages of production of this popular children's book — written and illustrated by Ian Wallace.

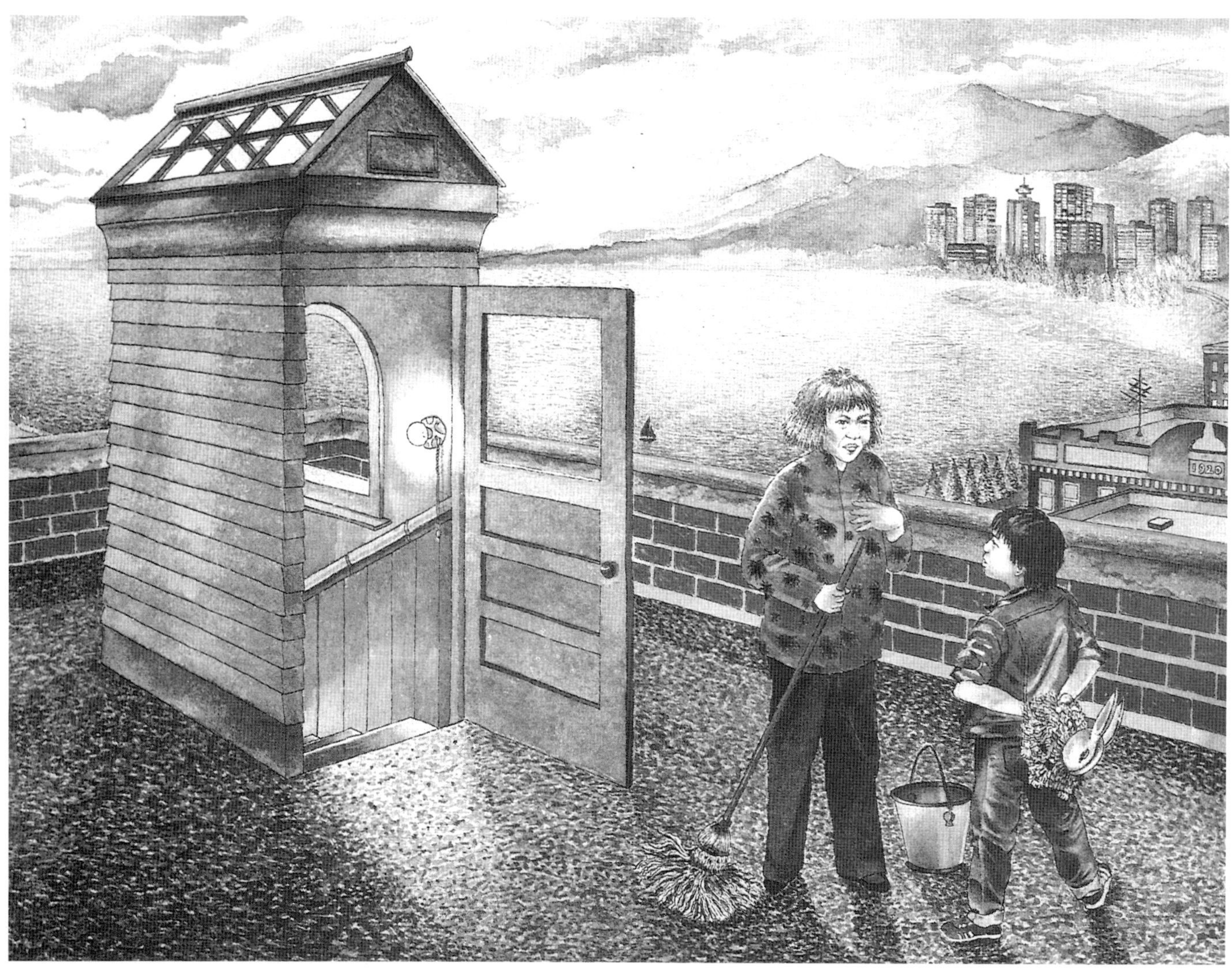